RSS and Atom

Understanding and Implementing Content Feeds and Syndication

Heinz Wittenbrink

BIRMINGHAM - MUMBAI

RSS and Atom
Understanding and Implementing Content Feeds and Syndication

First published: October 2005

Published by Packt Publishing Ltd.
32 Lincoln Road
Olton
Birmingham, B27 6PA, UK.

ISBN 1-904811-57-4

www.packtpub.com

Cover Design by www.visionwt.com

Authorized translation from the German Edition:

"Newsfeeds mit RSS und Atom"
© 2005 by Galileo Press

GALILEO COMPUTING is an imprint of
Galileo Press, Fort Lee, NJ (USA), Bonn (Germany).

German Edition first published 2005 by Galileo Press.

Credits

Author
Heinz Wittenbrink

Technical Editors
Ajayesh Srinivasan
Niranjan Jahagirdar

Editorial Manager
Dipali Chittar

Proofreader
Richard Deeson

Production Coordinator
Manjiri Nadkarni

Cover Designer
Helen Wood

About the Author

Heinz Wittenbrink was born in 1956 in Mülheim (Ruhr region). He studied literature and philosophy and worked as an editor and then a senior editor for the Bertelsmann Group. He was responsible for several CD ROMs with encyclopedic content, and later, for the development of the first free German encyclopedic website http://www.wissen.de. In 2000 he moved to a Munich-based web agency, and in 2002, founded his own company for online publishing. Since 2004 he has been a professor for web publishing at the University for Applied Sciences in Graz/Austria. He has written books and online teaching material on XML, HTML and CSS.

Heinz used RSS for the first time when he developed a news service for a major German magazine publisher. He sees the ease of use and the extensibility of modern syndication formats as their major advantages. He is convinced that RSS and its successors will soon develop from syndication formats used in special contexts (news publishing, weblogs, and so on) to general formats for publishing and archiving online content.

Table of Contents

Foreword

Do we need a book about newsfeeds, RSS, and the new format, Atom? After all, they are pure online formats, and there is a multitude of sources available on the Web to obtain information. Why should someone want information available on the Web on paper? The reason why only a few books on newsfeeds currently exist is because the formats themselves are easy to use; there is not much need for explanation. The complexity of RSS becomes evident only if one actually compares the different formats for newsfeeds. It is then that one realizes that the differences between the formats lie in the different ideas of the Web's architecture, its future development, as well as the role of technological standards.

With this book, I would like to try to explain these connections, and thereby explain why there are different formats for a task that is actually easy to achieve. In addition, a book offers the chance to deal systematically with this technology, to get an overview of the different formats, and to compare them synoptically. Linear and three dimensional at the same time, the book as a medium offers opportunities for insight and overview, which are superior to the two-dimensional screen.

It has been some time since I was first confronted with newsfeeds. The great potential hidden behind the three letters "RSS" became obvious to me when I had to provide a client with up-to-date news on online media. I subscribed to feeds of a great number of news sources and was able to analyze a lot more material than would have been possible through traditional websites. Also, RSS was a useful format with respect to my own deliveries to my clients. RSS documents have the structure needed for up-to-date messages which reference sources on the Web, and they are easy to transform into different formats. I knew RSS because I had been reading weblogs—Dave Winer's ScriptingNews, Doc Searls's weblog, David Weinberger's "Joho the Blog!," the "Schockwellenreiter," and "langreiter.com"—daily for a few years already.

I was preparing a presentation on RSS as a technology and its possibilities for online publishing, and that's when I realized that there is no book on RSS available on the German market. That was when the idea for this book was developed.

Because I was also observing the American market concerning online media for my client, I realized the enormous commercial possibilities that newsfeeds, and services that are based on newsfeeds, open up. Moreover.com established itself very successfully as a provider of generated newsfeeds on the news market; Daypop and Feedster went online as the first search engines that specialized in RSS feeds and weblogs.

Like in most areas of online publishing, here, too, it was a long time before Europe discovered the possibilities of the new format. The first feed formats didn't include much more than headlines, links, and short descriptions of news on HTML pages.

Atom, the newest feed format can, however, transport any kind of content. Additionally, Atom includes a "publishing protocol" or API, defining a complete provider-neutral publication environment for periodically updated Web content. Furthermore, Atom allows the archiving newsfeeds and their parts and to clearly and permanently identify them. With Atom, newsfeeds have finally become a publication format in its own right. It doesn't need a lot of imagination to see that that the classical HTML page will soon play an inferior role compared to continuously updated feeds, as a format for static content like tutorials, scientific texts, reference material, and presentations.

While I was working on the book it dawned on me that newsfeeds are much more than a practical means and a basis for business ideas in online publishing. Newsfeeds—together with formats like RSS and Atom—have already changed our idea of online publishing as a whole, and will change them even more radically in the future. Since the first years of the Web, our image of online publishing has been determined by the HTML page—a format similar to a book page that is presented static and square on the screen and can be upgraded through newspaper-like layouts to a "portal." In the beginning, newsfeeds had a secondary task; they were developed as guideposts for HTML pages, and allowed for headlines and contents of a page to be built into other pages as a teaser. Step by step, they themselves conquered more and more functions of HTML pages: they incorporated Web content including the typography and the images.

With newsreaders and aggregators, a kind of software established itself that enabled a user to read newsfeeds outside of browsers. Through APIs, they turned into a format that makes it very easy to publish weblogs, thereby losing the status of a secondary product. Newsfeed formats made a pivotal contribution to making the vision of the "Writable Web" become reality for the every-day Web user—a few clicks in a weblog system and every Web user could be a Web author. Since the introduction of podcasting in 2004, newsfeeds have become the format for Web-compatible broadcasting of audio and video content.

During the process of writing the book I learned a lot about the possibilities newsfeeds have to offer for online publishing. I hope that the book will help you, the reader, to evaluate what the different formats can do for you today, and what role they are likely to play in the development of the Web in the years to come.

My wife Regina and my sons Samuel, Jonathan, and David put up with not being able to talk to me at all for months, or only about XML and web architecture, if at all. I would like to dedicate this book to them.

– Heinz Wittenbrink, Graz, 20 May

Introduction

The field of information technology has seen an advent in the number of new businesses and startups. It is, however, important to take a realistic look at the needs as well as constraints of such a setup before investing in a solution—to not get extravagant, and also stay practical. This is the thought that has gone behind the development of the Small Business Server 2003—to provide a server with a range of functions specially optimized for efficiently running such businesses.

What This Book Covers

The book focuses on a description of the three major syndication formats RSS 1.0, RSS 2.0, and Atom. It explains the common tasks and the problems these formats have to solve: What structure can be used to describe a large variety of different time-based online content? What are the essential metadata? How can the format be extended and customized? How can content in other formats (especially HTML/XHTML) be cited or transported?

Chapter 1 gives a general introduction to online syndication and sketches the history of the new syndication or feed formats.

Chapter 2 is about the most popular syndication format RSS 2.0 and its predecessors from RSS 0.91 to 0.94. This part of the book describes the semantic elements (author, date, rights, and so on), which are common to the other feed formats where they are expressed differently to RSS 2.0. The chapter covers the use of RSS for podcasting, a phenomenon currently revolutionizing audio and video distribution. It describes new extensions to RSS used for the publishing of media and search results by companies like Amazon and Yahoo!.

Chapter 3 is devoted to RSS 1.0 and its foundations in the **Resource Description Format (RDF)**. Its gives an introduction to the structure of RDF statements and tries to explain the syntax of RSS 1.0 in detail by relating it to RDF semantics.

Chapter 4 is about the newest syndication format, Atom. Atom is much more "general purpose" than RSS and it has been developed in a long and thorough process by leading XML experts. Since August 2005 the Atom Feed Format has been an official standard approved by the the Internet Engineering Steering Group. The Atom Editing Protocol should be finalized by November 2005. Both are covered in this book with a focus on the technical motivations of the features of this format.

Conventions

In this book, you will find a number of styles of text that distinguish between different kinds of information. Here are some examples of these styles, and an explanation of their meaning.

There are three styles for code. Code words in text are shown as follows: "The rdf:RDF element acts as a container for several so-called "top-level" elements".

A block of code will be set as follows:

```
<rdf:Description rdf:about="http://www.example.com/weblogs/lisa">
  <dc:creator>
    <rdf:Description
     rdf:about="http://www.example.com/persons/lisa"/>
  </dc:creator>
</rdf:Description>
```

When we wish to draw your attention to a particular part of a code block, the relevant lines or items will be made bold:

```
<rdf:Description rdf:about="http://www.example.com/weblogs/lisa">
  <dc:creator>
    <rdf:Description
     rdf:about="http://www.example.com/persons/lisa"/>
  </dc:creator>
</rdf:Description>
```

New terms and **important words** are introduced in a bold-face font. Words that you see on the screen, in menus or dialog boxes for example, appear in our text like this: "clicking the Next button moves you to the next screen".

Tips, suggestions, or important notes appear in a box like this.

Reader Feedback

Feedback from our readers is always welcome. Let us know what you think about this book, what you liked or may have disliked. Reader feedback is important for us to develop titles that you really get the most out of.

To send us general feedback, simply drop an e-mail to feedback@packtpub.com, making sure to mention the book title in the subject of your message.

If there is a book that you need and would like to see us publish, please send us a note in the SUGGEST A TITLE form on www.packtpub.com or e-mail suggest@packtpub.com.

If there is a topic that you have expertise in and you are interested in either writing or contributing to a book, see our author guide on www.packtpub.com/authors.

Customer Support

Now that you are the proud owner of a Packt book, we have a number of things to help you to get the most from your purchase.

Errata

Although we have taken every care to ensure the accuracy of our contents, mistakes do happen. If you find a mistake in one of our books—maybe a mistake in text or code—we would be grateful if you would report this to us. By doing this you can save other readers from frustration, and help to improve subsequent versions of this book. If you find any errata, report them by visiting http://www.packtpub.com/support, selecting your book, clicking on the Submit Errata link, and entering the details of your errata. Once your errata have been verified, your submission will be accepted and the errata added to the list of existing errata. The existing errata can be viewed by selecting your title from http://www.packtpub.com/support.

Questions

You can contact us at questions@packtpub.com if you are having a problem with some aspect of the book, and we will do our best to address it.

1

What are Newsfeeds?

RSS and Atom are XML formats for messages and other information that is updated frequently. The documents that are written in these formats are called "newfeeds" or "feeds".

Scenario 1: Weblogs

M. writes a weblog. She composes new entries several times a week. M. writes for a group of friends, some of whom are webloggers as well. M.'s friend Peter learns about M.'s new postings through his newsreader (see Section 1.1).

M.'s audience reads her newsfeed primarily in newsreaders and aggregators. M. would like her feed to be easy to subscribe to, and to look as good in the interface offered by these programs, as in a browser. Besides this, it is important for M. to be able to easily inform weblog communities that she has written a new weblog.

Scenario 2: Publishing of Metadata

N. is in charge of a gallery's website. The gallery regularly offers new drawings to its clients. The website of the gallery is based on a database that continuously incorporates new information. N. wants to inform clients and colleagues through a newsfeed about every information update in his database.

For N.'s newsfeed, it is crucial that the content can be processed. The receivers of the newsfeed are to be alerted automatically as soon as a new work of a certain artist, with a certain subject or from a certain epoch is put up for sale in the gallery.

Scenario 3: Aggregating and Archiving of Newsfeeds

T. is a journalist. Her contract includes the writing of a daily news service for a publisher. This service is based on two types of sources: on pre-existing newsfeeds and on websites that don't make newsfeeds available.

The purpose of T.'s service is not only to be read on a daily basis. The messages are archived in a database. They are supposed to be saved there with information about their original source. Above all, T. is interested in aggregating news from different feeds, that is, to write a new feed from those that already exist. Besides this, T. also depends on the messages being permanently accessible.

Scenario 4: Asynchronous Broadcasting

P. works for a district radio. Part of the broadcast includes interviews with artists and authors. These interviews are available on the Web as podcasts. Interested listeners can download them to their MP3 player and listen to them while traveling.

Like M., P.'s main interest is that his audience can subscribe to his feed. For P.'s feed it is also important that the audios can be downloaded automatically and as easily as possible by the users to the terminal of their choice. They only listen to P.'s online broadcasts regularly if they don't have to endure long download times. For that, audio data has to be downloaded at the time when the listeners' computers are idle, for example, early in the morning.

Content and Metadata

Scenarios 1 and 4 are already everyday experience; 2 and 3 can soon become reality. M., N., T., and P. all share and distribute information. Their feeds consist of the content itself and of metadata, that is, information about the data that makes up the content. Newsfeeds give users access to web content in different contexts and on different devices, and allow various services to inform users about updates through the metadata. The range of these services extends from simple headline news to the beginnings of the Semantic Web, which is the automated processing of web content.

When Do We Talk about Syndication?

The technical term for the regular exchange of up-to-date information between websites is "content syndication". The first form of syndication was to regularly integrate news from one website, or newsfeed, into another site. Newsfeeds can also be directly subscribed to and read with special programs called "newsreaders". At the same time, newsreaders serve as "aggregators"; aggregators give an overview of various newsfeeds. They show what information the feeds contain, which feeds have been updated, and which feeds' content the user hasn't read yet. Often, they also allow users of an online community to share newsfeeds.

One of the specifications of newsfeed formats defines syndication as "making data available online for further transmission, aggregation, or online publication" (http://web.resource.org/rss/1.0/). Syndication of web content means that the content is distributed at different locations on the Web. In this context, "location" is to be understood in a figurative sense, like a web address, which also doesn't refer to a place in real space.

Often, syndicated content is accessible through different URIs, not only through the URI of the website where it was originally published. We also talk about syndication when content is published in only one location, yet the users can decide how they want to combine it with other content on their terminal. In this case, the content is taken out of its original context and adapted to the graphical interface that the user has chosen.

1.1 Applications

Syndication or feed formats were developed in the 1990s to exchange content between websites and to integrate the content into portals. For that purpose, software on the server subscribed to feeds from other websites. The first portal of this kind, Netscape's My Netscape, gave registered users the option to compile feeds from different sources for their own purposes.

Aggregators

Soon after these portals, independent online aggregators became available. UserLand developed the first aggregator (`http://radio.userland.com/newsagg`) in 1997. Initially it was a simple directory of newsfeeds, but it soon developed into a web interface that allowed the user to subscribe to newsfeeds and share his/her own feed with others. Online aggregators spread as a tool for personal publishing. UserLand's aggregator, for example, was integrated with the weblog editor Radio UserLand. With a few clicks, users could transfer messages from another feed to their own feed to cite, comment on, or just spread. Radio UserLand is also prototypical of later developments insofar as members of a community could display the feeds to which they have subscribed. Like a hit parade or bestseller list, the ranking helps the further spread of the most popular feeds. The author of a weblog can find out who has subscribed to his/her feed. The reader finds sources of the authors he or she is specifically interested in.

In many cases, those applications that compile feeds and filter them according to certain criteria are also called aggregators, for example, O'Reilly's Meerkat service (`http://www.oreillynet.com/meerkat`). Usually, aggregators of this type automatically generate metafeeds from the compilation of feeds of several individual topics or from different sources.

Newsreader

Newsreaders like Feedreader (`http://www.feedreader.com/`), RSS Bandit (`http://www.rssbandit.org/`), FeedDemon (`http://www.bradsoft.com/feeddemon/`) and NetNewsWire (`http://ranchero.com/netnewswire/`) are desktop tools to subscribe to newsfeeds. They frequently offer a more sophisticated interface than online aggregators. In addition, users can read newsfeeds with them while offline and newsfeeds can be saved and searched locally. Newsfeeds can be subscribed to and read with newer browsers and e-mail programs as well.

Meanwhile, some offline newsreaders can synchronize themselves with online aggregators like Bloglines (http://www.bloglines.com) while online, so that users can take advantage of both worlds. Microsoft's next operating system, "Windows Vista", will allow users to subscribe to the results of web searches on their computers or other machines as newsfeeds. It is certain that for the user, the difference between online and offline use, especially in the area of newsfeeds, is growing narrower and narrower.

1.2 Feed-Based Services

Aggregators and newsreaders helped newsfeeds to have their breakthrough. Recently, numerous services have developed on the Web that process and analyze newsfeeds, or offer specific feeds themselves. Among the first of these services were feed directories like NewsIsFree (http://www.newsisfree.com) and syndic8 (http://www.syndic8.com). Special search engines like Feedster (http://www.feedster.com) and Daypop (http://www.daypop.com) scan feeds to find up-to-date information.

Today, UPS clients can track the status of their packages via RSS feed (http://www.simpletracking.com/). Google's Gmail users receive the content of their e-mails via RSS (http://gmail.google.com). Players of Microsoft Halo2 can keep track of their rank through the posts on the players' ranking list (http://bungie.net).

Very soon the advantages of RSS for companies' intranets became obvious as well. Companies like Moreover.com (http://w.moreover.com/) specialized in creating aggregated newsfeeds for commercial clients. RSS is easy to combine with knowledge management technology in this particular environment. Newsfeeds can also be used as a tool to observe the media, an example in this case being RSS Radars such as (http://www.masternewmedia.org/news/2005/02/06/create_enterprise_rss_rada rs_rss2exchange.htm).

RSS search engines can indicate new information with great precision, because the newsfeed itself tells them what was updated and when this was done. For this reason they are much more reliable in searching for news than common search engines.

Collaborative Filtering with RSS

The idea of collaborative filtering of newsfeeds already forms the basis of Radio UserLand. In its simplest form, the author of a weblog publishes in a "blogroll" which feeds he or she subscribes to. The more unmanageable the amount of information on the Net becomes, the more interesting are the possibilities of recommendations from people with the similar interests. Interesting attempts in this direction are Rojo (http://www.rojo.com) and Nearest Neighbor News Network (http://www.nearestneighbor.net).

Publication of Geocoded Information

Newsfeeds also have important applications in connection with localized services. The generation of newsfeeds from geocoded information with tools like worldKit, for example, allows the user to receive regularly updated information concerning certain regions or places (`http://www.brainoff.com/worldkit/index.php`). After the tsunami disaster in the Indian Ocean at the end of 2004, services were developed that spread seismographic information via newsfeed (`http://lists.oasis-open.org/archives/emergency/200501/msg00039.html`).

Feed Combinations as Website Metaphors

There is a lot of evidence to suggest that the success of feed formats will continue. Newsfeeds are not just an important part of the infrastructure of the "Semantic Web" but they might soon change the common concept of a website—and with it the content management systems as well. More and more, websites themselves could become aggregators, in which different feeds with specific common interests or characteristics are produced, combined, and recombined (Jason Kottke: *Some "Web as platform" noodling*, `http://www.kottke.org/04/08/web-platform`).

1.3 RSS Requirements

Up to now I have only introduced some application scenarios for newsfeeds and referred to certain exemplary programs and services that are based on newsfeeds. Most users don't know that these programs and services are made possible through common document types for newsfeeds, which clearly differ from HTML. These documents have become widely accepted as the first XML formats on the Web.

The abbreviation RSS has established itself as the collective term for these newsfeed formats. The name "RSS" encompasses a number of closely connected technologies that identify and find updated or updatable information on the Web, and show and exchange that information. The term RSS developed from an abbreviation that can be interpreted in different ways: the three letters, depending on your interpretation, stand for "RDF Site Summary", "Rich Site Summary", or "Really Simple Syndication". "Atom" is the name of an attempt to formulate RSS in a new way, more precisely and in close synchronization with other up-to-date web technologies.

A document format is an important precondition to syndicate content. The exchange of these documents on the Web needs communication protocols to be already considered in the definition of the format. However, these protocols don't necessarily have to be RSS specific. As you will see, RSS usually uses HTTP, the standard communication protocol of the World Wide Web.

Advantages of a Standardized Syndication Format for Users and Providers

A standardized syndication format makes it possible to receive precise information on which of the information objects, accessible through a URI, were changed and when that change occurred. A user can use this information to not only decide which parts of the updated web offering he or she wants to have a look at, but he or she can also get the new information with the feed itself. Software can process the appropriate elements automatically.

For both the content providers and the receivers, feed formats have important advantages:

- **Bandwidth Advantage**
  One important advantage of a syndication format can be that the transferred data needs less bandwidth than the original documents. In practice, however, this advantage plays only a secondary role, because today many documents in syndication formats contain the entire content of the original page.

- **Clear Semantics**
  More importantly there is a second advantage: the simple and clear semantics of the language medium, which can be defined to carry information about the latest changes to a website. An HTML document doesn't indicate which of its h1, h2, or h3 elements contains the headings of up-to-date information, and where these messages originate. In a syndication document each of these messages can become an information object, which has a title and further attributes.

- **Time Saving**
  To visit more than 20 websites a day regularly is not easy for anyone, with regard to the time this would entail. Without a standardized exchange format; I would have to actively search for the information that an aggregator or newsreader provides, or I would be dependent on subproviders. The syndication format would give me easy access to many different news sources. I don't need an entity between the provider of the information and myself as the receiver; be it software, a specific server, or a company.

A standardized syndication format makes the user more independent; he or she can make a much better decision on what news to receive and when to receive it. At the other end, a syndication format increases the range of the news producer. The provider of news is not dependent on interested users checking their website for news; users can be actively informed about all changes on the site.

RSS is an example of the end-to-end principle (http://web.mit.edu/Saltzer/www/publications/endtoend/endtoend.txt), and in this it is similar to many other successful Internet technologies.

With RSS, an intermediate or switching level is no longer necessary. However, RSS is a purely technical tool; the task of choosing and assessing the content still remains with the user.

Requirements of a Standard Format

In the first section, we have seen examples of what feed formats are used for. These formats achieve the biggest impact because they have established themselves as standards. As such, they have advantages that were unimaginable with just a syndication format, however good it might have been. A shared format and standardized publication processes make it easier to:

1. Find updated information
2. Display it
3. Exchange and further publish it

The requirements of a standardized feed format can be described on two levels:

- What information does an RSS document have to transmit (functional requirements)?

- How does it work together with other formats and protocols (formal requirements)?

The first level deals with application and use. These functional requirements are manifold: the users want to keep an overview of a large amount of different information; the information providers want to easily distribute information about different topics and in different formats and to provide their audience with up-to-date news. For that purpose, many platforms and many different types of content have to be considered (such as photo and video blogs, and the transfer of data for automatic processing).

Formal requirements have to be met, so that a feed format can be standardized. The chances that a feed format establishes itself are best if it goes back to previously established technology, which it complements and modifies only for its specific purposes. With a format for sharing content, standardization is not only nice to have, but a must: the wider the technical base is spread, the better syndication works.

Only a solution that is effective, abstract, and simple at the same time can be used as a standard: **effective**, because otherwise it could not manage the job; **abstract**, so that it can be adapted to different situations; and **simple**, so that it can be applied by many users. Furthermore, it has to fit into the "ecological" system within which it is used, that is, it has to match the architecture and infrastructure of the World Wide Web.

Functional Requirement: Finding Updated Information

Newspaper sites like `http://news.ft.com/home/us`, news sites like
`http://www.slashdot.org`, portals like `http://www.yahoo.com`, and weblogs like
`http://scripting-news.com` are updated on a regular basis, often hourly. Other
operators update their sites with new information with a lower frequency. When and
which components of a website have been updated is clearly recognizable; software can
search for these specific elements.

In fact, the HTTP protocol also allows the user to find out if and when a web document was
updated, but a server can inform a client via HTTP only of changes to the document as a
whole, not of individual components that have been added or modified. The client can find
out through the information in the HTTP header that the homepage of a daily newspaper
has changed, but can't discern *which* messages and articles were added or modified.

Functional Requirement: Presentation of Information

Primarily, RSS is processed to better present RSS documents, that is, to make them
readable. The information has to be structured in such a way that it can be easily shown,
and that it offers an overview of the content. Without conventions for a standardized
presentation of updated web resources, users have to surf the Internet for individual
documents and to direct themselves within their internal navigation.

In fact, HTML is also a standard to present information in a standardized way. However,
HTML doesn't have the semantics for news or news-like information, because it was
developed as a language for all kinds of information as a sort of lowest common
denominator for laying out web documents.

In contrast, standardized information about what is new on a site makes software possible
that searches many sources for news and compiles the updated information. It is not
specified, though, how much of the updated information is enclosed in an RSS document
and how much in a source to which that document refers.

Functional Requirement: Exchange and Processing

Publishing information about changes on a website doesn't actually become interesting
until that information can appear on other websites as well.

In this case, a website can subscribe to other websites and integrate their content, just as
genetic material from one cell can be inserted in DNA strings of other cells. Without a
standard for web news, such exchange operations can become complex and unstable.
Users have to know the exact structure of the content they want to integrate, and then
change it into their own publication format. The scripts necessary for this integration
have to be rewritten for every change in the source structure. A standard, however, makes
it possible to use material of any kind—aside from any legal problems.

Publishing and republishing also includes the commenting on, citing, and changing of information. An intention of the first web developers was to create a medium for users to publish and write, as well as receive and read. This "Semantic Web" needs rules for integrating and republishing if it is supposed to work worldwide, and be accessible for everyone.

Functional Requirement: Publishing and Editing of Information

Feed formats can also be used to publish or edit documents. In this case, the document reaches the web server in a feed format—publication protocols or APIs (Application Programming Interfaces), regulate how the data on the server is to be interpreted. Here, too, the combination of RSS with other XML formats and web protocols plays an important role. On the one hand, HTML fragments often belong to the content of the documents that are to be published. On the other hand, technologies like HTTP, XML-RPC, and SOAP are used for publishing.

Functional Requirement: Extracting and Processing Metadata

Another type of requirement is the extraction of information for automatic processing. Here in particular, the connections between RSS and the resource description format are of relevance. Magazine publishers, for example, can provide within their newsfeeds, the bibliographical data of all articles in machine-readable form. A feed with seismographic data can be analyzed for disaster warnings.

Functional Requirement: Extensibility

The history of the development of feed formats along with the applications that are based on them suggests that feed formats are likely to face numerous further challenges. Often it is particularly important to combine data in these formats with other forms of data. That is why feed formats need a standardized extension mechanism. Such a mechanism makes sure that new applications can be developed without the need to change existing formats and applications, or making them obsolete.

Formal Requirement: Integration in the Architecture of the Web

Added to these requirements, which can be derived from the challenges of the format, there are further requirements that arise from the environment that the format will mainly be used in: newsfeeds and documents on the World Wide Web that have to work in this specific environment. This means:

- Feed formats have to work in a similar fashion to other universal web technologies; they have to be simple and stable. This requirement concerns all aspects of feed formats: the syntax, semantics, and their application.

- Content is published in newsfeeds. Their format has to work with other web content formats. That is why the connections to these formats have to be well defined. This requirement concerns not only the syntax of feed documents, but also that of documents that use feed formats together with other vocabularies. HTML markup, for example, occurs in many newsfeeds. One demand for the specification of a feed format is to determine the relationship between these two vocabularies: whether an HTML passage in the content of a feed document is also a logical part of the document (belonging to the same document tree), or whether it is just cited.

- Newsfeeds contain information about other information or what is known as metadata. In many cases, feed formats are even considered metadata formats. That is why the connections to metadata formats have to be clarified. It also has to be clarified whether data in feed formats can coexist with other metadata. This requirement not only affects the syntax, but also (more importantly) the semantics of the documents.

- Feed formats belong among the publication technologies of the World Wide Web. Therefore, they have to consider the common procedures of the Web to transfer and publish messages, either by referring back to them or by specifying how and why they differ from them. This requirement concerns more the use of feed formats than the document structure. Without it, however, the syntax and semantics of the documents can't be determined.

1.4 Semantics: The RSS Model

The common basic functions of the syndication formats can be divided into four categories:

- **Architecture**: structure of information
- **Content**: description and reproduction of information
- **Identification and linking**: relocating to other information on the Web
- **Metadata**: description of important characteristics of the information

These requirements are so general that they could as well be listed for other, possibly for almost all, text formats on the Web. Specific to syndication formats, are restrictions within each requirement group.

Even if the different RSS versions clearly differ from each other, the semantics of the most important features of the language are similar. The model of a collection of updated information objects belonging to a resource that is identifiable on the Web forms the basis of all syndication vocabularies. The feed document is a snapshot of the resource.

The term "resource" is used here in the language of the World Wide Web consortium and the URI standard: "every object that can be identified through a URI (Uniform Resource Identifier)" is a resource. Roy Fielding has made the concepts behind this usage transparent in his dissertation "*Architectural Styles and the Design of Network-based Software Architectures*" (http://www.ics.uci.edu/~fielding/pubs/dissertation/top.htm).

Independence of Topics and Original Formats

Most importantly, a feed document contains information about which information objects are to be found under a URI and when they were updated. In addition, it can include a description of the resource and the individual information objects, the specification of a unique identifier for the objects, information about the editor-in-charge and the webmaster, and other information. It is also possible that the information object described may be completely embedded in the feed document.

All feed formats have a basic model in common. This basic model, however, is serialized—that is, translated into strings of characters—differently in the syntax of the feed formats. You can consider the formats that are described in this book as modifications, specifications, and extensions of this basic model.

The RSS model generalizes all the specifics of the updated information; it works independently of the internal structure of the information, and the topics it concerns. It is so universal that RSS feeds of all kinds of content are possible. Newsfeeds can refer to a wiki as well as to a weblog, an information portal, a compilation of software updates, or new multimedia data. Any collection of information that is updated at any point in time can be the object of a feed document.

At this point, I would like to introduce the basic model of the various feed formats. For this purpose, I will use the names of the XML elements in the existing feed formats, such as channel or title, as the names for the components of the feed documents.

1.4.1 Minimal Information

Structure: channel and item or feed and entry

There are two kinds of information objects in all RSS formats, that is, collections of new information items and new individual items of information. The collections are called a channel (RSS 1.0, RSS 2.0) or a feed; an object within a collection is called an item or an entry. On both levels—that of the channel or feed and that of the item or entry—there is content information, metadata, and information about the identification and linking of information objects.

Description: title—link—description

Apart from the two levels of the information channel and the individual information object, that is, the channel and the item respectively, all feed formats are characterized by three pieces of information. The RSS elements that hold this information are called title, link, and description. They can be found on both the channel and the item level.

Usually, a feed document describes another web resource, namely, the resource that is identified by the content of the link element. Because the feed document is not only the representation but also the description of a web resource; feed formats can be called metadata formats, even if the difference between data and metadata is difficult to grasp precisely.

The obligatory presence of an element called link, and with it, the ability to identify a document it refers to, distinguishes feed documents from other web formats like HTML. An HTML document element and a feed document, together with all other data that can be reached on the Web through the HTTP protocol, both represent a resource that is identified by the URI through which it can be reached. [1]

The link element only states what the RSS document describes; it is not the description alone. Also, RSS defines the description as generally as possible: just simply as a description. All syndication vocabularies have an element that stands for the description as such; in RSS 1.0 and 2.0, it is called description. The only additional requirement is a title that identifies to people what the URI in link identifies for machines. These three elements then repeat themselves for the individual information objects that are described in the newsfeed as components of the resource. These objects can, but don't have to, refer to the information they describe through a link element of their own.

All syndication vocabularies repeat at the level of the item, and also at the component part of a feed, the minimal description of the entire feed. All additional elements are extensions; they build on the foundation of a model that could hardly be reduced any further. These additional elements make it possible to describe resources with "rich metadata" in a feed document and to transfer content within it.

---

[1] This resource is not identical to the data that the server delivers to the client, but abstract in nature. This is most obvious with URIs such as www.yahoo.com that clearly identify something, but never directly refer to particular data and/or a specific server. But the URI of an individual image also identifies the image, independent of a particular location in the data system on a server; rather, a mechanism has to be defined in all cases to resolve the URI and to send the data to the user.

Presentation of Newsfeeds in Feed Readers and Aggregators

Documents with this simple basic structure—channel and item for the organization and title, link, and description for the descriptive content of a feed document—contain the minimum information a feed reader or aggregator needs.

The following screenshot shows how a feed document is presented by a common newsreader (the document source can be found in section 2.2.1).

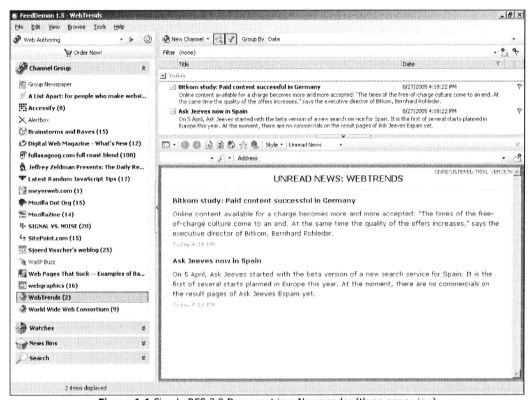

Figure 1.1 Simple RSS 2.0 Document in a Newsreader (three-pane view)

On the left side you see a list of different newsfeeds, from which a sample document was chosen for display. On the right, in the upper field, the header (the content of the title element) and other features of individual messages are shown. The lower field displays the message that was chosen. Above are the news items, which are displayed one below the other including the headline of the message (again, the content of the title element); the content of the description element follows. Below the description the feed's title is shown; the date that follows was generated by the newsreader.

This so-called "three-pane view" is not the only possible way to reproduce RSS documents. The news items can also be displayed one below the other:

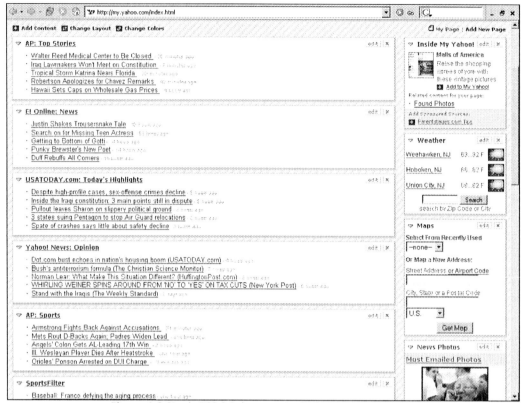

Figure 1.2 Simple RSS 2.0 document in the list view of MyYahoo!

Several other features of the entire channel are shown if the user opens the presentation of the feed's features in a context menu as the following screenshot demonstrates:

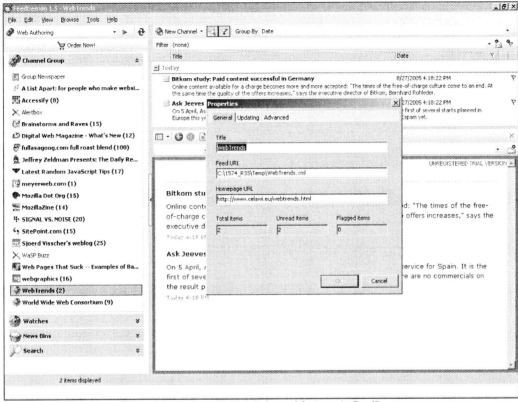

Figure 1.3 Display of RSS 2.0 channel features in FeedDemon

The pop-up window on the right shows the contents of the `link` and `description` elements of the `channel`. The window on the left displays the titles of several RSS feeds, which are preset in the newsreader that we use (FeedDemon). (The newsreader also works as an aggregator at the same time. With this program, it is also possible to share one's own subscriptions with others.)

You can see that the basic functions of a newsreader and a news aggregator can be realized, even if only a few elements of the feed vocabulary are used.

1.4.2 Other Content and Metadata

Content: Quotations and Pointers

Syndication formats are not content formats; they use existing formats for content: simple text, HTML, XHTML, other XML vocabularies, and also other text and binary media formats. These formats are used for titles, summaries, and the partial or complete reproduction of the content.

One of the characteristics of newsfeed models is that the description itself is defined in as generic a nature as possible. For this reason, it is possible to include any type of content in that description. In a syndication feed, any kind of web content can be sampled and further distributed. That is why RSS and its relatives are also suitable as a universal publication format on the Web.

Metadata in Syndication Formats

Syndication formats serve to exchange information and make it available in different forms. For this reason, they describe the information they contain in a way that allows other users to use it; at the same time, they also inform the users of the legal and other limits connected to using their information, like the identification of publication and update data, the categorization of content, and the identification of writers, authors, and copyright holders.

RSS as a Publication and Syndication Format

Even though all existing feed formats require an element called `link`, it is possible that the information in a news stream isn't to be found outside the RSS feed, meaning that the RSS feed not only refers to another resource, but also contains the original information. The description model of an addressable collection of updatable information objects on the Web, on which RSS is based, works no matter whether these objects exist *only* in the RSS document, or are referred on other resources on the Web. In principle, every resource on the Web that can be modeled as a collection of updated information objects can be the subject of an RSS feed.

1.5 Syntax: RSS as an XML Format

Many websites identify their newsfeeds through an orange-colored button labeled "XML." For many users and also for many developers "XML" and "RSS" are synonymous. In fact, all versions of the RSS feed format and Atom are XML applications. Since XML itself is a metalanguage to define languages for the exchange of information on the Web, the feed formats are also often called "XML dialects" or "XML vocabularies". To date, RSS is the most successful XML vocabulary—except for maybe XHTML, the XML version of HTML.

Standardization and Openness of XML

The biggest advantage of XML in the field of syndication is that XML is a simple, open, and standardized format to exchange information on the Web.

RSS has spread so successfully in recent years not only because it is a particularly effective format, but also because it has established itself as a standard. It acts like a lowest common denominator for updatable information of all kinds, and from the beginning it was accepted as such. Due to the fact that millions of Internet users use RSS to spread and receive information, applications are possible that profit from network implementation and become more useful, the more users use them.

This success would not have been possible without the fundamental features of the underlying technology, XML. XML is a text-based format: people can read XML documents without any great difficulty. The content of XML documents can easily be extracted. In addition, XML is not a proprietary technology that is controlled by any software provider. RSS has inherited these advantages from XML; without them, it would have not been able to spread explosively on the Web. The use of a binary format or a proprietary text format would have complicated the development of software that produces or processes RSS, and limited the market for RSS applications. XML makes it easy to define a format for specific needs. All RSS formats consist of a very small group of XML elements and attributes defined for this purpose, and of rules for the hierarchical connections between these elements. Due to this set of rules (executed as a Relax NG or XML schema), limits for the permitted content of RSS elements can be specified, such as for the format that provides calendar dates.

Separation of Content and Presentation in XML

XML allows for the content and the presentation of documents to be separated. Many XML formats are content formats; they contain no information about how the documents are supposed to be reproduced visually or acoustically. The DocBook vocabulary for technical documentation, for example, uses an emphasis element for important passages and terms. DocBook doesn't specify, however, how such sections are to be emphasized in print. Other XML languages are description or presentation vocabularies. SVG (Scalable Vector Graphics) describes graphics, SMIL (Synchronized Multimedia Interface Language) describes time-structured presentations, and XSL-FO (eXtensible Stylesheet Language-Formatting Objects) describes the layout of printed pages in detail.

Semantic Distinctions

RSS is a pure text format. An RSS document doesn't contain information about how a document should be presented to the user. RSS uses XML to semantically distinguish information. Additionally, it uses the possibility provided by XML to separate content and presentation.

All RSS formats are pure source-text-based content formats. This means that it is necessary to provide them with additional presentation instructions that can be adapted to the respective presentation medium. The presentation instructions make it easy to present RSS documents in different media or in different contexts.

Transformability

The simplest method to present RSS is to convert it into HTML and then use an HTML browser or a toolkit to display the HTML. On the one hand, XSLT (XSL Transformations; http://www.w3.org/TR/xslt) can be used with this method to transform XML data into HTML; on the other hand, HTML fragments are frequently included as a part of the content of RSS documents, so an HTML Rendering Engine is necessary anyway to display them. Like all XML documents, RSS documents can also be formatted directly with Cascading Style Sheets. Moreover, there are many other presentation methods; Flash can be used, for example. One example of an RSS document using the latter is Gush (http://www.2entwine.com).

Ability to be Validated

As XML documents, RSS feeds can be checked with standard procedures to determine whether they comply with the rules of the respective format. A document type definition or a schema contains the formal description of the rules that should be checked for compliance.

Internationalization

A document format that is defined as an XML format can use the methods typical to XML to solve problems of internationalization. XML consistently specifies Unicode as the default coding format for the character set. The Unicode standard assigns all the characters from all known alphabets, a number; and by doing so, is able to reproduce texts in any language. [2]

If it is important for the process to specify the language in which a document is created, the xml:lang attribute can be used XML-wide. The newer feeds make use of this option.

Extensibility and Namespaces

Extensibility is one of the key aims of XML; the acronym XML doesn't stand for "Extensible Markup Language" without a good reason. First of all, XML is extensible in that every user can define new element types and attributes, whereas a format like HTML determines the scope of the language.

---

[2] In order to present Unicode texts, the characters have to be coded, then, the numbers that are determined by the Unicode standard are designated a certain string of bits. All XML applications have to support UTF-8 coding. UTF-8 assigns one byte to the first 128 characters, and two or more bytes to the following characters. In the coding of Latin letters, UTF-8 doesn't differ from the more popular ASCII coding. XML applications assume that an XML document is coded according to UFT-8, if the XML notification at the beginning of the document doesn't state a different coding format.

The developers of all the RSS versions used this feature of XML to define element types like `rss` (the document or root element of an RSS document), `channel`, and `item`.

However, elements and attributes won't be defined freely any more, if vocabularies like RSS 1.0, RSS 2.0, and Atom are determined and standardized for certain tasks. The formulated and consequently stipulated rules for such vocabularies—in the form of a DTD (Document Type Definition) or a Relax NG or XML schema—allow only certain elements and attributes with determined identifiers in a determined hierarchical order.

The regulation of the content that is permitted for the elements (content models) can nevertheless at the same time, allow embedding elements of other vocabularies in certain locations of a document. This is fundamental for feed formats, in order to allow the inclusion of sections that are formulated in XHTML in a document.

In order to extend documents created in such a vocabulary by adding elements from other vocabularies, a method called the **namespace mechanism** was developed. All the feed formats described in this book use this mechanism. You need to understand it in order to be able to work productively with these vocabularies. The appendix contains a short introduction to the namespace mechanism (see appendix, section A.3).

1.6 Feed Formats and other XML Formats

Syndication Formats are not News Formats

A comparison of news-specific formats used by news agencies and commercial publishing houses shows that RSS simply can't be called a news format. The combination NITF/NewsML is increasingly establishing itself there. NITF stands for "News Industry Text Format". NITF is an XML dialect to identify the components of news content, such as headlines, introductory texts, and names of people and organizations (`http://www.nitf.org`). NewsML which stands for News Markup Language, is a format for the "wrapper" of news, with information about release dates, the legal situation, etc. (`http://www.newsml.org/pages/index.php`). NewsML and NITF are based on the model of news in a journalistic sense. For feed formats, these semantics don't play an important role; their semantics are considerably more abstract.

NewsML and NITF are neither formats for information about the state of a—modifiable—web resource, nor formats for feeds, that is, for documents that summarize different information objects. RSS differs from NewsML and NITF in that all RSS messages refer to resources on the Web, which are identifiable through a URI. It is characteristic for an RSS document to be linked to a complete resource and that the individual information objects may or may not contain links as well.

Essentially, an RSS document is nothing more than a simple, two-level hierarchy of links that are provided with a title and a description. This pattern is so general that it refers to every resource on the Web that is identifiable, that is: which has a URI, which has components that can be labeled, and which changes with time.

Distinction of Message Formats

RSS can also be distinguished from those message formats that have been developed for the purpose of machine-readable data recently. Well-known formats of this kind are XML-RPC and SOAP. These formats mainly serve to exchange Web data that is normally seen by no one. XML-RPC addresses functions of program operation on distant computers (See `http://www.xmlrpc.com/spec/`). SOAP is a format for enveloping any complex message, for example, documents that are exchanged in e-business processes. For example, SOAP serves as a format for covering ebXML messages. (See `http://xml.coverpages.org/ebXML.html` and `http://webservices.xml.com/pub/a/ws/2001/04/04/ebXML.html`.)

Surely it is no coincidence that the American developer Dave Winer significantly influenced RSS as well as XML-RPC and SOAP. These three XML vocabularies are formats for messaging on the Web. They both don't need any exchange technology other than the HTTP protocol; SOAP and XML-RPC, as well, can be called end-to-end technologies. For Winer, especially, XML-RPC and SOAP are complementary to RSS in creating complete publication solutions.

RSS is a format for documents that are accessed by people, whereas SOAP is a format for data that is to be processed by machines. Due to their extensibility, all new RSS versions can in fact be used as envelopes for data. At the same time, the semantics of RSS remain: the messages inform about the state of a web resource that can be modeled as a collection of similarly structured information objects.

1.7 The Versions of RSS and Atom: Their Evolution and the Future

If I use the term "RSS" in this book without the version number, it acts as a collective term for "the different RSS versions and Atom" as a group, that is, as a synonym for "feed format". If I only talk about one of these formats, I use "RSS" with a version number, or the name "Atom."

In an ideal world, this book would just be an essay that describes a format for the syndication of content, which is easy to use and explain. In fact—apart from the various predecessors—we are dealing with at least three and a half newer formats, which were developed as alternatives for each other, namely, RSS 1.0 and RSS 1.1 (an RSS 1.0 update), RSS 2.0, and Atom.

Many websites still offer feeds in the predecessor formats of RSS 2.0; these feeds have version numbers 0.91, 0.92, and 0.93. In this book, I describe them along with RSS 2.0. The development and discussion of these formats isn't over; it is frequently discussed in a passionate and fierce manner. After all, because it concerns a key area of the Web's future development, it also involves influence and money.

Almost all RSS applications can process every, or at least the relevant, form of RSS feeds. The most important reason for this is the fact that the semantic models, which are the basis for the different syndication formats, overlap for the most part. In addition, documents in the syndication formats have a flat structure; they don't involve any deep and complex hierarchies. (Where do deeper hierarchies happen?—for example with quoted HTML markup—applications can usually leave the processing to an HTML Rendering Engine.)

The following table includes data in respect of the most important feed and news formats. With this, I follow:

- Dave Winer: *RSS History*,
  `http://blogs.law.harvard.edu/tech/rssVersionHistory`;
  Mark Pilgrim: *The myth of RSS compatibility*,
  `http://diveintomark.org/archives/2004/02/04/incompatible-rss`;

- Sam Ruby: *Really Simple Syndication*,
  `http://www.intertwingly.net/stories/2002/09/02/reallySimpleSynd ication.html`;

- Edd Dumbill: *XML in News Syndication*, `http://webservices.xml.com/pub/a/ws/2000/07/17/syndication/newsindustry.html`, and the news section on XMLNews.org, `http://www.xmlnews.org/`.

Name	Publication Date	Author	URI of the Specification
MCF (Meta Content Format)	1995	R. V. Guha/ Apple Computers	`http://www.xspace.net/hotsauce/mcf.html`
CDF (Channel Definition Format)	9 Mar 1997	Castedo Ellerman/ Microsoft	`http://msdn.microsoft.com/workshop/delivery/cdf/reference/CDF.asp` (Suggestion for W3C-Standard: `http://www.w3.org/TR/NOTE-CDFsubmit.html`)

Name	Publication Date	Author	URI of the Specification
Meta Content Format Using XML	6 Jun 1997	R. V. Guha/ Netscape Tim Bray/Textuality	`http://www.w3.org/TR/NOTE-MCF-XML/` and `http://www.textuality.com/mcf/NOTE-MCF-XML.html`
Scripting News	27 Dec 1997	Dave Winer/ UserLand	`http://davenet.scripting.com/1997/12/15/scriptingNewsInXML`
ICE (Information and Content Exchange Protocol) 1.0 Note a	26 Oct 1998	Neil Webber/ Vignette et al.	`http://www.w3.org/TR/1998/NOTE-ice-19981026`
RSS 0.90	15 Mar 1999	Netscape	`http://www.purplepages.ie/RSS/netscape/rss0.90.html` (Previously found at: `http://my.netscape.com/publish/help/quickstart.html`)
XMLNews Meta Tech Spec.(N.b)	5 Apr 1999, 1 Dec 1999	David Megginson	`http://www.xmlnews.org/docs/story-spec.html`; and `http://www.xmlnews.org/docs/meta-spec.html`
Scripting News 2.0b1	15 Jun 1999	Dave Winer/ UserLand	`http://my.userland.com/stories/storyReader$11`
RSS 0.91	10 Jul 1999	Dan Libby, Netscape	`http://my.netscape.com/publish/formats/rss-spec-0.91.html`
RSS 0.91 (UserLand-Version)	6 Apr 2000	Dan Libby/ Netscape Dave Winer/ UserLand	`http://backend.userland.com/rss091`
ICE 1.1	1 Jul 2000	Jay Brodsky/ Tribune Media Services et al.	`http://www.icestandard.org/Spec/SPEC-ICE1.1.htm`
RSS 1.0	14 Aug 2000	Rael Dornfest/ O'Reilly et al.	`http://web.resource.org/rss/1.0/`

Name	Publication Date	Author	URI of the Specification
OPML (Outline Processor Markup Language)	15 Sep 2000	Dave Winer/ UserLand	`http://www.opml.org/spec`
NITF 2.7 Note c	20 Sep 2000	International Press Telecommunications Council	`http://www.nitf.org/IPTC /NITF/2.5/dtd/ nitf-2-5.dtd`
NewsML 1.05 Note d	11 Oct 2000	Daniel Rivers-Moore/ RivCom et al.	`http://www.newsml.org/IP TC/NewsML/1.0/specificat ion/NewsML_1.0-spec-functionalspec_5.html`
RSS 0.92	25 Dec 2000	Dave Winer/ UserLand	`http://backend.userland. com/rss092`
PRISM (Publishing Requirements for Industry Standard Metadata) 1.0 Note e	9 Apr 2001	Donald Alameda/ Sothebys et al.	`http://www.prismstandard. org/specifications/PRISM1 %5B1%5D.0.pdf`
RSS 0.93 (draft)	20 Apr 2001	Dave Winer/ UserLand	`http://backend.userland. com/rss093`
NITF 3.0	12 Oct 2001	International Press Telecommunications Council	`http://www.nitf.org/IPTC/ NITF/3.0/dtd/nitf-3-0.dtd`
PRISM 1.1	19 Feb 2002	Donald Alameda/ Sothebys et al.	`http://www.prismstandard .org/specifications/PRIS M1%5B1%5D.1.pdf`
NITF 3.1	4 Jul 2002	International Press Telecommunications Council	`http://www.nitf.org/IPTC/ NITF/3.1/dtd/nitf-3-1.dtd`

Name	Publication Date	Author	URI of the Specification
RSS 3.0 Note f	6 Sep 2002	Aaron Swartz	`http://www.aaronsw.com/2002/rss30`
RSS 2.0	18 Sep 2002	Dave Winer	`http://blogs.law.harvard.edu/tech/rss`
NewsML 1.1	October 2002	Daniel Rivers-Moore/ RivCom et al.	`http://www.newsml.org/IPTC/NewsML/1.1/specification/NewsML_1.1-spec-functionalspec_6.html`
NewsML 1.2	October 2003	Daniel Rivers-Moore/ RivCom et al.	`http://www.newsml.org/IPTC/NewsML/1.2/specification/NewsML_1.2-spec-functionalspec_7.html`
PRISM 1.2	12 Mar 2004	Donald Alameda/ Sothebys et al.	`http://www.prismstandard.org/specifications/Prism1%5B1%5D.2.pdf`; or `http://www.prismstandard.org/specifications/1.2/modularized/index.asp`
ICE 2.0	1 Aug 2004	Jay Brodsky/ Tribune Media Services et al.	`http://www.icestandard.org/specification/`
RSS 1.1 (draft)	23 Jan 2005	Sean B. Palmer, Christopher Schmidt	`http://inamidst.com/rss1.1/`
Atom 0.4 (draft)	18 Apr 2005	Mark Nottingham, Richard Sayre et al.	`http://www.ietf.org/internet-drafts/draft-ietf-atompub-format-08.txt`
Atom 1.1 (spec.)	15 Aug 2005	Mark Nottingham, Richard Sayre et al.	`http://www.ietf.org/internet-drafts/draft-ietf-atompub-format-11.txt`

Notes for the table:

1. ICE is an industry standard for the automatic exchange of content. You can find more information on the ICE website `http://www.icestandard.org/`, and on the Cover Pages at `http://www.oasis-open.org/cover/ice.html`.

2. David Megginson defined XMLNews as a format for news content and metadata. The content format is a subset of NITF; the metadata format uses RDF. You can find more information on the XMLNews homepage `http://www.xmlnews.org`, and on the Cover Pages at `http://xml.coverpages.org/xmlnewsORG.html`.

3. NITF is used in the news business as the format for news items content on a large scale. You can find more information on the NITF website at `http://www.nitf.org/` and on the Cover Pages at `http://xml.coverpages.org/nitf.html`.

4. NewsML is a format used for exchanging news in text and multimedia formats; it can be used together with NITF. You can find information on the NewsML website `http://www.newsml.org/pages/index.php` and on the Cover Pages at `http://www.oasis-open.org/cover/newsML.html`.

5. PRISM is an industry standard for the exchange of metadata between commercial content providers. You can find information on the PRISM website at `http://www.prismstandard.org/` and on the Cover Pages at `http://xml.coverpages.org/prism.html`. There is also an RSS 1.0 extension module available for the PRISM metadata vocabulary: `http://www.prismstandard.org/resources/mod_prism.html`.

6. RSS 3.0 is a text format for newsfeeds with no serious intention behind it. You can find information on the website `http://www.aaronsw.com/weblog/000574`.

In this book I discuss only the following three families of formats:

- RSS 2.0 and its predecessors (RSS 0.91, RSS 0.92, and RSS 0.93)
- RSS 1.0 and RSS 1.1
- Atom

The news industry formats in the strictest sense (NITF, NewsML, ICE, and PRISM) have tasks different to that of the feed formats of the RSS and Atom family. They serve to exchange content and trade data between commercial partners. All remaining formats either didn't establish themselves or are irrelevant. This doesn't mean that they are not interesting. The appendix contains an overview of the Outline Processor Markup Language, OPML, which is used by many aggregators and newsreaders as an addition to RSS (see section A.2, *Outline Processor Markup Language*).

1.7.1 The Beginnings: MCF, Scripting News, and CDF

The disparate influences that subsequently led to the development of different RSS versions are pretty obvious in the history of the formats. A metadata format—the "Meta Content Framework" MCF—and news channel formats like the Scripting News format and Microsoft's Channel Definition Format (CDF) were the predecessors of RSS. For the description of RSS's case history, I follow primarily Ben Hammersley, *Content Syndication with RSS*, O'Reilly, 2003. In 2005, the second edition of the book was published (see bibliography).

The World Wide Web was developed as a net of texts, linked to each other. The protocols and standards to which the Web owes its astronomical rise, namely HTML and HTTP, describe how web documents are structured and how they are published, modified, and accessed. HTML doesn't take into account that many of these documents are often, and in many cases regularly, changed and updated. In the Web's infrastructure, which established itself in the first half of the 1990s, software developers and their clients were concerned with the demands posed by constant changes and updates in resources on the Web. In this manner, the first content management systems and browser add-ons, like the Netscape Sidebar and Java Applets with stock ticker messages, emerged. In the process, it became clear that common formats and protocols that support the constant updating of web resources, would simplify publishers' and users' lives and work on the Net. Such formats were developed in the mid 1990s.

Meta Content Format and Channel Definition Format

The origins of RSS reach back to at least 1995. At the time, Ramanathan V. Guha designed the Meta Content Format or MCF. Apple used the Meta Content Format in an experimental project called ProjectX, and later HotSauce. MCF makes it possible to describe sites with metadata that is found in an MCF file of its own. HotSauce presents this metadata in a format that allows three-dimensional navigation. In 1995, Guha switched over to Netscape and met Tim Bray, one of the most important developers behind the XML standard. Together they transformed MCF into an XML-based format. From this collaboration, the **Resource Description Format (RDF)** was developed—the basic technology of the Semantic Web.

Simultaneously, Microsoft, together with Pointcast and other companies, also developed an XML-based format to describe websites, which was called **Channel Definition Format (CDF)**. CDF allowed the description of content, publication plans (scheduling), logos, and metadata of a site. It was incorporated in Internet Explorer 4 and acted as the technology basis for Microsoft's so-called Active Desktop.

UserLand's Scripting News Format

Perhaps the oldest syndication format in today's sense is the Scripting News format from UserLand.com (`http://my.userland.com/stories/storyReader$11`). Dave Winer described it in December 1997 and implemented it publicly. A number of sites still offer newsfeeds in this format, in which every entry is a section with links. Winer tried to form the basic characteristics of writing on the Web, instead of offering only headlines, as in earlier RSS versions. In 1999, Winer included important elements of RSS 0.9 in version 2 of the Scripting News format.

RSS 0.9

In 1999, Netscape introduced RSS 0.9 as a format to describe information channels and aggregate content. RSS made it possible to publish snapshots of content in the portal "My Netscape". RSS soon proved to be an effective, simple XML format for the syndication of content beyond this application.

Initially, RSS channels contained only news, but soon new types of content were added. For example, RSS feeds started describing articles in discussion forums, wikis, and new software versions (`http://web.resource.org/rss/1.0/spec`).

RSS was initially an abbreviation for "RDF Site Summary". (For information about RSS as "RDF Site Summary" see Chapter 3. For a detailed explanation of the term, see section 3.1 *RDF Basics*.) With RSS, it is possible to integrate headlines from other sites with links to these sites in the portal. The user could personalize the portal and subscribe to a number of sites that offered RSS data. In this manner, My Netscape had at its disposal a great amount of additional content, which kept users on the site longer; the providers of RSS data received additional traffic—the most important goal of many websites in the times of the dot-com boom. Since it is easy to convert RSS to HTML, other sites soon started using the same technology. Slashdot soon used RSS instead of its own headline format, and tools were developed to create and process RSS in the common scripting languages.

The first desktop headline viewers were released in 1999 (Carmen's Headline Viewer; compare `http://www.xml.com/pub/r/91`; `http://www.headlineviewer.com/`; with Ben Hammersley's article in the Guardian: `http://www.guardian.co.uk/online/ story/0,3605,781838,00.html`). These applications made it possible to download RSS information and then read it without being connected to the Internet. Likewise, RSS directories like syndic8 and other aggregators were developed at about the same time.

Dan Libby developed the first version of RSS as a pure RDF application. At Netscape, however, that format was soon considered too complicated, and it was replaced by a simpler vocabulary, which was not usable RDF, but wasn't a really simple format either. Soon after, Netscape completely abandoned RDF in RSS 0.91. This decision provoked the first split in the development of the syndication formats, a split that lasts until today. One group of developers considers RSS an XML format to exchange news and other content that is updated often. The other group regards it as a metadata format, that is, an instrument to represent knowledge. The debate over whether newsfeed documents should be RDF documents at the same time isn't over yet.

In the first year of their existence alone, there were 4,000 different RSS feeds to be found on the Web. In 2002, the RSS directory syndic8 broke through the symbolic 10,000 feeds barrier.

1.7.2 RSS 0.91

Soon after, Netscape published RSS 0.91 under the name of Rich Site Summary. RSS 0.91 wasn't an RDF format anymore; it took on some elements from UserLand's Scripting News format, most importantly the description element. This allowed RSS to evolve into a format for spreading content, for which it was developed in the first place. Netscape wasn't involved in further development of the format for very long. UserLand and especially its founder, Dave Winer, successfully propagated RSS as an element of the syndication framework and soon after published version 0.91 under their own copyright. Winer is among the founders of Weblogging and also belongs among the pioneers of the "Semantic Web".

RSS 0.91 and all its subsequent versions, as well as XML-RPC and the MetaWeblog API, owe their origins to UserLand and Winer. UserLand products like the content management system Manila and the service EditThisPage.com "brought together the world of content syndication and weblogs": to use the quote given in the introduction of the RSS 1.0 specification.

An important novelty of the Netscape RSS 0.91 version compared to RSS 0.90 is the possibility of validating documents of this format against a DTD. Abandoning the RDF characteristics, which couldn't be used any more at that point, simplified the language compared to its predecessor. The abbreviation RSS now stood for Rich Site Summary or Really Simple Syndication (for more information on the XML elements see also section 2.5.1).

1.7.3 RSS 1.0

In the following years, the split came to a real head in the RSS developer community. Dave Winer's company, UserLand, controlled RSS 0.91. UserLand was above all interested in keeping the format simple and using it for personal publishing, particularly for the new publishing form of Weblogging.

Other important developers, however, among them Rael Dornfest, who was working as a chief technology officer at O'Reilly's, wanted to expand the scope of RSS to use it for other purposes and connect it with additional formats. Therefore, they reintroduced RDF and also introduced a new mechanism, the XML namespace. A related specification was published in December of 2002; the developers called the format that was described, RSS 1.0.

RSS 1.0, which is in no way just an additional RSS version, but an alternative language on its own, is more formally specified than RSS 0.91 and its successors. RSS 1.0 is defined not only as a syntax, but also as a data format. Due to its compatibility with RDF, the metadata framework of the W3C, RSS 1.0 makes the exact description of the relationship between RSS data and metadata of other RDF formats possible.

However, RSS 1.0 and RSS 2.0 don't differ much with respect to the embedding of content in other formats and the description or non-description, respectively, of the relationship between document formats and publication environments. (Chapter 3 gives a detailed description of RSS 1.0. You will find a reference of its XML elements in section A.4 in the appendix.)

1.7.4 RSS 0.92

Winer answered the publication of RSS 1.0 with RSS 0.92, within two weeks. RSS 1.0 was a modular and extensible syndication vocabulary that could be easily combined with other XML vocabularies and RDF formats. RSS 0.92, on the other hand, was an easy-to-use vocabulary whose limited features were sufficient for the needs of most users of syndication technologies.

From the users' perspective, RSS 0.92 and RSS 1.0 were compatible. Most RSS parsers could and can process documents in both formats. Parsers for the 0.9x formats, however, can't understand the RSS 1.0 extension modules, let alone extract RDF data from RSS documents.

All attempts to develop another RSS format, acceptable to representatives of both versions failed. Several RSS 1.0 fans held Dave Winer responsible for this. Not only did Winer refuse to define RSS as an RDF format or design it to be RDF compatible, but he also didn't accept the common practice of discussing a format on a mailing list in order to reach the widest possible consensus with other developers.

Instead, Winer wanted to turn weblogs into discussion forums for the further development of RSS. This procedure allowed him and UserLand to filter the articles. (For more information on the XML elements used by RSS 0.91, see section 2.5.1.)

1.7.5 RSS 0.93

RSS version 0.93, which was published by Winer a year later, already contained most of the elements that belong to today's up-to-date RSS 2.0. But RSS 0.93 doesn't have an extension mechanism. This format remains popular even today. (For more information on the XML elements used by RSS 0.93 see section 2.5.3.)

1.7.6 RSS 2.0

In September of 2002, Winer published the specification for RSS 2.0, again without making an effort to reach a consensus with those who participated in the rss-dev mailing list and helped develop RSS 1.0. (Just prior to this, he had published the same RSS 2.0 format as RSS 0.94.) At the same time, Winer declared RSS 2.0 a frozen standard; successor formats weren't supposed to be published under the name RSS any more. A little later, Winer assigned the rights of RSS to Harvard University—RSS was to be exempt from the suspicion of serving personal or business interests.

Today, RSS is the most widely used feed format. It is characteristic of this format to not specify, or to leave it to the application developers to specify: the connections between RSS data on the one hand, between other content formats, data/metadata formats, and publication environments on the other hand. Essentially, RSS 2.0 defines syntax, whereas meaning and use were determined through the use of examples. The supporters of RSS 2.0 consider this low level of specification one of the format's biggest advantages, whereas the supporters of alternate RSS versions see it as its prime weakness.

Other formats owe their existence to the fact that RSS 2.0 ignores a lot of problems. The enormous problems encountered during the formal definition of these formats are an argument for, as well as against, this strategy; an argument for it, because RSS 2.0 works in many different applications and is by far the most popular version, including its predecessor formats. The argument against it is the fact that, in practice, problems arise wherever the RSS 2.0 specification is unclear, for example, in the case of document validation. (Chapter 2 gives a detailed description of RSS 2.0. You find a reference list of the XML elements of RSS 2.0 in the appendix in section A.3.)

1.7.7 From a Syndication to a Publication Format: Atom, the New Alternative

In June of 2003, the Atom roadmap was published. (See `http://intertwingly.net/wiki/pie/RoadMap`; concerning the date: `http://virtuelvis.com/archives/2003/06/index`. Initially, the format was called "Echo" and "Pie".) The goals of this format were to be "100% vendor neutral, implemented by everybody, freely extensible by anybody, and cleanly and thoroughly specified". Previously, there had been intense debate about RSS 2.0 and the political implications of the fact that Dave Winer had control over the format. (Links for background material: `http://diveintomark.org/archives/2003/06/23/a_fresh_start`).

At that point, it was clear that "weblogging would become an industry of its own", as Mark Pilgrim put it: in the future, interoperation would require more than "calling a friend or sending an e-mail". Mark Pilgrim and Sam Ruby developed the FEED Validator, which checks the newsfeeds of almost all known feed formats with respect to standard compatibility (`http://feedvalidator.org/`). In the process, they came across deficits of the RSS 2.0 specification and its predecessors. The specification is unclear on several important points, so in some cases it can't be decided whether a document complies with it or not. Winer's attempts to stay in control seemed to be "FUD" to the group of future Atom developers. (Fear, Uncertainty, Doubt: open-source supporters like to characterize this acronym as a generic strategy—used deliberately, but often in vain—to make someone insecure.) At that time, Mark Pilgrim considered RSS 1.0 more or less a failure, or even dead, and some of the people who had backed RSS 1.0 up to that point, supported Atom from then on as a new format.

In March of 2004, Dave Winer—unsuccessfully in the end—suggested combining RSS 2.0 and Atom into one format and naming the document element `rssAtom` (`http://blogs.law.harvard.edu/crimson1/2004/03/08`). The new format would "differ from RSS as little as possible" and would be developed by an open IETF work group. The specification, which the Atom developers were promising, and the validation service could be used together. Winer's suggestion differs from the goals of the Atom developers only in the fact that he placed value on maximum backward compatibility towards older RSS versions. At that point, however, the discussion had advanced too far already, and Winer didn't participate. In fact, the Atom developers chose the IETF as the standard body. As the only feed format so far to be backed by an organization that is in part responsible for the development of the Internet, Atom has a good chance of becoming a standard.

The Atom work group followed the path of an exact syntactical specification that clearly defines the connections of Atom-specific information to other information included in the document. Atom is explicitly defined as both a syndication format and a publication format. The "Atom Publishing Protocol" will belong to the Atom standard as well, once it is completed. On the other hand, the connection with metadata formats is not the center of the Atom developers' attention. The Atom standard as such is independent of the specifications of the Resource Description Format; however, for some developers it is especially important that Atom and RDF stay compatible. (Chapter 4 gives a detailed description of Atom. You can find a reference list of the XML elements for Atom in section A.7 of the appendix.)

1.7.8 Which Format for Which Purpose?

All three—or four—up-to-date RSS versions offer the same basic functions for the user. The differences with respect to these tasks are easy to balance with modifications and extensions. The formats, however, vary notably in the amount of detail in the specifications, the processing of documents in these formats, and the additional functions they offer:

- RSS 2.0 and its predecessors were defined by referring to the latest technological implementations. The specification doesn't depend on the way RSS is treated, but—explicitly or implicitly—it refers regularly to the current practice. This is supposed to make the specification simple and easy to implement, and restricts the creativity of software developers as little as possible. (It is for this reason that it is so easy to accuse Dave Winer, one of the format's founders, of using the format definitions for personal interest or the interests of his company UserLand. It is a design principle of RSS 2.0 to abide primarily by the current practice; as a pioneer of this practice, Winer can't do anything other than to refer to his own developments.)

- RSS 1.0 and its successor RSS 1.1, on the other hand, are specified in such a way that the content of documents can be automatically processed. An RSS 1.0 or 1.1 document is nothing but a serialization of statements which follow the rules of the Resource Description Format (RDF). The format uses a semantic model that makes the formal description of the document's meaning possible. Information that is available in an RSS 1.0 or RSS 1.1 document can be easily connected with other RDF information and used together.

- Atom was defined considering the technological requirements of newsreaders and authoring systems for weblogs. (See also the site of the Atom Wiki concerning Use Cases: `http://www.intertwingly.net/wiki/pie/UseCases`.) However, in the specification the format is described abstractly and independently of how such systems are implemented. It is the goal of the Atom specification to describe the format and the rules completely and clearly for users. Software developers are supposed to be able to decide for certain what is allowed in an Atom document and how documents are exchanged between the client and the server. (This doesn't mean the importance of the language elements for a human user, that is, their social function, is clearly determined. It also doesn't mean that Atom meets its own expectations one hundred per cent. If it can't be decided in Atom and RSS 1.0 whether a certain construct in a document is possible or not, it means that there is a bug in the specification.) Another important difference between Atom and RSS 2.0 and 1.0 is the fact that Atom was also developed as a format for authoring documents. For that, the format is used in the context of the architecture of the web as described in the current specifications of the W3C.

If you read this book, you are probably using RSS yourself, or at least you will want to use it in the future. Considering the different RSS versions used on the Web, you will ask yourself sooner or later which one is right for you.

You will find here a long and a short answer to this question. The long answer is the book itself. As you will see, the advantages and disadvantages of the different syndication formats can't be summarized in just a few sentences. If it involves more than producing a simple newsfeed, several aspects have to be considered, like the existing software, the necessity to combine RSS with other vocabularies, the way of validating data, future extensibility, and the requirements that result from the use of web services.

The short answer is: users who want to use RSS only as a syndication format have to analyze what data they want to offer. The most important content elements are found in all RSS versions. Those who restrict themselves to these core elements can use any of the formats and automatically convert it into one of the other formats—either with software on their own system, or with a service that is offered on the Web, like, for example, Feedburner (`http://www.feedburner.com`).

Those who are looking for more ways to express themselves have to evaluate, which one of the versions offers the features they are looking for and is at the same time supported by software that is supposed to process the data. In respect of the possibilities of expression, the modules of RSS 1.0 are still unmatched at the present time. Anyone who wants to offer multimedia data, for example as a podcast, depends mostly on RSS 2.0 and its expansion modules. It is to be reckoned that the corresponding modules of both formats will soon be integrated in Atom as well.

2

Really Simple Syndication: RSS 2.0 and Its Predecessors

RSS 2.0 is the most popular and simplest version of the newer syndication formats. The functions of this format are the benchmark for the alternatives RSS 1.0/RSS 1.1 and Atom.

2.1 Overview

For the great majority of newsfeed providers today, RSS 2.0 is the syndication format of choice. Together with its predecessors RSS 0.91 to 0.93, it reaches a market share of about 80 percent among the RSS versions. (See also the statistical information of the newsfeed directory syndic8 at `http://www.syndic8.com/stats.php`. However, there are no reliable statistics. In addition, weblog systems as well as other tools that generate newsfeeds, frequently offer several formats at the same time.) All common aggregators and newsreaders process RSS 2.0 and its predecessors without any problems. If you want to offer a newsfeed yourself, you can be sure that the software of your potential readers can understand this format. RSS 2.0 has not been developed by a formal standards body, but the format is open and free. Dave Winer assigned his copyright of the RSS 2.0 specification to the Berkman Center of Harvard Law, which republished it under a Creative Commons license. The RSS 2.0 homepage of Harvard University is `http://blogs.law.harvard.edu/tech/`.

2.1.1 RSS 2.0: Lowest Common Denominator of the Feed Formats

The fact that few feed providers forgo RSS 2.0 isn't the only reason why I present it as the first of the common syndication formats. RSS 2.0 is well suited for an introduction into the world of syndication formats, because it forms their lowest common denominator. The common elements of the other formats mean—entirely or partially—the same as their counterparts in RSS 2.0. For all the RSS 2.0 elements, there are equivalents in RSS 1.0 and its numerous modules. In many cases you can follow the explanations of the RSS 2.0 elements to understand the language of other feed formats.

The so-called core elements of RSS 1.0 have the same name and the same function as their counterparts in RSS 2.0. The Atom work group explicitly set themselves the task of formulating equivalents for all RSS 2.0 functionalities.

2.1.2 Important New Developments: Podcasting and Further Extensions

Because RSS 2.0 is so popular, big commercial providers put products on the market that are based on this format. They not only publish RSS 2.0 feeds of their content, but also complement this vocabulary with modules that fit their new services. The year 2005 saw RSS 2.0 extensions proposed by large commercial providers: Amazon presented the OpenSearch module, which allows subscription to search results as RSS feeds. With RSS Media, Yahoo! initiated an RSS extension for the metadata of broadband offers. Microsoft will make RSS a part of its upcoming operating system Windows Vista, and has adopted OpenSearch RSS for Internet Explorer 7; Microsoft engineers have proposed the "simple list extensions" to allow the ordering of items in an RSS feed. The section on extension modules describes these new complements to the RSS 2.0 standard vocabulary.

Since 2004, the neologism "podcasting" has outstripped terms like "syndication", "newsfeeds", and even "RSS" in the media. It describes the spreading of audio and video data in an extension of an RSS entry. Podcasting makes asynchronous broadcasting possible; users download the feeds with the media to an MP3 player or some similar device and play them when they are in the mood. The procedure is named after Apple's iPod. The technical basis of podcasting will be described in *2.4 Adding Multimedia Data with enclosure*.

2.1.3 Design Principles

Primary Syndication Format

Dave Winer and his colleagues consider "RSS" the abbreviation for "Really Simple Syndication". Beginning with the UserLand version of RSS 0.91, they designed and propagated RSS as a means to syndicate news and weblog entries. Newsreaders and aggregators are the most important types of software to use this format. Winer created RSS 2.0 neither as a broad extensible metadata format like RSS 1.0, nor as a format to edit and archive newsfeeds like Atom.

Simplicity

Simplicity is the characteristic that distinguishes RSS 2.0 from RSS 1.0 as well as from Atom. Thanks to their technical simplicity, RSS 2.0 and its predecessors established themselves as a synonym of "syndication" on the Web. Anyone who is looking for the best among the available syndication methods first asks whether the advantages of the RSS 2.0 version's simplicity make up for its disadvantages.

"Literary XML"

Dave Winer, the author of the specification, talks about people who consider XML a "literary space". Winer wishes for XML documents as understandable as literature (*Two XMLs, sliced and diced*, http://essaysfromexodus.scripting.com/2003/08/03). With RSS 2.0, he created a textbook example of "XML for authors". The names of almost all RSS elements are intuitively understandable. Basic HTML skills are enough to change a text with a few tags into an RSS document. The documents have a flat structure. Attributes occur only infrequently, namespaces only in extensions. HTML markup can be integrated in the content of the describing elements, if the markup delimiters are escaped.

Flat Document Structure

The structure of an RSS 2.0 document is similar to that of an essay with an introduction and paragraphs. A simple outline with only two hierarchy levels can describe this structure. Except for rss and channel, it has only three obligatory elements: text, link, and description. Most of the metadata elements of an RSS 2.0 document describe the whole channel, that is, all entries of a feed. Data with different functions, like metadata and data items that include content, for example, aren't differentiated from one another in the document format. RSS 2.0 doesn't know recursive structures like those suggested for Atom. It also doesn't need, like RSS 1.0, namespaces of its own for frequently used element types.

Easy Extensibility

Unlike its predecessors, RSS 2.0 has mechanisms to extend the vocabulary by adding elements. Extension elements have to stem from a defined XML namespace. However, the specification doesn't say anything about the relationship between elements from other namespaces and RSS elements. An author or user can use elements from extensions in any desired location of a document. He or she has to make sure that the addressee—be it a human user or an application—can understand these data items.

In the case of RSS 1.0 and 1.1, however, the RDF data model determines how an RSS parser is supposed to correlate the elements from the different namespaces. Atom allows complements from other namespaces only in certain locations of a document and differentiates between simple and structured extensions.

Simplicity of the Specification

The RSS 2.0 specification requires only minimal technical skills of its reader. Winer doesn't go back to other XML specifications and hardly to other standards to define the format's syntax, and he doesn't make the semantic preconditions of the RSS 2.0 specification explicit. In order to explain what the individual language components mean, he uses news sites and webloggers (the common practice with RSS feeds), describes the meaning of the elements in common language, and simply gives examples. Like the British and American judicial systems, he follows precedents instead of a universally valid model.

Backward Compatibility

The effort to maintain compatibility with its predecessors (RSS 0.91, RSS 0.93; see sections 1.7 and 2.5) explains many characteristics of the RSS 2.0 design. Every RSS 0.91 document is also supposed to be a valid RSS 0.92 document, and every RSS 0.92 document is supposed to be a valid RSS 2.0 document. The additional features of the later versions are always optional; later versions mark some obligatory elements of earlier versions as optional.

Frozen Specification

In contrast to its predecessors, Dave Winer explicitly declares the RSS 2.0 specification frozen. New versions are possible only as bugfix releases (version 2.01 is current). Either modules or entirely new syndication formats with new names are to be used in order to further develop the format.

2.2 The RSS 2.0 Vocabulary

How is an RSS 2.0 document organized? The tree diagram in the following figure shows all the element types of the RSS 2.0 vocabulary. (The textinput element, which RSS 2.0 keeps only for historical reasons, isn't included.)

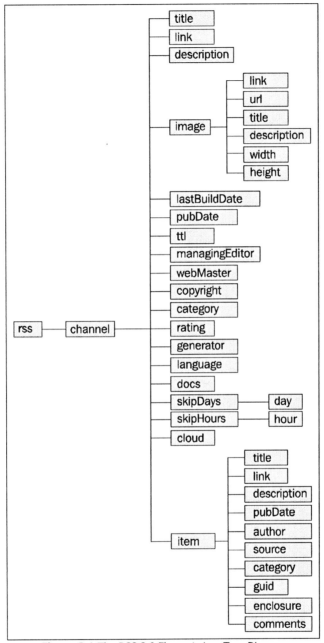

Figure 2.1 The RSS 2.0 Elements in a Tree Diagram

The diagram illustrates the main characteristics of RSS 2.0:

- The document element is called `rss`. The elements `channel` (for a feed) and `item` determine the structure of the document (for an entry in a feed).

- On both the `channel` and the `item` level, the elements `title`, `link`, and `description` play the most important role.

- Additional metadata concerning the author, the publication date, etc., can characterize `channel` and `item`.

- A `channel` can be additionally characterized by an image.

I would like to start this introduction to the organization of an RSS 2.0 document with the elements that are included in almost all RSS 2.0 documents and that determine their basic structure. After that I will continue with the presentation of the different kinds of metadata and their formats. Finally, I'll discuss the `enclosure` element, through which RSS turns into a publication format for multimedia content.

2.2.1 Basic Structure of an RSS 2.0 Document

The following document example includes only those elements that no feed in this format can omit.

```
<?xml version="1.0"?>
<rss version="2.0">
   <channel>
      <title>Webtrends</title>
      <link>http://www.celawi.eu/webtrends.html</link>
      <description>News about commercial websites and
            online advertising</description>
      <item>
      <title>Ask Jeeves now in Spain</title>
      <link>http://www.celawi.eu/webtrends/20040415_01.html</link>
      <description> On 5 April, Ask Jeeves started with the beta
            version of a new search service for Spain. It is the
            first of several starts planned in Europe this year.
            At the moment, there are no commercials on the result
            pages of Ask Jeeves España yet.</description>
      </item>
      <item>
      <title>Bitkom study: Paid content successful in Germany</title>
      <link>http://www.celawi.eu/webtrends/20040415_02.html</link>
      <description> Online content available for a charge becomes more
            and more accepted: "The times of the free-of-charge
            culture come to an end. At the same time the quality of
            the offers increases," says the executive director of
            Bitkom, Bernhard Rohleder.</description>
      </item>
   </channel>
</rss>
```

Listing 2.1 Simple RSS Document

Figures 1.1 to 1.3 show how this document is reproduced in offline and online newsreaders.

The document has a very simple and straightforward structure. The names within the tags often explain the meaning of the elements. The figure that follows shows this structure in a tree diagram.

Six elements belong to the core of RSS 2.0: rss, channel, item, link, title, and description. Three of these elements determine the structure of the document; the other three form its content.

You have already heard about the elements channel, item, link, title, and description in the first chapter; they accomplish tasks that are essential for any kind of syndication. Due to these elements, a newsfeed works like a snapshot of the current state of a resource on the Web. In addition, they allow for different newsfeeds to be combined, that is, to be "aggregated". The other syndication formats have language tools that correspond to these RSS 2.0 elements in their meaning. In RSS 1.0, these elements have the same names as those in RSS 1.1; Atom has the element types feed and entry instead of channel and item.

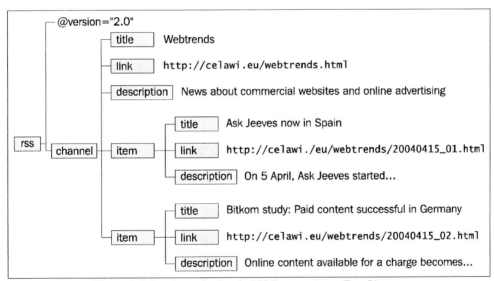

Figure 2.2 Structure of a Simple RSS Document as a Tree Diagram

- **Structural Elements of the RSS Document**

  RSS has three structural elements, namely, rss, channel, and item. The entire content of the document is allocated to either the whole channel or one element with the name item. The term channel suggests that the content of an RSS document is similar to a news or broadcast channel. An item stands for any information object that is included in such a channel. The document element rss is the ancestor of the channel element in the hierarchy and also has the version attribute.

- **Descriptive Elements of the RSS Document**

  The rest of the RSS 2.0 elements describe either the whole channel or the individual item elements. These descriptive elements are ranked successively without identifiable order. The example shows that in the process some elements can repeat themselves on both levels. The elements title, link, and description belong to channel as well as to the individual item elements.

XML Declaration and Specification of the RSS Version: Definition of the Language

The document starts with an XML declaration. The XML declaration is not obligatory with XML documents, but it is recommended. As with almost all existing XML documents, version 1.0 is used. (In the meantime, an XML version 1.1 has been released, which differs only minimally from version 1.0.) The RSS 2.0 specification demands that an RSS document complies with the rules of the XML 1.0 specification.

The rss Element (Document Element)

Like every XML document, the RSS document has a root or document element; this element is called rss. The root element merely informs the processing software that its content includes RSS information. The value of the version attribute expresses which version of RSS is in use. In this way, the RSS processor learns that the content of the element follows the rules of the RSS 2.0 specification.

For its own elements, RSS 2.0 ignores one of the most important XML specifications, namely, XML namespaces (*Namespaces in XML*: http://www.w3.org/TR/REC-xml-names/). For RSS 2.0 as with its predecessors, no namespace is specified. However, extensions are possible with the help of the namespace mechanism. (For more information on rss see also section A.3.1 in the appendix.)

The Structure of an RSS 2.0 Document Through the channel and item Elements

The channel and item elements have three functions:

- They structure an RSS document.
- They represent a web resource as a whole (channel) or as its parts (item), respectively (the parts normally being web resources themselves).
- They are containers for the description of the characteristics of the resource and its parts.

Every RSS document describes an individual channel, which can consist of any number of item elements. A channel element is a container for elements that describe the resource as a whole. It is left to the author how many item elements are descendants of channel. Documents that contain no item element at all are also possible.

As you could see in the example, the channel element is always embedded in an rss element. Basically, the channel element doesn't contain any information beyond the rss element. Other elements don't represent the language type on the one hand, and the feed as a whole on the other in two different elements, because they can specify with a namespace attribute in the document element which vocabulary they use. In Atom, for example, the root document is called feed.

Further structuring levels are neither necessary nor possible. The order of the elements below the containers channel or item isn't regulated.

All descendants of channel except item describe characteristics of the feed; all sub-elements of item describe characteristics of the individual entries. The English element name almost always explains the information it is concerned with.

RSS 2.0 allocates many more possible sub-elements to a channel than to an item. channel and item have in common not only the obligatory sub-elements for a channel, namely, title, link, and description, but also the elements category and pubDate.

The elements author, comments, enclosure, guid, and source refer only to an item. The elements language, copyright, managingEditor, webMaster, lastBuildDate, docs, cloud, ttl, image, rating, textInput, skipHours, and skipDays occur only as descendants of the channel element. (For more information about channel see also section A.3.2 in the appendix.)

The item Element

When explaining the function of the item element, the RSS specification is vague. The individual item can refer to an existing information object, or can serve to publish an object in the first place that does not exist beforehand. The specification says that an item can either contain the description of a "story" or be self-contained. In the former case, Dave Winer talks about a story similar to that in a newspaper or a magazine. Here, the description is an abstract and link points to the complete version. In the latter case, the description contains the complete text, so that the link and the title are not needed. As a consequence, RSS 2.0 knows only optional descendants of item; however, every element of this type either has to have a child with the name title or one with the name description. (For more information about item see also section A.3.4 in the appendix.)

2.2.2 Basic Information of an RSS 2.0 Document: title, link, and description

channel must always include the elements title, link, and description. These obligatory descendants of channel are the minimal elements required in order to characterize the collection of information as a whole: the URI of the resource, its name, and a short description.

As you have already learned above, on the `item` level only `title` and `link` or `description` are necessary. The elements `title`, `link`, and `description`, however, mean the same on both the level of the `channel` and the level of the `item`.

The title of the individual message, that is, the content of the `title` element as a descendant of `item`, corresponds in most cases with the sub-headline in an HTML version, which can be marked, for example, as an h2 or h3 element.

The RSS 2.0 specification characterizes the content of the element `title` as follows: "The name of the channel. It's how people refer to your service. If you have an HTML website that contains the same information as your RSS file, the title of your channel should be the same as the title of your website." The explanation in the specification can be interpreted as follows:

"If an HTML document exists under the URI that is specified in the `link` element of the RSS document, the content of the `title` element of the RSS document and the `title` element in the HTML head are to be consistent."

However, this specification is an interpretation; the specification itself is vague here, as in many areas. In common speech, "title" can also be understood as the title of a website, which isn't always identical with the content of the HTML `title` element.

Usually, feed readers and aggregators use the URI that is specified in `link` to create a hyperlink for the respective document.

Feed readers use the title as the headline of the respective channel. If an `item` is quoted in a different `channel`, the `title` of the original `channel` identifies the resource it stems from.

`description` is one of the obligatory elements to characterize a `channel`. The specification defines it vaguely as a "phrase or sentence describing the channel", that is, a short description of the channel.

Consequently, the `description` gives brief information about a feed or a channel (analogous to a `meta` element with the attribute `description` in the head of an HTML document). This information can be presented in a feed reader, but often stays hidden. The information appears in the NetNewsWire reader in a slide-out window to help choose channels. Otherwise you have to specifically click on "information" in the context menu to get this information. In Bloglines, the content of `description` is presented above the individual entries. On the channel level, `description` clearly has a "meta function": it collects information about other information, namely, the channel. On the `item` level it is different: here also, `description` can serve to briefly describe the content of the `item`. However, it is also possible that `description` holds the content of the `item` entirely or partially. Atom, on the other hand, has on the level of the individual entry two elements called `summary` and `content`, and on the level of the feed an element called `subtitle`. (For more information about `title` see also section A.3.3 on in the appendix. Information about `description` can be found in section A.3.6.)

The link Element

The third obligatory element below `channel` is called `link`. As you have seen in the introductory chapter, this element makes it possible to interpret an RSS document as a description of another document. Within `item`, `link` is optional.

The specification establishes that `link` is to hold the URI of the HTML website that corresponds to the `channel`. With this, the specification assumes that the channel is always allocated to an HTML site. The examples that are given for the `link` element as a descendant of `item` also refer to HTML documents. An RSS `channel` as a whole and the individual `item` refer to an HTML document or its fragments.

link as Sub-Element of channel and of item

Dave Winer identifies the content of `link` as being the URL of the HTML site to which an RSS channel refers, and the content of a `link` that belongs to an `item` as being the "URL of the `item`".

This connection clearly indicates that the URL of the `item` means the URL of the "full story" that is described in the `item` element. If the complete story is included in the `description` of the `item`, the `link` element, as well as the `title` element, can be omitted on this level. (For more information about `link` see section A.3.5 in the appendix.)

2.2.3 Text or HTML as the Content of title and description

One of the basic problems of the RSS 2.0 format is connected with the two elements `title` and `description`: the specification doesn't clearly regulate whether and how markup can be used as content of these elements. Finding a solution for this problem became one of the motives for the formulation of Atom later on.

The question of how HTML markup is to be treated within an RSS document comes up because RSS has turned from a syndication format into a publication format. In the first years of RSS only pure text occurred within the elements. However, it soon became acceptable to use text with HTML markup for the titles and descriptions of `item` elements. (In some cases, this markup wasn't protected by entity references, which is absolutely necessary with XML.) This is the only possible way to include the entire content of an HTML fragment in an RSS document. Aggregators and feed readers can then decode the information back to HTML and interpret it with technologies known to the browsers. In the specification of RSS 2.0, Dave Winer doesn't clearly state which kinds of data should make up the content of these elements. It is just explicitly permitted to use "entity-coded HTML" within `description`.

HTML as Content of RSS is Illegal

One technique, to use RSS with HTML markup, is incompatible with the rules of XML in any case: it is not allowed to simply insert HTML in the RSS elements. Standard-compliant HTML is not well-formed XML, unless it is XHTML. In contrast to HTML elements, XML elements have to be closed with an end tag. The capitalization of identifiers is relevant. The common "abbreviated" writing of attributes possible here and there in HTML by omitting the attribute value is forbidden, and the attribute value has to appear in quotation marks. HTML contradicts these and other XML rules. If an XML processor works correctly, it reacts to a document that contains such markup with an error message and cancels the processing.

Escaping Markup

Markup that doesn't comply with the rules has to be "protected" or "escaped," in which case an XML parser interprets the characters that usually limit markup—the markup delimiters—as normal text content. This effect can be achieved with two techniques:

- It is possible to declare an entire section of text as a CDATA section. The characters <, >, &, and ; that otherwise delimit markup are simply understood as character data (CDATA). Thus, there is only information about characters in the info set, which the parser extracts from the XML document. A CDATA section begins with the character string <![CDATA[and ends with the character string]]>.

- Individual characters can be masked using entity references. An entity reference is a reference to an abbreviation that represents a character. The character <, for example, is reproduced by the entity reference < and the character & by &.

The two examples that follow show how HTML markup can be inserted in an RSS document with these techniques. In the first case a CDATA section is used, whereas in the second case entity references are used for individual characters:

```
<item>
...
    <description><![CDATA[Online content available for a charge
becomes more and more accepted: <blockquote> The times of the free-
of-charge culture come to an end. At the same time the quality of the
offers increases,</blockquote> says the executive director of Bitkom,
Bernhard Rohleder...]]></description>
</item>
<item>
...
    <description> Online content available for a charge becomes more
and more accepted: &lt;blockquote&gt; The times of the free-of-charge
culture come to an end. At the same time the quality of the offers
increases,&lt;/blockquote&gt; says the executive director of Bitkom,
Bernhard Rohleder...</description>
</item>
```

The following screenshot shows how these examples are reproduced in the newsreader FeedDemon:

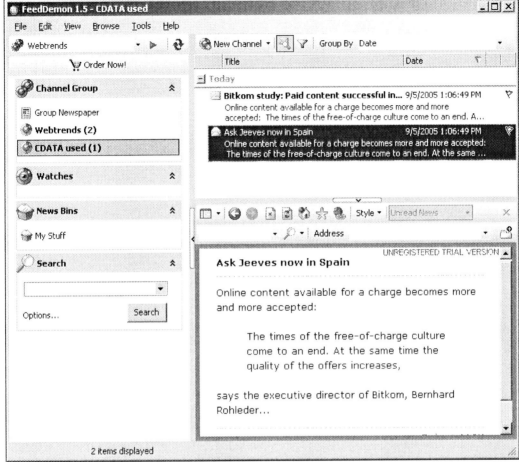

Figure 2.3 Reproduction of escaped HTML markup within the description element

All common newsreaders and aggregators support this method to embed HTML markup in a `title` or `description` element. They don't have to specify which version of HTML or XHTML, respectively, they use. (Since RSS is extensible through namespaces, it should be possible to use XHTML with the right namespace identifier within the `description` element. Newsreaders and validators, however, don't support this method.) The RSS specification allows only entity-coded HTML markup in its text, but in the attached examples it accepts CDATA sections as well. This differentiation is not necessary if one proceeds from the rules for the correct processing of XML, which were established by the W3 consortium. The parser extracts from a well-formed document the info set that includes information about which kinds of characters are to be found where in the content of the elements. Whether this information is produced by CDATA sections or by entity references is irrelevant; the processing software "doesn't notice it".

"Escaped Markup Considered Harmful" (Norman Walsh)

Using protected markup to enable the software that processes the feed to reproduce it as HTML results in syntactically correct XML; however, this process doesn't comply with the rules for this format. It is expected, after all, that the character string with the escaped markup delimiters be interpreted as HTML markup rather than as a character string. This procedure is considered a "hack" that encourages developers to program software that breaks the basic rules for processing XML.

This practice has rightly been criticized again and again, most clearly by Norman Walsh (`http://www.xml.com/pub/a/2003/08/20/embedded.html`); if these examples set a precedent, it would be superfluous to create a standard for markup languages with XML that can be used everywhere on the Web.

If markup is quoted within the HTML document, that is, it is already masked in the "decoded" HTML content, there is no rule for the processing software on how to deal with the respective passages. In practice this problem is solved through double escaping. If the content of `description` is "`description of the element <br/>`", it is specified as follows:

```
<description>description of the element
&amp;lt;br/&amp;gt;</description>
```

If an angle bracket is quoted within a `description` element, there is no rule at all that the processor can depend on. In regards to the following element content, the processor has to "know" that no markup is meant:

```
<description> In scientific references URIs are put in angle
brackets, e.g.: &lt;http:www.example.com&gt;.</description>
```

In contrast to RSS 2.0, Atom defines in detail a method to embed HTML and XHTML in newsfeeds. (Atom too can't do completely without masked markup.)

2.3 RSS 2.0 Elements for Rich Metadata

With the core elements of RSS 2.0, a resource can be characterized only very rudimentarily. Several other RSS 2.0 elements are used to describe an entire feed and its components in detail. Only with these elements does an RSS feed become a container for rich metadata.

With the elements for metadata you can characterize a feed and its aspects from different perspectives: concerning the origin and the kind of content; the authors and rights; and the technology and publication frequency. Some elements support aggregators in downloading only new and changed information. As far as syntax is concerned, there are three groups among these elements:

- Elements that can only be descendants of `channel`: `language`, `copyright`, `managingEditor`, `webMaster`, `lastBuildDate`, `generator`, `docs`, `cloud`, `ttl`, `rating`, `skipHours`, and `skipDays`.

- Elements that can only be descendants of `item`: `comments`, `enclosure`, `guid`, and `source`.

- Elements that can appear on both levels: `pubDate` and `category`.

  The vocabulary of RSS also includes elements by means of which one can provide a feed with an image and a text input field and also describe the characteristics of these features: `image`, `textInput`, `url`, as well as the `title` and `description` elements that you already know, as descendants of `image` and `textInput`. (The `textInput` element for a text input field is a historical relict.)

In the RSS 2.0 specification, Dave Winer describes the meaning of elements that can be descendants of different elements in two different places at the same time. The semantics of `title`, `description`, `pubDate`, and `category` can differ if the ancestors are not the same. (You can find detailed information about the correct use of the elements as well as examples in the overview in the appendix.)

Definition of Date Formats in RSS 2.0

For the correct processing of RSS documents, it is of great importance *which* formats are used for the content of the different elements. Only the `title` and `description` elements contain a simple string; the remaining elements contain among other things URIs, language codes, and calendar dates. The RSS 2.0 specification usually doesn't include references for formal definitions of the formats for content. Only in regards to formats for time and date as well as for language specification are standards referred to. You have already seen that "underspecified" content formats can cause problems when we were dealing with HTML within `title` and `description`.

2.3.1 Dates: Time Specifications and Updating

Except for the title and the content of the `item` elements, no other information in a newsfeed is probably as important for the user as the date specifications. If the feed and the entries are dated, they can be automatically organized according to time. Furthermore, it is possible to display only new or changed feeds and items. Conversely, if the information about the date of an article is missing, the feed reader or user can't decide whether an item has just been published, or is already months or years old.

Besides the publication date, an update date can be relevant as well. An indicated update date allows searching specifically for updated feeds and entries. It is also possible to report if news items that a user has already read are updated.

The elements `pubDate` and `lastBuiltDate` refer to publication dates. They have been included in the RSS vocabulary since RSS 0.91. (The three elements `skipHours`, `skipDate`, and `ttl` are connected to the specific requirements of aggregators and will be dealt with separately.)

The Date Format of RSS 2.0

A peculiarity of RSS 2.0 and its predecessors is the format that specifies the date. Dates have to be formatted according to RFC 822. RFC 822 is an old standard from the early days of the Internet. The explanation for it can be found in another document (http://blogs.law.harvard.edu/tech/2004/05/16). RFC 822 is widespread because it is used for dates in e-mail traffic. Besides, it is easy for people to read. (Apart from that, this document refers almost apologetically to the fact that the decision for this format was already made in 1997. For information about the resulting problems for developers see, for example, http://weblogs.asp.net/lhunt/archive/2004/03/01/82201.aspx.)

How are Dates Created According to RFC 822?

Two examples will show what this date format looks like: Tue, 2 Feb 2005 08:15:48 +0100; Tue, 2 Feb 05 07:15:48 GMT.

The first entry is always the day of the week, which is indicated with one of the English abbreviations Mon, Tue, Wed, Thu, Fri, Sat, or Sun. It is followed by the day of the month in one or two digits, and the month, again in the English abbreviation (Jan, Feb, Mar, Apr, May, Jun, Jul, Aug, Sep, Oct, Nov, or Dec). For the year that follows next, two or four digits can be used, although four digits should be preferred. Hours, minutes, and seconds are indicated with two digits each separated by a colon. The difference from GMT can be indicated with four digits (for hours and minutes). As an alternative, a time zone can be defined (UT, GMT, EST, EDT, CST, CDT, MST, PST, or PDT). The day of the week and the seconds may be omitted.

The pubDate Element

The author is to decide which date will be indicated within pubDate. In its function, pubDate corresponds to the publication date that is mentioned in a printed edition, or noted with a signature. Updates or different versions of a feed or an entry should differ from this date. A publication date can be indicated for an entire feed document as well as for individual news. If an item element lacks the pubDate, the publication date of the whole channel applies.

The specification points out that the publication date of news articles of the New York Times, for example, changes every 24 hours. Consequently, pubDate doesn't record the actual original date of a feed. The publication date of a channel or item isn't always the same as the date that the user sees. It is quite possible that the feed reader has converted it according to the system time of the user's computer. (For that purpose it is necessary that the time zone of the date be correctly indicated in the RSS feed.) Often, the feed reader simply shows the date on which the information object was downloaded for the first time.

The specification explicitly allows for the publication date to indicate a future point of time. A date that refers to the future was intended to display the respective information object only from that date on (so-called scheduled publishing).

In the following example the time zone is indicated in two different ways:

```
<channel>
<pubDate>Tue, 2 Feb 2005 08:15:48 +0100</pubDate>
  ...
  <item>
    <pubDate>Tue, 2 Feb 2005 07:15:48 GMT</pubDate>
    ...
  </item>
</channel>
```

Listing 2.2 Example of the use of pubDate

(For more information about pubDate see also section A.3.11 in the appendix.)

The lastBuildDate Element (Sub-Element of channel)

The date within lastBuildDate refers to the last version of the channel itself, that is, the document. (However, the specification isn't completely precise here either. It talks about "The last time the content of the channel changed".) It can clearly differ from the publication date, because an RSS document can describe other dated content as well.

RSS 1.0 uses the Dublin Core vocabulary for dates. With that vocabulary, a distinction can't be made between the publication date and the date of the last version—however, the time of the feed's creation should be identifiable through the HTTP header. The format of the date string corresponds with the ISO standard ISO 8601 http://www.w3.org/TR/NOTE-datetime. Because RSS 2.0 allows extension through namespaces, it is possible to use the Dublin Core date element instead of the RSS 2.0 date element in an RSS 2.0 document. (See also Mark Pilgrim: *History of RSS Date Formats*, http://diveintomark.org/archives/2003/06/21/history_of_rss_date_formats. For more information about lastBuildDate see also section A.3.12 in the appendix.)

Generated Time Information

Implicit time information is part of every feed. Apart from the dates that are indicated in the document, processing software can use the point of time when it received the information. In addition, the HTTP header provides information about when a document was created and when it was modified. Since the client software often processes only that content, the times and dates that are displayed in a newsreader aren't always identical with the times and dates indicated in the feed.

2.3.2 Specification of Persons and Authors

author, managingEditor, and copyright tell the consumers of a feed about the people who are responsible and the copyright holders. In RSS 2.0, these elements are also supposed to allow contacting the author or the people in charge via e-mail.

On the channel level the responsible editor and the copyright holder(s) can be listed with managingEditor and copyright; on the item level the author can be listed with author. The specification requires an e-mail address as the content of the author and managingEditor elements. The examples in the specification show that after this the name of the author or the editor in charge can be mentioned in brackets.

The copyright Element

This element contains the copyright notice for the content of the feed. (For more information about copyright see also section A.3.8 in the appendix.)

The managingEditor Element

The content of this element is the e-mail address of the person who is responsible for the content of the feed. managingEditor and author overlap in their meaning. The author element is required only if a feed has several authors. A feed with just one author indicates the author as managingEditor. (For more information about managingEditor see also section A.3.9 in the appendix.)

Writer Specification with the author Element

The authors of an item are identified through their e-mail address too; their name can follow in brackets. (For more information about author see also section A.3.23 in the appendix.)

2.3.3 Identification and Description of the Content

The guid Element

In regards to its meaning, the guid element is related to link. It primarily serves to uniquely identify an item and, furthermore, to create a link to this item. guid makes it possible to permanently identify an individual entry. The content of guid can, but doesn't have to, differ from the content of link. In contrast to guid, link can have a short-lived reference; for example, the URI of a weblog's homepage with a fragment identifier.

guid is to include a "globally unique identifier", but it is left to the producer of the feed to make sure that the identifier is really unique. The best-known examples of such identifiers are the **permalinks** that are already provided by most weblog content management systems. A permalink is the URI under which a weblog entry is permanently archived.

The RSS specification specifically states that the content of guid doesn't have to be a URL. However, RSS processing software is to assume that it is a URL. In order to prevent this interpretation, the isPermalink attribute with the value false has to be used to indicate that a different construct is involved.

Supporters of the Atom standard heavily criticized the definition of the guid element for being imprecise. On the one hand it isn't specified how the content should be formed. Consequently, there is no binding mechanism to make sure or to check whether this element really includes a unique identifier. Much more problematic is the fact that the data type of the element is not specified, which means that a URI as well as a string can be involved. URIs and strings, however, have different identity conditions, because a URI parser can read two different character strings as the same URI.

guid is an optional element that is omitted by many RSS feeds. It doesn't exist in older versions. (For more information about guid see section A.3.26 in the appendix.)

The rating Element

The main purpose of introducing rating was to provide information on whether the content of a feed is G rated or not. In order to achieve this, it can be specified how, according to the Platform for Internet Content Selection (PICS; http://www.w3.org/PICS/), the content of the channel is to be classified. (For more information on rating see also section A.3.19 in the appendix.)

Categorization with the category Element

With this element an entry can be assigned to a category. The content of the element specifies the name of the category. Such an allocation, however, makes only limited sense if the category doesn't belong to a system of categories with known specifications, that is, a taxonomy. Within an RSS document such a system of categories can be referred to through the optional domain attribute of the category element. The value of domain is a string that clearly identifies the chosen system of categories. This string can be a URI.

The content of category is made up of a list separated by forward slashes that refers to the hierarchical location within the chosen taxonomy. An element of the type item can include any number of sub-elements of the type category. It is possible to assign an entry to various categories in the same (as well as in different) taxonomies. (For more information on category see also section A.3.13 in the appendix.)

Most weblog systems use categories to structure content. The labels of these categories are used as content of the category RSS element.

Services like Technorati, flickr, and del.icio.us are built around this element and its equivalents in other syndication formats (dc:subject and atom:category). category makes it possible to exchange tagged content and to aggregate items based on content categories. It is an easy but very effective tool to make web content searchable by semantic metadata.

Source Information with the source Element

The source element contains the name of the original channel that an item or its core information was gathered from.

This element can be best understood by considering the common practice in weblogs to quote and to redistribute messages from other blogs—the classical case of content syndication. In this case, a message with the `source` information shows where it originated from. In doing so, the text content of `source` is to be identical with the `title` content of the quoted `channel`, and not with the title of one of its `item` elements.

The `url` attribute is obligatory when using the `source` element. The value of this attribute is specified—in one of the most mysterious terms of the whole RSS 2.0 specification—as linking "to the XMLization of the source", that is, the RSS feed of the respective resource. The example of the specification, `<source url="http://static.userland.com/tomalak/links2.xml">Tomalak'sRealm</source>`, demonstrates the fact that the URI of the entire channel is meant, not the URI of the individual message—that is to say, a permalink on the message.

`source` stems from RSS 0.92 and was developed for software that is used as a weblog tool and an aggregator at the same time, that is, for programs that allow users to read weblog entries and, based on them, to post their own entries. An indication of the source is then generated with the content of `source` (`http://blogs.law.harvard.edu/crimson1/2003/05/17`). It was only later that the element `guid` was introduced. It was suggested to use the content of `guid` as a value of `source` if it is a permalink. However, `source` is clearly defined in the way that the resource title forms the content, and the value of the attribute `link` is the URI of the whole feed, not just that of an individual entry. (For more information on `source` see also section A.3.27 in the appendix.)

2.3.4 Technology

The docs element serves to describe the specific format. The content of this element refers to the documentation of the RSS 2.0 format. In addition, `generator` specifies the software that generated the feed.

The docs Element

`docs` refers to the documentation of the RSS version that created the feed. Winer thinks of the addressees as people in a distant future who no longer know what RSS actually is. (For more information on docs see also section A.3.15 in the appendix.)

The generator Element

`generator` specifies the program that generated a feed. This information can be used for statistical analysis. Above all, though, it is needed if mistakes occur in a feed. It can be determined whether the mistakes happen regularly in feeds that were created by a certain program, and the developers in charge can be informed. (For more information on generator see also section A.3.14 in the appendix.)

The webMaster Element

webMaster includes the e-mail address of the person who is in charge of all technical questions connected with the feed. (For more information on webMaster see also section A.3.10 in the appendix.)

2.3.5 Internationalization

RSS 2.0 introduces here the language element, which is used for the channel as a whole.

The language Element

A code in the content of the language element indicates in which language the channel is written. Allowed language codes are values specified by RFC 1766 (http://www.ietf.org/rfc/rfc1766.txt) or according to the list at http://blogs.law.harvard.edu/tech/stories/storyReader$15 (initially determined by Netscape). (For more information on language see also section A.3.7 in the appendix.)

2.3.6 Elements for the Support of Publication and Subscription Tools

Several RSS 2.0 elements support aggregators, the model for which was probably always the functionality of Radio UserLand. These elements make it easier to subscribe to newsfeeds. In addition, they save bandwidth through mechanisms for notification about changes.

The comments Element

comments contains the URI under which comments concerning an entry can be found. comments also only appears within item. This element demonstrates once again the desire for simplicity that is expressed in the RSS 2.0 specification. *Where* comments can be made is not indicated, nor are there language tools to subscribe to a separate feed of comments concerning an entry. (For more information on comments see also section A.3.24 in the appendix.)

2.3.7 Characterization of a Feed with an Image: The image Element

image is one of the oldest RSS elements. With image you can insert an image that can be used as a logo or icon of the feed. image has several sub-elements to indicate the URI of an image, a title, and the target to which the image is supposed to refer. In the hierarchy of an RSS document, image is on the same level as item. Like item, it has the three sub-elements title, link, and description. (For more information on image see also section A.3.18 in the appendix.)

Support for the Functions of Aggregators: cloud, ttl, textInput, skipHours and hour, skipDay, and day

textInput is a relic from the beginnings of the syndication formats. RSS 2.0 and 1.0 have been carrying it along up to today. RSS 1.1 and Atom have eliminated this element. textInput was supposed to allow the user to interact with the server from which a feed was received. The element works like a simplified HTML form. The Netscape developers included it primarily to start searches. The element has four descendants: link contains the URI of a CGI script, name correlates with the HTML attribute of the same name, description contains an explanation, and title includes the label of the submit button. (For more information on textInput see also section A.3.20 in the appendix.)

cloud is one of the few RSS 2.0 elements whose use isn't explained by its name. Originally, the element was introduced for the aggregator of Radio UserLand; RSS 2.0 generalized it. Cloud means a "cloud" of members of a community that can be informed together about content updates. It is inseparable from the rssCloud interface (sometimes called cloud API) proposed by Userland Software (http://blogs.law.harvard.edu/tech/soapMeetsRss#rsscloudInterface).

This interface reduces bandwidth consumption: It makes possible for a machine to be informed about updates of a channel without having to download the complete feed document more than once. The machine can register with the "cloud". The information needed for the registration is provided by the obligatory of cloud attributes: domain indicates the host where the registration is realized, port the port number, path the path to the procedure, registerProcedure the name of the procedure used to register the client, and protocol the protocol (allowed values are xml-rpc, soap or http-post). (For more information on cloud see also section A.3.16 in the appendix.)

ttl stands for "time to live". The element indicates in minutes for how long the feed cannot change, so that the data can be cached for this time. (For more information on ttl see also section A.3.17 in the appendix.)

skipHours tells software during which hours it should not check a feed for updates. The content of the element consists of up to 24 elements of the type hour. (More hour elements than this are not allowed in the content of skipHours.) In each of these elements a number between 0 and 23 indicates an hour during which the content of a feed doesn't change. The function of skipDays and day corresponds with those of skipHours and hour, with the exception that within day the English names of the weekdays are used to indicate days during which a feed won't be updated at all. (For more information on skipHours, hour, skipDays, and day see also section A.3.21 and A.3.22 in the appendix.)

2.4 Adding Multimedia Data with enclosure

With the RSS enclosure element, a miniature RSS success story has been repeating itself since 2004: developers discover the enormous potential that is included in simple language elements, and prototypical applications spark the interest of the market and trigger an avalanche of products and business ideas. Meanwhile, "podcasting" has established itself as the catchword for the new publication formats that are based on enclosure. The preconditions of the success story include the availability of both inexpensive broadband connections almost everywhere, and popular devices for media that are received from the Internet—first and foremost Apple's iPod, the godparent of podcasting.

Dave Winer already extended RSS in version 0.92 by adding enclosure. (Winer describes the idea of podcasting in Payloads for RSS, http://www.thetwowayweb.com/payloadsforrss.) The element serves as a container for references to audio, video, and other multimedia data within an RSS feed. By virtue of this element, RSS can be used as a format to publish digital media online in a very easy way. RSS documents can collect the data with which applications find multimedia content on the Internet, access these data, organize and present them on the user's computer, and exchange and further publish them.

If an aggregator is used to receive multimedia data, the data can be automatically downloaded at times when the computer is not in use. Feeds are subscribed to instead of "clicking and waiting". In addition, media from the same resources can be received on a regular basis. Conversely, a publisher can regularly reach the subscribers of a feed through enclosures. Consequently, enclosure allows asynchronous broadcasting for standardized software at the client end.

In the RSS vocabulary, enclosure has functions for binary data that are similar to those that description has for text data. Unlike description, an enclosure element always belongs to an item, never directly to a channel. And while description doesn't have attributes to describe the kind of content, enclosure demands the indication of the type of data that are referred to.

enclosure is always an empty element. It has three obligatory attributes:

- url: Indicates the address under which the embedded file is to be found.
- length: Indicates the size of the embedded file in bytes.
- type: Contains as its value the MIME type of the embedded file.

An item is only allowed to contain one element of the type enclosure. There were discussions about lifting this restriction. However, that would've meant that the advantages RSS offers couldn't be used any more—it wouldn't be possible to separately indicate the metadata like author and publication date for the connected data. (Dave Winer: *Multiple enclosures on RSS items?* http://www.reallysimplesyndication.com/2004/12/21#a221.)

```
<item>
   <enclosure url="http://triest.fh-joanneum.at/SDR25FEB.mp3"
     length="1024" type="audio/mpeg"/>
   ...
</item>
```

Listing 2.3 Example for the Use of the RSS enclosure Element

BitTorrent via RSS

It is also possible to receive the enclosure element through the BitTorrent protocol. (Andrew Grumet describes the easiest method in *Experimenting with BitTorrent and RSS 2.0*, http://blogs.law.harvard.edu/tech/bitTorrent.) The value of type has to be indicated as "application/x-bittorrent", and the length is the size of the .torrent file. If a complete file as well as a BitTorrent seed is offered for download, the BitTorrent extension element should be used (see also section 2.6.2).

Broadcatching

The combination of RSS and BitTorrent can also be used to receive TV or radio broadcasts via RSS on a regular basis. The end device can be a television or a multimedia PC with television functionality, which is operated by a remote control. In that case, the RSS feed works like a TV guide, and the aggregator like a program selection. This technique is frequently called "broadcatching". (For more information on enclosure see also section A.3.25 in the appendix.)

An Alternative to enclosure

For the publication of media via RSS the element enclosure is the most known, but is not the only alternative. Media RSS, an extension of RSS proposed by Yahoo in 2005, has a similar functionality but allows addition of more media-specific metadata. In section 2.6.6 you will lean more about this newcomer to the RSS family.

Apple took another approach for its iTunes software. A publisher who wants to make his podcasts available via iTunes can use the enclosure element and a set of extension elements that are specific for this software (complete list available at http://phobos.apple.com/static/iTunesRSS.html). On the W3C website you find a comparison of media RSS and Apple's iTunes extensions (http://www.w3.org/2005/07/media-and-rss.html).

2.5 The Predecessors of RSS 2.0

The UserLand version of RSS 0.91 was the first direct ancestor of RSS 2.0. Every document in one of the predecessor formats of RSS 2.0 is a valid document of the formats with higher version numbers (with certain restrictions). All documents of the RSS versions 0.91, 0.92, and 0.93 are also valid RSS 2.0 documents. From version to version, new elements were added. In the process, more and more metadata was allowed not only for a whole `channel`, but also for individual elements of the `item` type. The development of functionalities and language elements for aggregated feeds in the current syndication formats continues this tendency. In addition, restrictions such as on the maximum number of `item` elements were lifted, and obligatory elements were declared optional. RSS 2.0 is an end point of this development; restrictions concerning maximum numbers or maximum length for document content no longer exist. The number of obligatory elements has been reduced to a minimum, and extensions are only to be carried out in namespaces of their own. Therefore, it is very consistent for Winer to declare the RSS 2.0 specification "frozen".

The overview of the individual RSS elements in the appendix lists for every element the versions of the format in which it is allowed. However, you shouldn't use these outdated versions of the format!

For most programs that process RSS, the RSS versions before RSS 2.0 (except for RSS 0.90 and RSS 1.0) are compatible. There are numerous small differences, however, which were not explicitly mentioned by Winer. These differences lead to the fact that documents in these formats don't have the same XML info set and, therefore, strictly speaking, aren't compatible. Mark Pilgrim described these differences in his essay *The Myth of RSS Compatibility*: `http://diveintomark.org/archives/2004/02/04/incompatible-rss`. (For more information on the history of RSS see also sections 1.7.2, 1.7.4, 1.7.5, and 1.7.6.)

2.5.1 RSS 0.91

An RSS 0.91 document was allowed to contain a maximum of 15 elements of the `item` type. Behind that restriction was the intention to save bandwidth, and the limitation in the presentational possibilities. Also, for every `item` element, RSS 0.91 already had the `title`, `description`, and `link` elements. However, the number of `metadata` elements was restricted and only existed on the level of the whole `channel`. Here, the elements `language`, `copyright`, `managingEditor`, `webMaster`, `rating`, `pubDate`, `lastBuildDate`, and `docs` were possible.

In addition, every feed could contain an optional text input field. Feeds were always received from a URI through the pull method; the publish-and-subscribe mechanism didn't exist at the time.

Probably the most noticeable difference compared to the later RSS versions is that the number of characters in every element is limited—a regulation that generally doesn't exist in the later XML formats. 100 characters are allowed for `title`, 500 for `link`, 500 for `url`, 100 for `copyright`, 100 for `managingEditor`, 100 for `webMaster`, 500 for `rating`, and 500 for `description`. Images have a maximum size of 144*400 pixels. The size 88*31 established itself as the standard. Only `html:` and `ftp:` are allowed as schema identifiers in `link` and `url`. HTML and entity-coded HTML isn't permitted in any of the elements.

The RSS 0.91 versions of UserLand (June 2000) and Netscape (July 1999) differ from each other in some important aspects. Netscape's hour element can contain numbers from 0 to 23; UserLand's equivalent includes numbers from 1 to 24. UserLand changed the name of the textinput element to textInput. The most important difference, however, is that UserLand omitted the DTD that belonged to the Netscape specification. For that reason, 96 entities that are defined in this DTD (e.g., aulm and Aulm) can't be used in the UserLand version.

2.5.2 RSS 0.92

RSS 0.92 omitted all length limitations, and the restriction on the number of item elements was lifted as well. The child elements of item became optional, and so did the language element. Important elements like source, enclosure, category, and cloud were added, and for the first time it was possible to provide metadata for individual item elements. Also for the first time, cloud allowed an optional publish-and-subscribe mechanism.

In the RSS 0.92 specification (December 2000), UserLand changed the content model of the description element. From then on it was possible to use masked markup, so that it can't be decided whether a masked less-than character is to be understood as a markup delimiter belonging to HTML or not.

2.5.3 RSS 0.93 and 0.94

Winer published RSS 0.93 to discuss several changes, but he never declared it a specification. (Some newsfeed providers used it anyway.) In RSS 0.93, an item element can contain several elements of the enclosure type. pubDate was introduced as an optional sub-element of item to indicate the point of time when content can be accessed. Furthermore, an additional element, expirationDate, was suggested for expiration dates of entries.

RSS 0.94 didn't become an official format either. Winer simply relabeled it RSS 2.0 with very minor modifications shortly after its publication. In the process he withdrew an interesting change. RSS 0.94 contained a type attribute for the description element. Its value was the identifier of the media type for the content; the default value was text/html.

description and description type="text/html" have the same meaning as description in the RSS versions 0.92 and 0.93; description type="text/plain" corresponds with description in RSS 0.91, which is missing in the later versions.

2.5.4 Differences Between RSS 2.0 and the Earlier Versions

The biggest difference of the versions 0.91 to 0.93 compared to RSS 2.0 is that it was impossible to extend the language through modules in their own namespaces. Besides, there were some elements missing, like generator and ttl on the level of the channel, and comments, author, pubDate, and guid on the item level.

Once more, the differences of the three RSS versions 0.91, 0.92, and 0.93 clearly demonstrate that RSS 2.0 developed in direct connection with the practical use of the syndication formats.

By the way, in version 2.0 of September 2002, the `rating` element, which had belonged to the language space since the two RSS 0.91 versions, was omitted. Moreover, Winer removed the `type` attribute as part of `description` to keep the vocabulary as simple as possible.

In the revised version of RSS 2.0, which was published in November as the specification of RSS 2.01, the content of `hour` was changed again. Once again, as in the Netscape version of RSS 0.91, only values between 0 and 23 were allowed. In January, the `rating` element was reintroduced into the already published specification.

2.6 Extension Modules

In contrast to its predecessors from the RSS 0.9x family, RSS 2.0 can be extended through modules. A module consists of XML elements that can perform additional functions. The elements of a module have to belong to their own defined XML namespace.

With the namespace mechanism, RSS 2.0 uses a technique that was introduced at an early stage of the development of XML to extend and to combine XML vocabularies. If you are not familiar with the namespace mechanism, you can learn as much about it as is necessary to read on from the appendix (see section A.1).

Modularization and extensibility are also characteristic of the other two syndication formats you see in this book: RSS 1.0 and Atom. Basically, modules that are used with RSS 2.0 can also be combined with these vocabularies. There are additional restrictions in RSS 1.0 and Atom, however, which do not apply to RSS 2.0.

For some time RSS 2.0 extension modules were used mostly by technically interested bloggers, and remained a rather esoteric feature of RSS. This changed in 2005, with OpenSearch RSS, Media RSS, and the Simple List Extensions—three extension modules proposed by Internet giants Amazon, Yahoo, and Microsoft. The companies started to promote RSS as a key component of their future offerings. It is significant that in this case these companies stick to the concept of RSS as an open, non-proprietary standard.

The vast majority of RSS 2.0 feeds do not use any extension elements In statistics about the popularity of the RSS elements, offered by Syndic8, most of them don't even appear (`http://www.syndic8.com/stats.php?Section=rss#TagUsage`).

Open Questions Concerning Extensibility

In the following chapters you will once more encounter the question of how extensions are to be interpreted by XML vocabularies. It could be formulated like this: is it possible to define general mechanisms for extensions, or is it necessary to define for every format extension individually how a target application should process the new elements? The discussions about RSS 1.0 and Atom make the problems concerning the extension of a syndication format explicit.

For now, it is sufficient to know that for many developers of other syndication standards, the namespace mechanism alone is not enough to define how a feed format can be extended.

All Non-RSS Elements Belong in a Namespace

An RSS 2.0 feed is allowed to contain elements from other vocabularies only if they belong to a defined namespace. There are no other restrictions. Extensions are only meaningful, however, if there is software to process the additional language elements.

In most cases, a prefix separated by a colon from the local name characterizes the element names that stem from an extension module. Examples are `ssr:rdf` or `dc:author`. Software that can't do anything with these element names is allowed to just ignore them. The namespace declaration tells the processor which namespace these elements belong to.

The processor allocates attributes without a prefix to the namespace of the element within which they appear. The XML namespace recommendation allows to combine attributes with a prefix with elements from other namespaces.

No Namespace for the RSS Elements Themselves

The RSS elements themselves are not allocated to a namespace—the use of namespaces would interfere with compatibility with the predecessor formats. If it were necessary for the validation of an RSS document to declare a namespace, RSS 0.91 and 0.92 documents would inevitably be invalid. Winer himself, however, suggested later experimenting with a namespace for the elements of the RSS vocabulary—but ultimately without result (Dave Winer: *Next Step in Syndication Technology*, `http://blogs.law.harvard.edu/stories /storyReader$419`; see also Sam Ruby's discussion about a namespace for RSS 2.0: *RSS Namespace Proposal*, `http://www.intertwingly.net/blog/1353.html`).

Risks for the Structure

Namespaces are used by the other syndication formats as well, although in a more restricted and explicit way than in RSS 2.0. Winer doesn't say anything in the specification about where in an RSS document extensions are allowed. Other authors like Morbus Iff (Kevin Hemenway's pseudonym; short biography: `http://www.oreillynet.com/pub/au/779`; see also `http://gamegrene.com/wiki/User:MorbusIff`) referred to the fact that extension elements that are not descendants of `channel` or `item` can change the structure of an RSS document and can lead to incorrect processing of the documents (*Extending RSS 2.0 With Namespaces*, `http://www.disobey.com/detergent/2002/extendingrss2/`).

In Regards to Extensions, Less is More

Again and again, Dave Winer has recommended using namespaces sparingly. Above all, he objects to the use of extensions where RSS 2.0 elements are sufficient (a practice he calls "funky"; `http://backend.userland.com/davesRss2PoliticalFaq#question whatDoesFunkyMeanInTheContextOfRss20`). The main interest here, again, is simplicity of the format for the user and the implementer. RSS achieves a lot, because it is a standard. Extensions that don't establish themselves widely are meaningless—with the exception of extensions that were developed for specifically defined software. Here, too, the motto "less is more" applies. Modules with few, simple, and clearly defined elements are easiest to implement and have the best chance to win recognition on a broader level. [1]

2.6.1 The blogChannel Module

Dave Winer defined the first of the extension modules himself; it is called `blogChannel`. The `blogChannel` module introduces three new elements `blogRoll`, `mySubscriptions`, and `blink`. All three are descendants of the RSS `channel` element. The URI that defines the namespace of these elements is `http://backend.userland.com/ blogChannelModule`. Under this address you will find documents that explain how the elements of the module are to be used.

The Elements of the blogChannel Module

The `blogChannel:blogRoll` element contains the URI of an OPML document with the blogroll of the weblog the feed belongs to. (OPML, or Outline Processor Markup Language, is a format for outlines. Like RSS 2.0 it was developed mostly by Dave Winer. Appendix A provides a short introduction to this format. OPML can be used for structured lists of URIs, and therefore to exchange information about subscribed feeds between applications. Many feedreaders can export and import subscription lists as OPML files.)

The `blogRoll:mysubscriptions` element contains the URI of an OPML document with the feeds the author of the weblog has subscribed to.

With the `blogChannel:blink` element—which shouldn't be taken completely seriously— the author of a weblog can advertise another weblog, the URI of which is the content of the element.

---

[1] Anyone who defines namespace URIs themselves should be aware that they end with a slash / or a hash #. RDF applications can easily use such URIs to interpret element names as unique identifiers of properties. (See the passages about the URIs of attributes in section 3.1 *RDF Basics*.)

The `blogChannel:changes` element is supposed to prevent aggregators from using too much bandwidth. The content of the element is the URI of a document called `changes.xml`. If a feed containing the `changes` element is updated, it sends a ping to the server on which the file is located. Consequently, aggregators can use this document to identify the feeds that were changed, and don't have to download all the feeds.

2.6.2 The BitTorrent Module

With the BitTorrent module (`http://www.reallysimplesyndication.com/discuss/msgReader$201?mode=topic`) the address of a BitTorrent seed can be indicated, through which data (mostly audio and video documents) that are also referred to in an enclosure element can be downloaded. The namespace for `torrent`, the only element of this module, is `http://www.reallysimplesyndication.com/bitTorrentRssModule`.

The default prefix is `bitTorrent`. The element should be used only in connection with `enclosure`, so that the remaining details within the parent `item` element refer to both. Dave Winer gives the following example (`http://static.podcatch.com/manila/gems/un/torrentRssExample.xml`).

```
...
<item>
    <title>Daily Source Code November 24 2004</title>
    <link>http://adam.opml.org/DSC20041124.mp3</link>
    <description>I finally got Patricia back on the mic to talk about
        another of her fabulous showbiz stories, today: Stevie
        Nicks.</description>
    <guid>http://radio.weblogs.com/0001014/categories/dailySourceCode/
        2004/11/24.html#a6900</guid>
    <pubDate>Wed, 24 Nov 2004 08:10:37 GMT</pubDate>
    <bitTorrent:torrent bitTorrent:url="http://torrents.podcatch.com/
        DSC20041124.mp3.torrent"/>
    <enclosure url="http://adam.opml.org/DSC20041124.mp3"
        length="16716621" type="audio/mpeg"/>
</item>
...
```

Listing 2.4 Example for the bitTorrent:torrent element

BitTorrent seeds can also be directly indicated within `enclosure`, if there is no alternative download address for the complete equivalent file (see also section 2.4).

2.6.3 The creativeCommons Module

Winer himself also developed the creativeCommons module. With the elements from this module it can be indicated on the level of the `channel` or the `item`, *which* of the different creativeCommons licenses is valid. The namespace `http://backend.userland .com/creativeCommonsRssModule` is defined for the creativeCommons module.

The module contains only one single element called `license`. If this element is used on the `item` level, it indicates only the license valid for that content. If, at the same time, a license that is valid for the whole channel is indicated, it will be overwritten for the relevant item.

The content of this element is formed by the URI of one of the Creative Commons licenses listed on the Creative Commons website (`http://creativecommons.org/`). It is specifically permitted, however, to refer to other licenses. The element can be used multiple times if a channel or element is published under more than one license.

2.6.4 The Easy News Topics Module

In recent years there have been repeated attempts to define the topics of newsfeeds more clearly and conveniently than is the case with the `category` element. (Although `category`, as well, allows the reference to a nomenclature.) Matt Mower and Paolo Valdemarin presented an interesting attempt in that direction with Easy News Topics (ENT; `http://matt.blogs.it/specs/ENT/1.0/`). The `category` element isn't sufficient for them, however, because it doesn't allow for the indicated topics to be linked to a classification. The namespace for the ENT module is `http://www.purl.org/NET/ENT/1.0/`.

This extension has two main goals:

It is supposed to facilitate indicating the topics of entries in such a way that intelligent aggregators can compile thematic feeds. For example, aggregators can filter and recombine feeds that are equipped with the ENT identifiers. All other developers who suggested extensions for topics or categories up to now pursued the same goal—with only moderate success so far, because none of the systems has been implemented to an extent worth mentioning.

In their second goal, the developers of Easy News Topics differ from other systems with similar tasks: through linking, the Easy News elements are supposed to allow the use of more powerful and flexible standards. The ENT developers assume that other modules with similar goals couldn't establish themselves because they are too complex and, for that reason, too difficult for most users.

The Elements of the Easy News Topics Module

The module defines only two elements, `cloud` and `topic`. The content of `cloud` is made up by any number of elements of the type `topic`.

The `cloud` element indicates a source for topics, and takes the form of a URI. This URI can refer to an RDF document, an OPML list, or a topic map that includes further information about the topics. ENT doesn't require the actual existence of a document under the URI. The application decides how to deal with a resource that can be found under the indicated URI. The element identifies the occurrence of a topic according to the topic map standard.

Topic maps are a standard for meta-information that overlaps in its functions with RDF. A topic map works like an index for any number of sources. The map doesn't indicate words, but terms and concepts, that is, topics. In regards to the book that you are reading right now, RSS extensions, for example, could be such a topic. A topic map is an XML document with information about where topics occur in documents. In the topic map terminology these locations are called "occurrences" of topics. Moreover, the relationship between topics is described in a topic map as well. The extensions of RSS 2.0, for example, are connected with the topic extensions in a way that can be called a subclass-superclass relation. In this way semantic nets that describe a great number of different sources can be built. (You can find more information about this highly interesting technology on the topic maps site of the Cover Pages: http://www.oasis-open.org/cover/topicMaps.html).

cloud has three attributes. The href attribute is obligatory, and the two attributes infoRef and description are optional:

Attribute	Description
href	Refers to the URI of the source of the topics.
infoRef	Can include a URI under which information about this source can be found: for example, human-readable documentation.
description	Serves the same purpose as the RSS 2.0 element with the same name, and can contain a short description of cloud, which is possibly displayed by a user agent.

In the topic element "a named representation of a subject" is indicated. The topic can be simply indicated as a character string (PCDATA). In connection with cloud, however, topic allows unique identification of the topic of the entry. The topic element also has three attributes. The id attribute, which is obligatory, and the optional attributes classification and href:

Attribute	Description
id	Has to be a fragment identifier according to the valid definition of URIs (or IRIs, their internationalized version). It can appear within the chosen cloud only once. Two topic IDs of a document are allowed to be the same, however, because they refer to their particular cloud's href. In this combination they are unique again and can be interpreted according to an XML topic map (XTM; http://www.topicmaps.org/xtm/1.0/).

Attribute	Description
classification	Contains the type of the topic. This attribute can only be used appropriately if a system that supports a classification is indicated as the cloud.
href	Holds the URI of a site that is human readable and refers to the topic.

The specification contains among others the following sample document:

```
<item>
    <title>
    <link>http://www.example.org/blog/2003/04/08.html#a855</>
    <guid>http://www.example.org/blog/2003/04/08.html#a855</guid>
    <pubDate>Tue, 08 Apr 2003 10:28:59 GMT</pubDate>
    <description>Here is the text of the item.</>
    <ent:cloud
        ent:href="http://matt.blogs.it/topics/
        resources/topicRoll.opml">
            <ent:topic
                ent:id="sf_giants">San Franscisco Giants</ent:topic>
    </ent:cloud>
    <ent:cloud ent:href="http://www.examples.com/mlb.xtm">
            <ent:topic ent:id="barry_bonds"
                ent:classification="player">Barry Bonds</ent:topic>
            <ent:topic ent:id="ray_durham"
                ent:classification="player">Ray Durham</ent:topic>
            <ent:topic ent:id="felipe_alou"
                ent:classification="manager">Felipe Alou</ent:topic>
    </ent:cloud>
</item>
```

2.6.5 The OpenSearch Module from Amazon

Amazon developed probably the most interesting new extension. Amazon's OpenSearch search engine called "A9" is further evidence of the considerable economic interest in RSS technologies—and certainly for the commercial possibilities of the format as well.

The extension "OpenSearch RSS" (http://opensearch.a9.com) serves to provide RSS 2.0 with language tools through which search results can be presented as RSS feeds, and can be received regularly. OpenSearch makes it possible to subscribe queries and to access their results in a feed reader or aggregator. The extension defines a standard format for the reproduction of search results. It is Amazon's expressed intention, however, that the OpenSearch extension elements can be ignored by existing RSS readers.

Amazon's search engine A9 (http://a9.com/) supports OpenSearch RSS 1.0. A draft of version 1.1 has been proposed; probably it will soon be finalized and implemented by A9.

OpenSearch provides an exchange format for search results. Sites that support this format can be registered with A9. A9 users can get search results from these sites in addition to default search results provided by A9's partner Google. They can, for instance, add the Wikipedia and the Amazon Book Store to their personalized version of A9.

The basic premise of OpenSearch RSS is very simple: Today the results of search engines on the Web are normally rendered as HTML and therefore cannot be exchanged between sites. There is no automated way to combine the results of the search engine of a bookstore with those of another search engine used, for instance, by a public library. Users interested in results from both sites have three choices (and none of them is satisfying):

- They can use a general search engine like Google, which may be outdated, incomplete, and less specific compared to the search engines offered by the sites themselves.

- They can browse through results of both engines one after the other—this might be no problem in case of just two sites, but nearly impossible for a search within, say, 20 or more resources.

- They can use a meta search engine that, in most cases, will not exist because it has to be tailored individually for each of the sites that it supports. (This would mean that programmers have to analyze the HTML produced by each of the search engines and to write a sort of parser that extracts the results.)

Enter OpenSearch: search engines can now put out their results in a standardized extended version of RSS instead of HTML; the lists in this format can be processed without taking care of the specifics of each search engine. OpenSearch RSS does for search results what RSS did for newsfeeds: it allows for isolation of the content from its presentation, and for encoding it in a simple format with defined semantics.

Many prominent websites are already supporting OpenSearch, among them newpapers like the New York Times and USA Today, and specialized search engines like Findory. OpenSearch will probably get even more momentum because Microsoft announced to support it in the upcoming Internet Explorer 7. Users of IE 7 will be able to subscribe to search engines just as users of other browsers already can subscribe to newsfeeds—a feature that IE 7 will adopt.

RSS extensions form the central part of OpenSearch, because they allow for the exchange of search results between sites and services. In addition to these extensions, OpenSearch defines an XML document type for the description of search services, and a standardized query syntax. An application that is OpenSearch-enabled uses this description and the syntax to address queries to search engines that support OpenSearch.

The query syntax is defined by URI templates for HTTP queries. The templates contain an array of parameters; the service description document of a search engine informs a client which parameters the engine supports; the client replaces the parameters in the URI template by values to start a query.

The Elements of the OpenSearch Module

OpenSearch version 1.0 introduces three new elements and a namespace of its own, `http://a9.com/-/spec/opensearchrss/1.0/`.

The search results themselves are characterized as RSS items. Within the `item` elements, `link` contains the link to the document that was found, `title` contains the title of the page, and `description` the beginning of the text. That is interesting, because this technology shows how common components of web presences can be semantically tagged with RSS. For this purpose, OpenSearch uses the already introduced RSS elements with the same name (which would remain in the RSS namespace if such a namespace were formally defined), but extends their frame of meaning.

With result lists of this kind, the name of the producer of the search results is to appear as the `title` of `channel`. Belonging to that information is the name of the search engine as well as the terms of the search. HTML markup should be avoided here.

The `link` element within `channel` refers to a website where the search results are to be found. The `description` element describes the search (and can contain simple protected HTML markup).

In addition, the extension introduces three new elements. The additional elements are descendants of the `channel` element and are located in the `openSearch` namespace.

The `totalResults` element indicates how many results the search engine has found:

```
<openSearch:totalResults>1000</openSearch:totalResults>
```

If the search came up with no results, 0 is supposed to be indicated. If the element is missing, the client can assume that all search results are included in the feed received from the search engine.

The `startIndex` element contains an integer as well:

```
<openSearch:startIndex>1</openSearch:startIndex>
```

It indicates which of the search results will be presented first. You know this procedure from all common search engines; the site usually starts with something like "1-10 of 1756 results". This element, like the other two, is optional.

The `itemsPerPage` element indicates the maximum number of results a page can contain:

```
<openSearch:itemsPerPage>10</openSearch:itemsPerPage>
```

In version 1.1 the extensions are called **OpenSearch Response elements**. The namespace is identified by the URI `http://a9.com/-/spec/opensearchresponse/1.1`. The elements are defined as an extension to RSS 2.0 and to Atom as well. A fourth element `openSearch:searchTerms` has been added; it is optional. As with the other OpenSearch elements, it can appear once at maximum. The extension is itself extensible; elements in other namespaces can be added as children of the OpenSearch elements.

The draft of the specification recommends using the `link` Atom element for extensions of the OpenSearch RSS elements. The specification proposes values for the `rel` attribute of this element to indicate the relation of a feed document to other documents. `rel="alternate"` and `rel="self"` need not be defined, as they appear in the Atom 1.0 specification. `alternate` points to an alternative representation of the same resource, usually to an HTML page. `self` points to the URI of the feed document. (The Atom specification states that all values of the element `atom:link` have to be registered at the IANA. `alternate` and `self` have already been proposed as value to IANA registry; see chapter 4).

The other values of `rel` proposed in the draft of the specification are specific to search results, and have still to be proposed to the IANA: `start` links to the first page of search results, `previous` to the previous, `next` to the next, and `end` to the last page. `description` refers to the description of the service in a special XML format.

Furthermore, the OpenSearch specification (`http://opensearch.a9.com/spec/opensearchrss/1.0/`) suggests methods to optimally use existing RSS 2.0 elements in connection with searches. Also, there is already the prospect of further versions of the OpenSearch technology with additional functions. The language choice, coding, spelling suggestions, multimedia results, and paid search listing are among the possible extensions mentioned. It is immediately obvious what possibilities such "saved searches" offer if they are combined with categories.

2.6.6 The RSS Media Module from Yahoo!

Yahoo! has publicly developed a media RSS specification (`http://tools.search.yahoo.com/mrss/`). (Dave Winer was irritated, and complained about how much of his work was used by Yahoo!—not only without mentioning him, but also without informing him.) Version 1.0 is used for Yahoo!'s video search (`http://video.search.yahoo.com/`). Meanwhile the developers have proposed a draft of a version 1.1 of the specification (`http://groups.yahoo.com/group/rss-media/files/`). The elements of the module are supposed to replace and complement the `enclosure` element and to allow a differentiated syndication of media. The module supports thumbnails, copyright information, and transcripts.

The namespace URI is `http://search.yahoo.com/mrss/`.

As a namespace prefix the specification itself uses `media:`.

Media RSS is adapted to the special requirements of movies and television shows and contains elements for the specific metadata items that frequently belong to such media. They are supposed to organize and indicate media content. Further describing attributes will be added in future versions.

The Elements of the RSS Media Module

If you want to incorporate references to media in an RSS feed, you have two alternatives: You can link to just one file or to several files with the same content adapted to different conditions of bandwidth and player software. With RSS Media you describe the individual files in both cases with the `media:content` extension element. If you offer several versions of the same content, use the element `media:group` as container for the descriptions of the individual files.

The `media:group` element is always a descendant of `item`. Its descendants are several elements of the type `media:url`, which refer to the same content, but to different representations of that content. The element is optional.

The extension element `media:content` is a descendant of `item` or `media:group`. Within an element of the type `media:group`, it can appear multiple times only if it refers to different representations of the same content. It is used to publish any kind of media. This element has the following attributes, almost all of which are optional:

- `url` indicates the URI of the medium. If this attribute is missing, an element of the type `player` has to be added.

- `filesize` indicates the size in bytes.

- `type` indicates the media type (as a MIME type).

- `isDefault` specifies whether, in a group, this is the medium that is played back if there is no expressed requirement for a different one. Permitted values are `true` and `false`.

- `expression` can have the values `sample`, `full`, and `nonstop`. The value indicates whether it is a sample or a full version; `nonstop` is chosen if the medium is continuously streamed. `full` is the default value.

- `bitrate` states how many kilobits per second are contained in the stream. With `bitrate`, streams with different download rates can be differentiated.

- `framerate` indicates how many frames per second are supposed to be shown for visual media.

- `duration`, `height`, and `width` indicate play-back time, size, and width.

- `playerwidth` and `playerHeight` indicate the window dimensions of the software that plays back the media, and `playerURL` indicates a URI that determines the play-back software.

- `samplingrate` is an optional attribute (since version 1.1) that can be used to declare how many samples per second were taken to generate the media object. The value is expressed in thousands of samples per second.

- `medium` declares (optionally) the type of the medium; allowed values are `image`, `audio`, `video`, `document`, and `executable`. The attribute was introduced in version 1.1. It helps the user to decide what he or she wants to do with a file and doesn't replace the declaration of the MIME type.

- `lang` indicates the language used in the media (introduced in version 1.1). As values, you can use the language tags defined in RFC 3066.

- `channels` serves to indicate the number of audio channels (introduced in version 1.1).

In principle, the two elements `media:content` and `media:group` can appear any number of times as descendants of the same element. However, the specification recommends sticking to the RSS rule that every item contains one "story", and within an `item` element to refer only to one item or one medium. As you may remember, in regards to the RSS `enclosure` element, a similar discussion is taking place about whether it can be repeated within `item` or not. If an `item` contains more than one medium, it can no longer be allocated to the URI that is indicated in `link`.

Further optional elements can describe `item`, `media:content`, or `media:group` (the latter in the namespace of the extension, labeled here with the prefix `media:`). They refer to a characteristic of this element.

- `media:rating` is used to declare the "permissible audience". It carries an attribute `scheme` with a URI do declare the rating scheme that is used. Examples for values used in the specification are `urn:icra`, `urn:mpaa`, and `urn:v-chip`. It is also possible to use `urn:simple` as value of `scheme`. In this case, the content of the element is simply `adult` or `nonadult`. In version 1.1 of the specification, `media:rating` replaces the `media:adult` element of version 1.0; `media:adult` is deprecated.

- `media:title` includes the title of the media object. There are no further rules. We don't get to know whether markup is allowed within the title or not.

- `media:thumbnail` contains information about an image that is to be used as a thumbnail of the media object. The three attributes `url`, `height`, and `width` indicate the URI, the height, and the width of the media object respectively.

- `media:category` indicates the category of the medium and is an example of an extension element that Dave Winer would call "funky". It doesn't have any other noticeable function than the `category` element, which already belongs to the RSS 2.0 language space. `media:category` has two attributes: `scheme` indicates which taxonomy the term that identifies the category derives from, and `label` gives an identification of the category that is human readable.

- `media:hash` indicates the hash according to the MD5 message digest algorithm. `hash` can be used to check whether a medium was fully transmitted or not.

- `media:player` is supposed to allow a media player in a browser to open the medium. `media:player` declares attributes as well: `url` for the URI of the player software, `height` for the height, and `width` for the width of the window.

- `media:credit` contains persons, companies, locations, etc., that have contributed to the creation of the medium. The optional attribute `role` indicates which role the person or company played during the production of the medium. In the specification you can find an entire list of such roles, among them `author`, `composer`, and `producer`. You can use the `scheme` attribute to declare the URI of the role scheme. As its default scheme Media RSS uses the European Broadcasting Union Role Codes; they are identified by the URI `urn:ebu`.

- `media:text` includes the transcript already mentioned above. The attribute `type` with the values `plain` or `html` indicates in which text format the transcription is available. `type` is an obligatory attribute. In the future it is also supposed to support text with a time code to allow subtitles for movies. In version 1.1 the `lang` attribute was added to indicate the language of the text.

- `media:description` is an element added by version 1.1 of the specification. It contains a short human-readable description of the medium. The attribute `type` with the possible values `text` or `html` indicates the format of the description.

- `media:keywords` can be used as a container for a list of human-readable descriptive keywords (since version 1.1).

Some of the language tools of Media RSS have functions you might recognize from the Synchronized Multimedia Integration Language (SMIL; `http://www.w3.org/AudioVideo/`). SMIL too allows indicating alternative media, incorporating transcripts, and displaying copyright information. However, SMIL was explicitly designed to control the timing of presentations on the Web. The functions of Media RSS are only rudimentary in comparison to SMIL. In the past, SMIL has been propagated above all by the company Real Networks, which, as a provider of media on the Web, is a competitor of Yahoo!. This maybe one reason why this language wasn't used to define a media module for RSS.

2.6.7 Microsoft's Simple List Extensions

RSS originated as a news syndication format; consequently the members (items) of a newsfeed are ordered by their date of origin. Meanwhile many other different uses of feed formats were discovered; in some cases it made more sense to order the items of a feed with regard to other criteria than date. Microsoft has published an extension module for RSS 2.0 that gives the publisher the power to decide over the order in which RSS items appear in a channel. (The URI of the specification is `http://msdn.microsoft.com/windowsvista/building/rss/simplefeedextensions/`.) With these extension elements you can, for instance, publish a photo feed and sort it by the names of the photographed persons or the subjects you like most—under the condition that the extension is supported by the software that consumes the feed.

Since Microsoft wants to make RSS a key feature of the next Windows version that is supported on the level of the operating system, it is highly probable that soon many applications will make use of this extension—notwithstanding that some prominent RSS and Atom developers remain skeptical about their usefulness (see `http://dannyayers.com/archives/2005/06/24/ms-rss/`). As for RSS in general, the applications can simply use the RSS-related functionality offered by Windows Vista.

The namespace of the Simple List Extensions is identified by the URI `http://www.microsoft.com/schemas/rss/core/2005`; the recommended prefix is `cf`. The element `cf:treatAs` (a child of `channel`) signals that a feed should be considered as a list. The specification states that it may be treated as a representation of a "complete, ordered list of content from the server".

The other elements describe properties that can be used to sort, group, or filter the content. The `cf:listinfo` element serves as a container for the information about the sorting or filtering criteria. It has the children `cf:sort` and `cf:group`. Both elements contain one or more children with a name that is also used as name of children of each item-element that belongs to the channel. `cf:sort` has an `data-type` attribute to indicate how the content used for sorting the members must be interpreted.

`cf:sort` and `cf:group` contain a text string with a human-readable name for the element used for grouping or filtering. This name will normally appear in an interface that allows the user to sort the items that belong to a feed. Thus you could, for instance, use an extension element with the name `project:meetingDate` to indicate that the items of a newsfeed contain information about meeting dates. As a child of `cf:sort`, it can serve to sort the items with respect to their dates even if they were published in another order. The content of the `data-type` attribute declares that the sorting should be based on the time-related content, not on the textual value of the element.

2.6.8 The Simple Semantic Resolution Module: RSS 2.0 as RDF

The Simple Semantic Resolution module developed by Danny Ayers plays a special role. I am introducing it as the last of the RSS 2.0 modules, because it leads on to RSS 1.0 and the RDF data model RSS 1.0 is based on. This module doesn't complement RSS 2.0 with additional functions; it only concerns the interpretation of a document. The only element of the module says: This document can be interpreted as a valid RDF document and it can be translated with an XSLT stylesheet into an RSS 1.0 document. If you don't know RSS 1.0, please read Chapter 3, which introduces this vocabulary in detail!

The SSR module belongs to the namespace `http://purl.org/stuff/ssr`.

Danny Ayers uses `ssr` as a prefix.

The module has only one element: `ssr:rdf`. If this element is included in an RSS 2.0 document, it tells the processor that it can be interpreted as RDF. Consequently, the processor can parse it in such a way that an RDF representation of the document is produced, that is, a directed graph with nodes and links. Furthermore, the module also uses one single attribute: `transform`.

The value of this attribute is the URI of an XSLT stylesheet. With this stylesheet the document can be transformed into the RSS 1.0 syntax.

Authors of other modules can use the module for Simple Semantic Resolution as well. If the semantics of their module is defined in a way that it can be presented as an RDF graph, they can communicate this information to a processor using the element `ssr:rdf`.

You will encounter the tasks of this module again in the next chapter. There, we will explain in detail what an RDF graph looks like, and when an XML document that doesn't contain RDF elements can be interpreted as an RDF document.

There are many other RSS 2.0 modules; you can find a complete list at `http://blogs.law.harvard.edu/tech/directory/5/specifications/rss20ModulesNamespaces`. Many of these modules couldn't establish themselves more widely; maybe they can be used as a starting point to develop future additions for this and for the other syndication vocabularies.

You will get to know one of the most important, and also most explored, possibilities for extending RSS in the next chapter: the Dublin Core vocabulary for bibliographical metadata. This module was developed in connection with RSS 1.0, but it can also be used together with the other syndication vocabularies without creating any problems. Some developers use elements like `author` from the Dublin Core vocabulary, because their semantics are defined more precisely than the language tools that are available to RSS 2.0.

As you can see, it is true that RSS 2.0 is "frozen", but the world of RSS modules is markedly active and becoming manifold. For several years, RSS 2.0 modules were developed apart from the mainstream and weren't used very often. Since 2005, however, Internet giants like Amazon and Yahoo! have adopted this technology and apply it for tasks that play a central role in their strategy.

2.7 Aggregation of Feeds and OPML

In an RSS 2.0 document only an element of the type `channel` can be a descendant of an element of type `rss`. In this way, the document always represents exactly one web resource.

This raises the question of whether and how the content of several feeds can be combined. This is not an academic question, because aggregated feeds play an increasingly important role in the face of growing information volume. For example, in an aggregated feed, information on a certain topic that derives from different resources can be combined.

RSS doesn't offer an element that would fulfill the task of a meta- or super-channel. It is not possible to embed several channel elements in one rss element. It is also forbidden to use the channel element recursively, that is, to embed one channel element in another channel element. (During the discussion in regards to Atom, Roy Fielding actually suggested recursive feeds, but he couldn't push through that suggestion.)

RSS 2.0 has an element, source, which is used to indicate the source of an item. This element can be employed to combine elements from several sources in one feed. However, source only has the function of a reference; it doesn't state anything about whether or how the resource was changed.

Approach in RSS 2.0: Outline Processing Markup Language

There is another tool in the environment of the RSS 2.0 technologies to combine several feeds in one unit, namely, the Outline Processing Markup Language (OPML). Dave Winer developed this language too. Outlines, that is, documentation structures, were the starting point of many UserLand developments. An RSS 1.0 document also has the structure of an outline, which can be filled with material in deeper levels. OPML is used whenever information about many feeds needs to be exchanged. Users of Bloglines and NetNewsWire can export a list of the feeds they subscribe to as an OPML document. I will describe OPML in more detail in the appendix. Of course, you can also list Atom and RSS 2.0 feeds in an OPML document.

Approach in RSS 1.0: mod_aggregation

RSS 1.0 has an extension module of its own for aggregated feeds, namely, mod_aggregation (http://web.resource.org/rss/1.0/modules/aggregation/). Its task is to include "aggregator-added information about the original source of the RSS item". In addition, RSS 1.0 included this function in the (non-official) mod_link module (http://web.resource.org/rss/1.0/modules/link/), where the attribute clearly refers to the resource for an individual item. It was also suggested to use the attribute to indicate the origin of an item in an aggregator.

Approach in Atom: Inclusion of Metadata of the Original Feeds in the Entry

Atom chooses a different path and allows the metadata information for a feed to be repeated within an individual entry, if this entry is to be integrated in another feed. In this way, feeds can be aggregated, the components of which contain information about their original feed. In older Atom versions an atom:origin element corresponded for the most part with the RSS source element.

3

RSS for the Semantic Web: RSS 1.0 and RSS 1.1

RSS 2.0 seems very simple, RSS 1.0 very complex. When scrutinizing the two formats more closely it becomes obvious that this impression is wrong: RSS 2.0 is simple because many problems are not explicitly mentioned. The complexity of RSS 1.0 is necessary to realize a very simple principle. RSS 2.0 defines only an XML format, whereas RSS 1.0 is based on a semantic model: the contents of documents consist of information about the resource characteristics.

RSS 1.0 (`http://web.resource.org/rss/1.0/`) not only has a lower version number than RSS 2.0, but it was also presented earlier (see section 1.7.3). The developers expand the abbreviation as "RDF Site Summary". Neither RSS 1.0 nor RSS 2.0 has a forum or organization in the background that develops the standards; the authors have full copyright. However, during the development of RSS 1.0, considerably more attention was paid to the compatibility of the format with other standards than was the case with RSS 2.0.

The most important means of communication for the development of RSS 1.0 and the continuing discussion of this format is the *rss-dev* mailing list (`http://groups.yahoo.com/group/rss-dev/`). RSS 1.0 includes several standard modules (`http://web.resource.org/rss/1.0/modules/`) and numerous proposed modules (`http://web.resource.org/rss/1.0/modules/proposed.html`).

Modularization

An important motive for the development of RSS 1.0 was that the existing formats were able to describe metadata only on a very limited scale. RSS 1.0 was supposed to allow the description of such different content as job offers, discussion lists, and wikis. The RSS 1.0 developers decided against the inclusion of new elements in the core of RSS in order to keep this core stable and to protect it from repeated revisions. For this reason, the specification is geared towards modularity—the core functions of RSS stay identical, and additional functions are offered in modules that are interchangeable.

In fact, RSS 1.0 is a relatively early example of a modularized standard; by now, modularized specifications for other important XML vocabularies are available. As a mechanism for the modularization, RSS 1.0 employs XML namespaces, which allows the use of elements from different XML vocabularies together in one document. Furthermore, as RDF modules, the different components of RSS 1.0 clearly refer to each other on the semantic level.

RSS 1.0 couldn't prevail against RSS 2.0 and its predecessors. Although there are many tools that generate RSS 1.0, the specific possibilities that this format offers are used sparingly. At present, only about one tenth of all newsfeeds are available in this format.

RSS 1.0 was the first extensible syndication format. It clearly defined how to deal with HTML markup, it offered a precise mechanism to identify RSS feeds, their components, and their objects, and it was open to any kind of content. But RSS 1.0 is more difficult than RSS 2.0—not necessarily for developers, but certainly for authors and consumers of newsfeeds. What seems to be the biggest advantage in the eyes of its supporters, proves to be the biggest disadvantage in the judgment of its critics: RSS 1.0 is an RDF format like RSS 0.9, which was the first of all formats called RSS. The syntax of RSS 1.0 is more complicated than that of RSS 2.0, and the semantics have so many preconditions that most descriptions of RSS 1.0 spare their readers from a detailed explanation.

Use of the Resource Description Format

From the formal or technical point of view, the significant difference compared to RSS 2.0 and its predecessors is the fact that RSS 1.0 documents correspond to the RDF data model, and use RDF/XML syntax. With regard to the content, RSS 1.0 is, as the name RDF Site Summary suggests, a metadata format: RSS 1.0 documents describe other documents. An RSS 1.0 document doesn't serve to publish information objects that don't already exist in other forms, for example, as parts of HTML pages.

Above all, the modularization of RSS is supposed to enable the differentiated and detailed description of existing information. The core elements are just containers for the explicit and extensible metadata. Syndication is declared to be one of the main purpose of RSS; it is to be understood as a means to access data for "retrieval and further transmission, aggregation, or online publication".

A feed about a discussion forum is supposed to give information about the previous entries that a new discussion entry refers to. A feed about sports results should contain information about which sport a message is referring to and in which country the competition took place.

In the introductory abstract of the specification, RSS is characterized as a "lightweight multipurpose extensible metadata description and syndication format". The "lightweight" characteristic differentiates RSS from syndication formats like ICE (see the table in section 1.7), which were developed for the media industry. At the same time, the specification assumes that RSS will be used in applications to be developed in the future. That's what is meant by the term "multi-purpose".

3.1 RDF Basics

RSS 1.0 differs fundamentally from RSS 2.0 and Atom, because it follows the rules of the Resource Description Format of the World Wide Web Consortium (`http://www.w3.org/RDF/`). RDF is supposed to allow machines to automatically correlate the information contained in an RSS document with the information from other RDF-conformant documents, and to process them together. This means that the machine behaves as if it could understand the information and draw conclusions. RDF belongs to the family of "artificial intelligence".

What should it look like when machines automatically correlate information from web documents? A simple example is the connection of information from RSS documents with information from Friend-of-a-Friend (FOAF; `http://www.foaf-project.org`) documents. Friend-of-a-Friend documents show relationships between people. (I use the analogy with FOAF only as a simple example for the combination of vocabularies. The problem described would be easy to solve.)

Consider this example: an FOAF document describes the net of relationships of a person called Lisa H. and shows that she is friends with Regina F. and Petra P., and that she is interested in music by the German group *Söhne Mannheims*. Lisa H. puts this document on her website. She also writes a weblog with an RSS 1.0 feed. This feed identifies Lisa H. as the author of the weblog. With RDF-capable software, a reader of Lisa H.'s weblog would be able to search for weblogs created by friends of Lisa H. The software finds the persons in the FOAF document. Using the RSS feeds of the weblogs, it can find out whether one of these persons is identified as the author. If additional information mentions that different entries of these weblogs talk about the *Söhne Mannheims*, they could make up an aggregated feed. If you modify this example, you will easily find more possibilities for combining information on the Web.

Why is a "regular" RSS 2.0 document and another "regular" XML document that describes the relationships of a person not enough to correlate the information they contain? Or, under which conditions is it possible to automatically combine the information they contain? An attempt to answer these questions results in a better understanding of the concepts RDF is based on. The application of these concepts is supposed to make sure that the RDF information is machine readable and that all identifiers of objects remain unique during the processing.

The Triple as an Information Model

If information is to be combined, it has to not only refer to the same objects, but also has to have similar—that is, in some way the same—structure. A sentence in a natural language and a data set in a database table can be processed together only if one of them can be transferred into the form of the other, or if both can be transferred into a common form. In the earlier example, both pieces of information, namely that Lisa H. is the author of the weblog "From Lisa's World" and that Petra P. is her friend, have to be transferred into a common machine-readable form. In RDF, this form is a "triple". An RDF triple includes two resources, that is, two objects, and the relationship that exists between them. The triples for the example are:

- "From Lisa's World" (resource) is created by (relationship) Lisa H. (resource)
- Lisa H. (resource) is the friend of (relationship) Petra P. (resource)

In RDF terminology, the first resource is called a "subject", the relationship is the "predicate", and the second resource is the "object", or, in other words, a subject, a trait or property, and a value. Subject, predicate, and object have the following tasks:

- The predicate assigns a property to the subject.
- The object determines a value for this property.

Identification through URIs

For the purpose of combining information from different documents, it is necessary to make sure that it refers to the same objects. That means in relation to our example, it has to be ensured that the Lisa H. who is described in the FOAF document is the same Lisa H. whom the RSS 1.0 document identifies as the author of the weblog. As a format that has to work on the Web, RDF chooses for this task the identifiers that the Web has at its disposal, URIs. In other words, whenever RDF data items refer to something outside themselves, they use URIs or URI references. URI references are URIs that include an optional fragment identifier.

Predicates and objects also have a URI to clearly identify them and differentiate them from other predicates. For that reason, every RDF triple can be written as a URI triplet, where the first URI stands for the subject, the second for the predicate, and the third for the object.

As URI triples, the two statements above can be expressed as follows:

```
http://www.example.com/weblogs/lisa
http://purl.org/dc/elements/1.1/creator
http://www.example.com/persons/lisa
```

and:

```
http://www.example.com/persons/lisa
http://xmlns.com/foaf/0.1/knows
http://www.example.com/persons/petra
```

Everyone who controls a URI, (e.g., who has reserved a domain name), can determine the URIs for persons or other resources. In the example, I simply used `http://www.example.com/` as a basis to form URIs for Lisa H. and Petra P. The URIs I used in the examples for the relationships derive from the RDF/XML vocabularies. In the first example the Dublin Core vocabulary is used, which is an important component of RSS 1.0. In this vocabulary, `creator` is the name for an element; `creator` indicates the relationship of a resource with its author. The namespace of the Dublin Core vocabulary has the URI `http://purl.org/dc/elements/1.1/`. In order to form the URI of the predicate, the element name has to be attached to the namespace prefix. In the second triple, the predicate stems from the FOAF vocabulary, the namespace of which is identified by the URI `http://xmlns.com/foaf/0.1/`. The FOAF vocabulary includes the element knows, which in the second triple describes the relationship between the two persons.

RDF Models Information as Graphs

If information is available in this form, it is easy to combine by making the object of one triple the subject of another triple.

The following graph is the result of the visual presentation of the relationships:

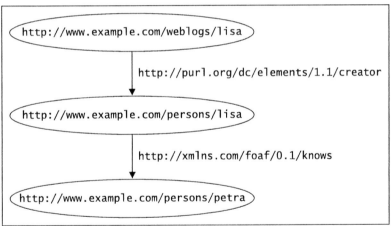

Figure 3.1 Graph of Two RDF Triples

The structure of RDF data can be described as a "directed labeled graph". A directed labeled graph consists of "nodes" (also called "vertices") and directional links known as "edges" or "arcs", each with a label. The mathematical discipline of graph theory deals with such graphs (`http://en.wikipedia.org/wiki/Graph_theory`). In an RDF graph, resources like those in the example (Lisa H., Petra P., and Lisa's weblog) are displayed as nodes, and the relationships as labeled arcs. The URIs `http://purl.org/dc/elements/1.1/creator` and `http://xmlns.com/foaf/0.1/knows` serve as labels of the arcs.

RDF Notation in XML

This graph model of RDF information is fundamental. The way it is represented, for example in XML, is secondary. According to the graph model, RDF statements can in principle be combined without limitations. The URI references, which clearly identify the components of the statements, ensure that machines can interpret the relationships between statements.

To summarize: RDF models information as directed labeled graphs, where the nodes represent resources, which are identified through URIs, and the arcs are also labeled through URIs. This conceptual model has nothing to do with XML syntax. It is possible, however, to describe RDF data—that is, data that corresponds with the RDF model—in an XML document, which is also referred to as XML notation of RDF data. The XML vocabulary that is used to denote RDF data is called "RDF/XML". It is described in the RDF/XML Syntax Specification (`http://www.w3.org/TR/rdf-syntax-grammar/`). RSS 1.0 follows this syntax.

The RDF/XML Syntax includes RDF-specific elements and attributes as well as rules for the structure of documents. I will explain the elements later to describe their function within RSS 1.0. The rules for the structure also state how elements from different XML vocabularies can be combined in an RDF document. The most important principle in this process is having a clearly mapped relationship between the RDF graph and the XML structure. To put it simply: in an RDF/XML document certain elements represent resources, whereas other elements represent properties.

There are two ways to tell the parser of such a document which elements represent resources and which elements represent properties:

- Through elements and attributes from the RDF/XML namespace
- Through the hierarchy of the XML elements which are embedded in each other

The RDF/XML version of the data for the example shows how these two methods cooperate:

```xml
<?xml version="1.0"?>
<rdf:RDF xmlns:rdf="http://www.w3.org/1999/02/22-rdf-syntax-ns#"
     xmlns:dc="http://purl.org/dc/elements/1.1/"
     xmlns:foaf="http://xmlns.com/foaf/0.1/">
   <rdf:Description rdf:about="http://www.example.com/weblogs/lisa">
      <dc:creator>
         <rdf:Description
          rdf:about="http://www.example.com/persons/lisa"/>
      </dc:creator>
   </rdf:Description>
   <rdf:Description rdf:about="http://www.example.com/persons/lisa">
      <foaf:knows>
         <rdf:Description
          rdf:about="http://www.example.com/persons/petra"/>
      </foaf:knows>
   </rdf:Description>
</rdf:RDF>
```

Listing 3.1 A Simple RDF Document

The document element rdf:RDF has no function in the structure of the RDF graph; it just tells the parser that it is dealing with RDF/XML data. The element rdf:description with the attribute rdf:about="http://www.example.com/weblogs/lisa" in the first triple and rdf:about="http://www.example.com/persons/lisa" in the second triple determines which resources the parser is supposed to use as subjects of statements (and thus as nodes within the RDF graphs). Embedded in these elements are the two elements that represent predicates, that is, the arcs of the RDF graph: dc:creator and foaf:knows. In the tree structure of the XML document, these elements are the descendants or child elements of those elements that represent the subjects. The successors or children of these elements again stand for nodes in the RDF graph. In our example, the successors are the other two rdf:Description elements. They are only wrappers for the URIs, which are indicated as values of the rdf:about attributes: http://www.example.com/persons/lisa and http://www.example.com/persons/petra.

Mapping of RDF Graphs on XML Trees

There is a mapping relationship between the RDF graph and the XML tree. One hierarchy level stands for nodes in the RDF graph, the second level for arcs, and the next deeper one again for nodes.

The following figure shows the tree structure of the document. You can easily imagine the mapping on the nodes of the graph. The RDF parser can combine the two branches of the XML document, because due to the URIs, it recognizes that two nodes represent the same resource.

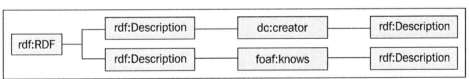

Figure 3.2 Tree Structure of a Simple RDF Document

If the levels of the nodes and the arcs in the RDF/XML document are differentiated from each other by using bold and normal print, a striped structure is the result, as in the following version of our example:

```
<?xml version="1.0"?>
<rdf:RDF xmlns:rdf="http://www.w3.org/1999/02/22-rdf-syntax-ns#"
    xmlns:dc="http://purl.org/dc/elements/1.1/"
    xmlns:foaf="http://xmlns.com/foaf/0.1/">
  <rdf:Description rdf:about="http://www.example.com/weblogs/lisa">
    <dc:creator>
      <rdf:Description
        rdf:about="http://www.example.com/persons/lisa"/>
    </dc:creator>
  </rdf:Description>
  <rdf:Description rdf:about="http://www.example.com/persons/lisa">
    <foaf:knows>
      <rdf:Description
```

```
                      rdf:about="http://www.example.com/persons/petra"/>
            </foaf:knows>
        </rdf:Description>
    </rdf:RDF>
```

Listing 3.2 A Simple RDF Document with "Striped Structure"

This structure is also known as the "striped RDF/XML syntax". (See Dan Bricklin's presentation: *RDF: Understanding the Striped RDF/XML Syntax*, `http://www.w3.org/2001/10/stripes/`.) By the way, in complying with the rules of this syntax, RDF documents can be created that don't include any elements or attributes from the RDF/XML namespace at all.

The W3C RDF Validator

The W3C offers an online validator (`http://www.w3.org/RDF/Validator/`) for checking RDF/XML documents and the triples they include for mistakes and shows, on request, a visual presentation of the graph. This validator created Figure 3.1. I will also use this validator to visualize the structure of the RSS data that I use as examples in the following sections.

Preview: More Complex RDF Graphs

By now you have gained an insight into the RDF data model and the function of the RDF/XML syntax. If you deal with RDF/XML data it is important never to lose sight of the triple or graph structure that is to be expressed through the XML document. You understand the syntax of the document once you realize that it projects an RDF graph onto an XML tree.

You will get to know several other distinctive features of the RDF/XML syntax in the following sections, which introduce RSS 1.0. In this context, tree features may occur that I haven't mentioned before:

- Character strings (literals) can be used as the objects of RDF statements as well. RDF knows plain literals and typed literals. Plain literals consist of a character string and a language identification that is optional. A typed literal connects a character string with the URI of a data type. (See also `http://www.w3.org/TR/rdf-concepts/#section-Literals`.)

- RDF maps collections through their own types of resources, which are called *sequence* (ordered list), *bag* (unordered list), and *alternative*.

- An RDF graph can include "anonymous" nodes as well—nodes that are not externally identified by a URI, but which can receive an internal identifier.

This technology makes it possible to model as RSS graphs information that can't be directly translated into the RDF triple structure. Without it, RDF as a data format would fail in almost every realistic scenario.

3.2 The Basic Structure of an RSS 1.0 Document

Even the simplest RSS 1.0 document uses elements that derive from different vocabularies. The following listing contains the information that is also present in the sample document for RSS 2.0, Listing 2.1:

```xml
<?xml version="1.0"?>
<rdf:RDF xmlns="http://purl.org/rss/1.0/"
    xmlns:rdf="http://www.w3.org/1999/02/22-rdf-syntax-ns#">
  <channel rdf:about="http://www.celawi.eu/webtrends">
    <title>Webtrends</title>
    <link>http://www.celawi.eu/webtrends.html</link>
    <description>News about commercial websites and online
     advertising</description>
    <items>
      <rdf:Seq>
        <rdf:li rdf:resource="http://www.celawi.eu/
         webtrends/20040415_01"/>
        <rdf:li rdf:resource="http://www.celawi.eu/
         webtrends/20040415_02"/>
      </rdf:Seq>
    </items>
  </channel>
  <item rdf:about="http://www.celawi.eu/webtrends/20040415_01">
    <title>Ask Jeeves now in Spain</title>
    <link>http://www.celawi.eu/webtrends/20040415_01.html</link>
    <description> On 5 April, Ask Jeeves started with the beta
     version of a new search...</description>
  </item>
  <item rdf:about="http://www.celawi.eu/webtrends/20040415_02">
    <title>Bitkom Study: Paid content successful in Germany</title>
    <link>http://www.celawi.eu/webtrends/20040415_02.html</link>
    <description> Online content available for a charge becomes more
     and more accepted:...</description>
  </item>
</rdf:RDF>
```

Listing 3.3 A Simple RSS 1.0 Document

This document has a simple structure. However, it is more complex than the structure of an RSS 2.0 document with identical content. Figure 3.3 shows the XML tree structure:

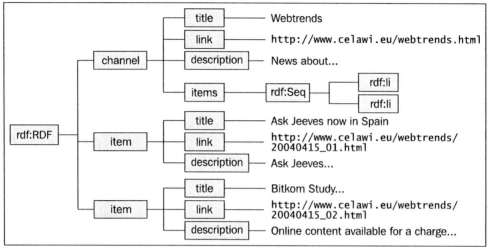

Figure 3.3 A Simple RSS 1.0 Document

The document and the diagram show two important differences between RSS 1.0 and RSS 2.0 very well. Both have to do with the fact that RSS 1.0 follows the rules of the RDF/XML syntax:

- The elements and attributes belong to different namespaces.
- The elements of the type item are also top-level elements beneath the document element; they are not embedded in a channel element.

3.2.1. Namespaces

Every RSS 1.0 document consists of elements that belong to different XML vocabularies. At the very least, the RDF/XML vocabulary and the vocabulary for the RSS 1.0 core elements have to be used for every RSS 1.0 document. Besides the root element rdf:RDF, the RDF/XML vocabulary includes the rdf:about attribute and the rdf:seq element, which will be introduced in the following sections. You already know the names of the elements that belong to the core vocabulary from RSS 2.0, for example, channel and item. Furthermore, elements from additional vocabularies occur in most RSS 1.0 documents, like those from the Dublin Core metadata set in the example above.

3.2.2 The Structure of the Document as a Consequence of the RDF Model

The document element rdf:RDF has no correspondence in the graph that an RDF parser creates from an RSS document. It contains information the parser needs to extract RDF triples from the contents of the document element. Part of this information is the fact that the document is an RDF document, and which namespaces are assigned to the descendants.

Moreover, the `rdf:RDF` element acts as a container for several so-called "top-level" elements, i.e., for several immediate descendants in the document hierarchy. An RDF parser interprets the descendants of `rdf:RDF` as **statements** about resources. (The term "statement" plays an important role in philosophy, above all in analytical philosophy. Statements are declarations, the truth of which is claimed by a speaker.) This means that for the example, the parser will create the RDF graph based on three statements about three resources.

Like all elements from the RDF namespace, `rdf:RDF` also occurs outside of RSS 1.0. Most RDF documents use `rdf:RDF` as a document element. It is possible, however, to use other document elements for RDF documents. RSS 1.1, which was suggested as the successor for RSS 1.0, makes use of this possibility.

The `rdf:RDF` element has three descendants: one `channel` element and two `item` elements. These three elements all have the `rdf:about` attribute, which is mandatory for all top-level elements of RSS 1.0. The URI that is the value of `rdf:about` in each case, indicates a resource that is the subject of the RDF statement. The descendants of the top-level elements—in the example, one `channel` element and two `item` elements—follow the rules of the striped syntax, which you already know: child elements of these elements represent basic properties. The URIs of these properties are formed from the element name and the URI of the namespace the element name is assigned to.

In order to understand how the parser creates triples from the elements of the sample document, you still have to know some additional rules of RDF and of the RDF/XML syntax, respectively. I will introduce them starting with the sample document.

The first rule concerns the RDF/XML syntax and reads as follows:

- XML elements with the `rdf:about` attribute indicate the type of the resource that is named as the value of the attribute.

The other two rules concern the RDF data model and state that:

- A character string can also be the object of an RDF statement.
- Statements about an ordered sequence (ordered list) are made as statements about a container of a certain type as well as a series of statements about the relationship between the container and its members.

I start with the first rule: it explains how the parser processes the information `<channel rdf:about="..."/>` and `<item rdf:about="..."/>`. It interprets the URI that forms the value of `rdf:about` as the subject of the statement, the predicate of which belongs to the RDF/XML namespace and is called `rdf:type`. That means that the subject is an instance of a class, and the object of the statement indicates the class (`http://www.w3.org/TR/rdf-schema/#ch_type`). The value of the property `rdf:type` is again a resource, namely, the class of which the subject is an instance. The parser identifies the URI of this resource from the element name and the URI of the namespace that is valid for this element name.

Consequently, from the top-level elements of the example the following triples can be built:

Subject	Predicate	Object
http://www.celawi.eu/ webtrends	http://www.w3.org/1999/02/ 22-rdf-syntax-ns#type	http://purl.org/rss /1.0/channel
http://www.celawi.eu/ webtrends/20040415_01	http://www.w3.org/1999/02/ 22-rdf-syntax-ns#type	http://purl.org/rss /1.0/item
http://www.celawi.eu/ webtrends/20040415_02	http://www.w3.org/1999/02/ 22-rdf-syntax-ns#type	http://purl.org/rss /1.0/item

By using namespace prefixes these triples can be abbreviated and written like this:

Subject	Predicate	Object
http://www.celawi.eu/webtrends	rdf:type	rss:channel
http://www.celawi.eu/webtrends/20040415_01	rdf:type	rss:item
http://www.celawi.eu/webtrends/20040415_02	rdf:type	rss:item

RSS as Representation of Knowledge

These first three triples already show where the big difference between RSS 1.0 and RSS 2.0 lies: an RSS parser extracts from an RSS 1.0 document statements about facts. In this case, that the resource that the URI http://www.celawi.eu/webtrends refers to, is an RSS channel. Consequently, in the broadest sense, RSS 1.0 serves to represent knowledge. It is clear, though, that the statement mentioning a resource is an instance of the class channel is of practical value only if it is known what the predicate "is an instance of the class" means, and if further statements can be made about the class channel itself. Such statements are possible within RDF; they can be made in RDF schemas and in so-called ontologies. I can't address this issue at this point. The statements that can be identified from the element names could be used, for example, to build a database with the properties of RSS channels and their entries.

There are more statements about the subjects of the first three RDF statements that can be extracted from the sample document. In order to form them, however, the two other rules that were mentioned have to be employed. The first of these rules states that instead of a resource (something that is identified with a URI) it is also possible to have a literal, that is, a character string, as the object of an RDF statement. The very first child element of channel, which has the type title, demonstrates such a case. From the rules of striped syntax it follows that the element name title identifies a property, because it is the name of the child element of an element that represents a subject. The value of this property is in this case simply the character string that is used as the content of the element. Consequently, the statement can be expressed as follows:

Subject	Predicate	Object
`http://www.celawi.eu/webtrends`	`http://purl.org/rss/1.0/` `title`	`"Webtrends"`

The contents of `link` and `description` are character strings as well. Thus there are the following four statements—written with namespace prefixes—about the resource that is represented in this document by the `channel` element:

Subject	Predicate	Object
`http://www.celawi.eu/` `webtrends`	`rdf:type`	`rss:channel`
`http://www.celawi.eu/` `webtrends`	`rss:title`	`"Webtrends"`
`http://www.celawi.eu/` `webtrends`	`rss:link`	`"http://www.celawi.eu/` `webtrends.html"`

`http://www.celawi.eu/`
`webtrends`
	`rss:description`	`"News about commercial`
		`websites and online`
		`advertising"`

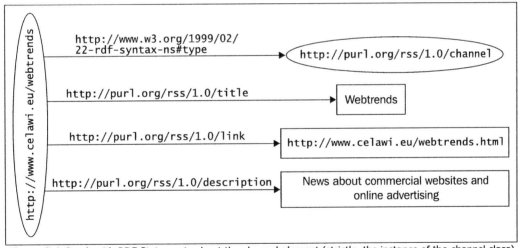

Figure 3.4 Graph with RDF Statements about the channel element (strictly, the instance of the channel class) of the Sample Document

The Relationships Between channel, items, and item

RDF containers are used if in an RDF graph more than one resource is to be indicated as the subject or the object. There are three types, namely, `Bag` (unordered list), `Seq` (for ordered lists or **collections**), and `Alt` (for lists of alternatives). For an introduction to RDF containers, please visit `http://www.w3.org/TR/2004/REC-rdf-primer-20040210/#containers`.

In the example, a container is the object of the predicate `items`. This container is a *collection* and, therefore, an ordered list. If a property was used instead—for example with the name `item`—the value of which was an individual resource, it would not be possible to indicate whether the set of individual `item` objects is an ordered or an unordered list. (Mark Pilgrim considers this semantic precision the main advantage of RDF, although he refuses to use the RDF/XML syntax for Atom: *Should Atom use RDF?*, `http://www.xml.com/pub/a/2003/08/20/dive.html`.) The following figure shows the graph the RSS validator creates from the element `items`:

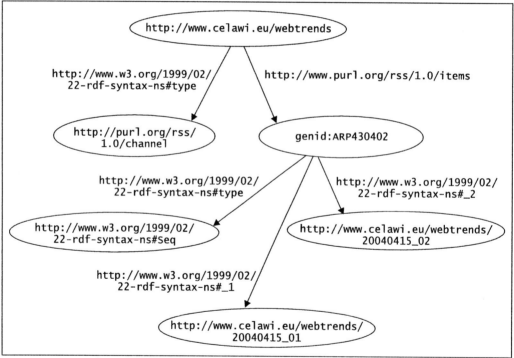

Figure 3.5 Visualization of an RDF Graph for the RSS 1.0 items Element

In this case the *collection* is a resource without a URI. Immediately an identifier, genid:ARP430402, is created for the corresponding node; a URI is not necessary, because this resource is not accessed from the outside. A statement of its own, represented by the left arc, states that this resource has the type rdf:Seq. For each member of the sequence a triple of its own is created with a specific property, namely, its position in the order of similar elements.

In this way, the subject rdf:Seq has the properties rdf:_1, rdf:_2, and so on in the RDF graph, the values of which again form resources. Later statements mention that the resources form instances of the class item. The visualization shows that the RDF/XML rdf:li element is the abbreviated indicator for the properties rdf:_1, rdf:_2, and so on.

The sequence itself is a so-called **blank node**; for an introduction to blank nodes please visit http://www.w3.org/TR/rdf-primer/#structuredproperties. RDF always describes structured information that belongs to a subject as a resource of its own, which is referred to by further statements. In the example the sequence is such a resource of its own. It is only intermediary, since it acts only as a connecting link to assign other resources to each other. Such intermediary resources are called blank nodes. The identifiers of blank nodes are not components of the RDF graph; they are just an aid to its notation.

Blank nodes are one of the methods that RDF uses to map relations, which are binary in nature, between one resource and several other resources. In the example, there is no relation between the resource channel and all the resources of the class item. Instead, there exists a binary relation between channel and the sequence, and further binary relations between the sequence—the blank node—and each of its members. The RDF/XML rdf:li element is only "syntactical sugar"; in the graph it is replaced by predicates that each occurs once (rdf:_1, rdf:_2).

Figure 3.6 shows the RDF graph of the complete sample document. The statements that refer to the item elements—more precisely, to resources of the class item—are represented on the lower right. Together with the statements about the channel they can be combined into a graph, because they refer to the resources that are the values of the properties rdf:_1 and rdf:_2.

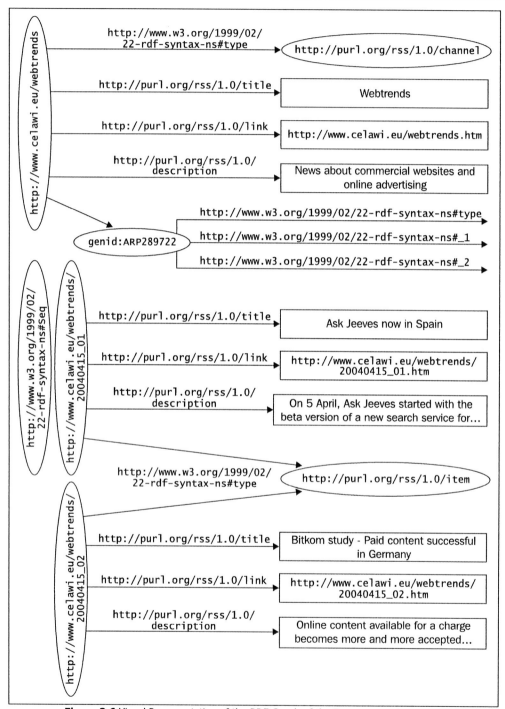

Figure 3.6 Visual Representation of the RDF Graph of the Document in Listing 2.1

3.3 The Core Vocabulary of RSS 1.0

3.3.1 Structure

It is also possible to distinguish between structural and descriptive elements in RSS 1.0. This distinction can be better justified in RSS 1.0 than in RSS 2.0 and its predecessors, because the semantics of the elements are clearly defined. The elements that have a structural function represent either nodes (resources) or properties, the value of which is a node. The descriptive elements stand for properties, the value of which is a literal, that is, a string of characters. Within the core vocabulary of RSS 1.0, there are exactly three descriptive elements, namely, title, link, and description.

The descendants of the document element rdf:RDF are one channel element and one or more elements of the type item. In contrast to RSS 2.0, the elements image and textinput in RSS 1.0 can be immediate descendants of the document element as well. Each channel, item, image, and textinput must have an attribute of the type rdf:about. The value of this attribute is the URI of the resource that is described by the element.

To put it less formally: in an RSS 1.0 document, channel, item, image, and textinput represent objects that exist independently of this document. Because these objects exist independently from the document, they can be identified with a URI.

On the Web, the URI allows access to these objects independently of the RSS document that describes them. (It could also involve objects outside the Net, for example, physical objects.) In this manner, it is possible, for instance, to receive every feed entry through the URI that is indicated in the feed as the value of rdf:about.

The only descendants of the channel element are the elements link, description, and items. Other elements are allowed but they have to be assigned to different namespaces. The architecture of the actual document, namely the structuring of the information in channel and item elements that are embedded in a document element, isn't changed by the extensions that are labeled using "external vocabulary".

RSS 1.0 complies with the rules of XML 1.0 and XML namespaces. The standard character coding is UTF-8. Quoted markup has to be escaped using entity references.

The order of the elements in an RSS 1.0 document is not of any relevance.

The RSS 1.0 channel element has an attribute, rdf:about, the value of which is a URI. This URI can be the value of the document itself, or the described homepage. In this respect, RSS 1.0 is as ambivalent as the other RSS versions. The role of the rdf:about attribute is to identify the subject of an RDF statement.

- `rdf:about`

    The value of the `rdf:about` attribute defines the URI of the element that contains it. It characterizes the subject of the statements that can be derived from RDF elements within the parent element. The elements within a parent element with this attribute are interpreted as descriptions of the element. Every resource that is described has to have this attribute.

- `rdf:resource`

    The role of this attribute is to indicate resources that function as values of properties within an RDF document. Thus it is used whenever a resource is used to indicate the value of the property.

The rdf:RDF Element

The document element of a valid RSS 1.0 document has the name RDF. This name is linked through the URI `http://www.w3.org/1999/02/22-rdf-syntax-ns#` to the namespace of the Resource Description Framework. The namespace for RSS elements is defined by the URI `http://purl.org/rss/1.0/`.

Normally, RSS 1.0 documents start like the sample document with:

```
<rdf:RDF
    xmlns:rdf="http://www.w3.org/1999/02/22-rdf-syntax-ns#"
    xmlns="http://purl.org/rss/1.0/">
```

The rules for XML namespaces also allow the use of a prefix other than `rdf`. However, the RDF specification recommends considering this prefix normative, so that in case of doubt the `rdf` part can also be interpreted as the component of a (local) identifier. Therefore, on the one hand, RSS 1.0 is compatible with RSS 0.9. On the other hand, it ensures that even programs that are not able to use the XML namespace mechanism can process the document. For such programs, the element name `rdf:RDF` is simply an ordinary identifier, which includes the (permitted) colon character.

Our example also declares the prefix `dc` in the first element. It is linked to a third namespace that was defined for the so-called Dublin Core elements:

```
<rdf:RDF xmlns="http://purl.org/rss/1.0/"
    xmlns:rdf="http://www.w3.org/1999/02/22-rdf-syntax-ns#"
    xmlns:dc="http://purl.org/dc/elements/1.1/">
```

If the namespaces in a document are declared as in our example, it means that all element names that don't have a prefix—that is, elements that don't have characters at the start of their name that are separated from the rest of the name by a colon—are considered RSS 1.0 elements. All elements that have the prefix `rdf` in front of their name are RDF elements. Attributes can also be provided with the prefix `rdf` and can be assigned individually to the RDF namespace. That is necessary if the accommodating element itself is not in this namespace. Thus the document element in the example states that the document embedded within it is composed using three XML vocabularies.

The descendants of rdf:RDF, namely, channel, items, image, and textinput, can't include any immediate child elements that repeat themselves. Repetitions are allowed only on deeper levels. The function of this restriction is to allow the construction of RSS triples, only with technologies that existed at the time the standard was developed. (For more information about rdf:RDF, see also section A.4.2 in the appendix.)

The rss:channel Element

The channel element is not, as in RSS 2.0, a container for all the data of the document. Its task is to describe the characteristics of the feed as a whole.

The only attribute that the specification requires is rdf:about. All top-level elements, that is, all elements of an RSS 1.0 document that are descendants of rdf:RDF, have to have this attribute. The value of rdf:about in channel is the URI of the channel.

The URI that is indicated here as the value of rdf:about (http://www.celawi.eu/ webtrends/ in the previous example) is the starting point to determine all other components of an RSS 1.0 document. It identifies the first node of the graph that a parser creates from the document.

In terms of the RDF syntax channel is a **typed node**, meaning that the node has an attribute type, the value of which is channel. (This can also be stated thus: the arc for the attribute type, the end point of which is channel, starts from the resource that is identified by the URI in rdf:about.)

The channel element must always include the elements title, rss:link, description, and items. Other subelements from RSS 1.0 modules that are identified through namespaces are possible.

The element names title, link, and description label characteristics of the resource that the URI identifies in rdf:about; title, link, and description are property elements. The rules of the RDF/XML syntax state that those elements that are embedded in an element that describes a node are property elements.

The elements description and link are also property elements with a literal as their value. The case of the items element is different: this element is also a property element, but its value is not a literal; it describes a resource instead. (For more information about channel see also section A.4.5 in the appendix.)

The rss:items Element

An RSS 1.0 document always includes a table of contents on the level of the channel. This table of contents links the channel with the different items that make up its content, as well as with an optional image and a text input field. Accordingly, an RSS 1.0 document explicitly contains information about which parts belong to a channel.

The `items` element contains the table of contents. You have already seen that according to RSS terminology, this element is a property element. The `items` element links the `channel` element with the entries that make up the contents of `channel`. (For more information about `items` see also section A.4.7 in the appendix.)

The rdf:Seq Element

The content of `items` is a resource of the type `rdf:Seq`, which is not identified by a URI, but forms a blank node. Each of the individual entries is the value of a property of this sequence that can be described as "first element", "second element", and so on. The order of the elements is also relevant; they can't be rearranged without a loss in meaning. (For more information about `rdf:Seq` see also section A.4.4 in the appendix.)

The rdf:li Element

Elements of the type `rdf:li` have an attribute, `rdf:resource`, the value of which is identical to the value of the `rdf:about` attribute of one of the `item` elements within the document. The use of `rdf:resource` allows statements to be made about the respective resource, which may be at a different location. These statements can be found within an `item` element that can be identified by the value of the `rdf:about` attribute as a resource assigned to the `channel`. (For more information about `rdf:li` see also section A.4.3 in the appendix.)

The rss:image Element

The `image` element corresponds in its function to the `image` element in RSS 2.0. There is no default size, yet the specification recommends a format that is supported by the majority of applications. The elements `title`, `link`, and `url` are the descendants of `rss:image`. The `url` element indicates the URI of the image. The content of `title` is used for the value of the `alt` attribute, if an RSS document is converted into HTML.

If an image is used in an RSS document, it has to be listed within `channel`. There, it is an empty element with the attribute `rdf:resource`. The value of this attribute is the URI of the image, that is, the URI that is indicated as the value of `rdf:about` in reference to the `image` element outside of `channel`.

Consequently, the `image` element appears twice with different functions. I will explain its meanings at this point to clarify again the specifics of the RDF/XML syntax: as a descendant of `channel` it is a *property element*. Its value is the resource, the URI of which is indicated in `rdf:resource`. As a descendant of `rdf:RDF` it represents the resource of the type `image`; in this case, it is also the container for the other characteristics of the image. (For more information about `image` see also section A.4.12 in the appendix.)

The rss:textinput Element

The `textinput` element is only mentioned here to be comprehensive. It is no longer used and it has already been omitted in RSS 1.1.

A `textinput` element includes the descriptive elements `title`, `link`, and `description`. The `name` element labels the input field like the HTML element of the same name; it may be passed on to a CGI script that analyzes the input. Like `image`, `textinput` would have to be listed within `channel`, if it were actually to be used.

The rss:item Element

Every `item` represents a resource of its own and, therefore, has a URI of its own. The `item` elements are typed nodes; they are interpreted by a parser in the way that you have just seen in relation to the `channel` type. In the RDF graph, the parser attaches the statements that refer to one of the `item` elements to the respective end nodes of the properties `rdf_1`, `rdf_2`, and so on, which it has created based on the value of the `rdf:resource` attribute. For this reason, the URIs of the individual `item` elements have to be identical with the URIs that are specified within the elements of the type `rdf:li`.

The specification very clearly states that an `item` can represent almost everything: "With RSS 1.0's modular extensibility, this can be just about anything: discussion posting, job listing, software patch—any object with a URI." (Section A.5 of the specification; for more information about `item` see also section A.4.6 in the appendix.)

3.3.2 Descriptive Elements

The descriptive core elements of RSS 1.0 have the same local names as their counterparts in RSS 2.0: `title`, `link`, and `description`. They are three property elements—in a graph they represent specified properties or predicates. The value of each of these properties is a literal—a character string that describes the resource the respective property belongs to. All subject nodes with a URI of their own, namely, nodes of the types `channel`, `item`, `image`, and `textinput`, have the properties `title` and `link`; `channel` and `item` have the additional property `description`. The `image` element has the property `url` as well.

The rss:link Element

The `link` element is a descendant of `channel` and of `item`, `image`, and `textinput`; it includes a URI. If the RSS document is converted into an HTML document, this URI indicates the destination of a link. The content of `title` is usually the origin of a link. The origin of an image is the address of the file indicated in the URI.

The content of link doesn't necessarily have to be identical with the URI, indicated as the value of the rdf:about attribute of the channel or item element. However, the specification recommends using the same URI with item, and that's how it is usually handled.

In order to be compatible with RSS 0.9, the specification restricts the content length of link to 500 characters. (For more information about link see also section A.4.9 in the appendix.)

The rss:title Element

The title element is used in RSS 1.0 the same way as it is in RSS 2.0: it contains the title of the feed, of an individual item or of an image or text input field. RSS 1.0 recommends—as the heir of older RSS versions—a limitation in size of 40 characters for the title of a channel and of 100 characters for the title of an item. Markup is strictly forbidden within this element.

A parser that understands the RDF schema (for an explanation of RDF schemas, see http://www.w3.org/TR/rdf-schema and http://www.w3.org/TR/2004/REC-rdf-primer-20040210/#rdfschema) that the namespace URI refers to can identify the title to be a specification of the title element that is derived from the Dublin Core metadata vocabulary. I will introduce the Dublin Core vocabulary in more detail later on when I address RSS 1.0 modules. In the graph the parser creates, it can therefore replace the property element title with dc:title. (For more information about title see also section A.4.8 in the appendix.)

The rss:description Element

The description element contains the description of the channel or the item. The value of description is also a literal, that is, a character string. This element is not allowed to have descendants, and also can't contain HTML markup—if HTML markup is to be inserted in an RSS 1.0 document, the Content module has to be used. A maximum length of 500 characters is recommended. Like title, the description is defined as a subset or sub-property of an element. (For more information about description see also section A.4.10 in the appendix.)

3.4 Modules for Metadata

As you have already seen in the introduction to this chapter, RSS 1.0 differs from RSS 2.0 and Atom insofar as its vocabulary remains restricted to the core of the language. However, it doesn't fall short in its expression, because it is extensible through modules in many ways.

The developers of the standard accepted three core modules with the RSS 1.0 vocabulary. These are components of the language although they belong to different namespaces. A considerable number of additional modules have been suggested until today. The modularization made RSS 1.0 a frontrunner among the XML vocabularies. It wasn't until years later that other XML dialects, like **Scalable Vector Graphics** (SVG; `http://www.w3.org/Graphics/SVG/`) and **Synchronized Multimedia Interface Language** (SMIL; `http://www.w3.org/TR/REC-smil/`), were separated into modules.

The XML namespace mechanism is one of the preconditions of this modularization. However, the namespace mechanism can't define the relationships between the vocabularies on its own.

The advocates of the Resource Description Format always come back to the point that RDF can describe the relationship between vocabularies explicitly and generally, whereas without RDF, the semantics of the combined vocabulary have to be redefined individually for every new extension. There are registered RSS 1.0 modules; furthermore, ad hoc extensions are possible as well.

RSS 1.0 facilitates the extension of the RSS basic model in terms of richer metadata. The extension occurs through modules, so that it isn't necessary to change the RDF core to make the language more expressive. The alternative would be to include new elements in the core. Above all, RSS 1.0 facilitates the expression of relationships between the elements, within a channel as well as between channels.

Naturally, you can also use the RSS 1.0 extension modules together with other syndication vocabularies. I mentioned the Dublin Core module in the introduction. Many aggregators support this module—even when it is used together with RSS 2.0. Authors like Mark Pilgrim recommend this combination, because the Dublin Core vocabulary is defined more precisely and comprehensively than its counterpart in RSS 2.0. Besides, the Dublin Core elements are a standard that has come to be used broadly and in many different areas.

For application developers, the combination of vocabularies leads to problems: their applications must, for example, master the namespace mechanism, if extension modules are to be used freely. Atom developers decided against the inclusion of Dublin Core elements in a namespace of their own; that is into the core of the vocabulary, to simplify dealing with the vocabulary. Users of Atom and RSS 2.0 can deal with just one single vocabulary in order to handle the tasks that arise in connection with their newsfeeds (at least as long as they do not use extensions).

The modularization of RSS 1.0 has the following advantages:

- It is not necessary to revise the core specification again and again. (These revisions would be necessary because the application area of RSS would be continuously extending.)
- No consensus is necessary on every element or every language detail. User groups can define the modules that are important to them. In this way, RSS can develop further in an evolutionary manner.

- There is no conflict between nomenclatures, because the identifiers are unique due to the namespace mechanism.

Namespace-Based Modularization

While RSS 2.0 allows the definition of extension modules in their own namespaces without further restrictions as a basic principle, RSS 1.0 defines rules for the developers of modules. The explicit regulation of a procedure for the extension of RSS doesn't mean that ad hoc extensions are impossible. However, they also have to use the namespace mechanism.

Every RSS 1.0 module is a compartmentalized extension bound to a namespace of its own. There is a distinction between standardized and proposed modules. However, only the Dublin Core, the Syndication module, and the Content module have been standardized. These modules make RSS 1.0 superior to RSS 2.0 and its predecessors with respect to its range of functionality—but also much more complex than these vocabularies.

Specification Documents

Every module has a specification document of its own under the URI `http://purl.org/rss/1.0/modules/`. Modules are supposed to combine functionalities that belong together and to be as narrowly defined as possible, without omitting any function that is necessary for the functionality of the module. Behind this rule lies the principle that many modules that are restricted in their functionality are easier to use and manage than a few extensive ones. The authors of the specification documents explicitly mention that it is possible to have simple as well as "rich" content models in the modules. Modules with a simple content model are vocabularies whose elements contain text, but no other XML elements.

In the Dublin Core module that is currently available, the value of the elements for authors and categories is simply a string, for example, `<dc:creator>Arthur Author</dc:creator>`. Such extensions are property elements. They represent properties whose value is a literal. In a future or alternative version, instead of the literal, a characterization could be inserted that is defined in a person description module of its own, for example:

```
<dc:creator>
  <pd:persdes
   rdf:about="http://www.example.com/authors/ArthurAuthor>
      <pd:firstname>Arthur</pd:firstname>
      <pd:lastname>Arthur Author</pd:lastname>
      <pd:email>arthur@author.com</pd:email>
  <pd:persdes>
</dc:creator>
```

Listing 3.4 A Resource as the Value of the dc:creator Property

RDF Compatibility of Extensions

RSS 1.0 modules should be written in such a way that an RDF parser is able to integrate XML fragments that comply with their rules in the graph that the RDF parser builds during parsing. If an extension module leads to XML that an RDF parser can't interpret as RDF-compliant, XML parsers should be alerted with the attribute parseType="literal", which makes them treat it as one single value. The content of an element that has the attribute parseType with the value literal is interpreted like the literals that you are already familiar with, for example, as values of title and description. An RDF parser doesn't analyze markup within the content of such an element, but an XML parser definitely does.

The parseType="literal" attribute is somewhat like a trick that you can use to make sure that certain XML fragments are not understood as RDF. This trick can only work, however, if the XML fragment that the parser has to interpret as a literal is the value of a property. Literals are allowed in a graph only as objects.

You have already seen that it is possible to interpret regular XML as RDF. Thus RDF can be written without knowing it—like Monsieur Jourdain in Molière's comedy *Le Bourgeois Gentilhomme*, who speaks prose without realizing it (http://www.site-moliere.com/pieces/bourg204.htm).

The condition for this is that an element on the first level of a document can be interpreted as a resource (that is, as a node), an element on the second level as a property (that is, as an arc), and the content of this element as the value of the property (that is, either as a node or as a literal).

This procedure is also called striping. If you remember the section about blank nodes, you will recall that an XML parser in such a "striped" document always finds anonymous nodes, if these are not assigned to a URI by the rdf:about attribute.

3.5 RSS 1.0 Modules

3.5.1 Dublin Core

The Dublin Core module belongs to the RSS 1.0 standard; even though it is defined explicitly as a module, and, therefore, has its own namespace. In this way, defining again within RSS things that already have an RDF version and an RDF/XML vocabulary can be avoided.

The integration of the Dublin Core module also allows for future extensions of this module to be used. The specifications of the modules also refers to the Dublin Core standard itself for the definition of the Dublin Core elements.

The Dublin Core is a set of metadata developed by a team of librarians who work on the Web. In 1995, the group met for the first time in Dublin (not Dublin, Ireland, but Dublin,

Ohio, in the United States!); that's where the name "Dublin Core Metadata Initiative" comes from. The development of the Dublin Core is continuing. By now, different extensions for different application areas are available. The RSS 1.0 module refers to the version 1.1 of the Dublin Core Metadata Set from 1999 (`http://dublincore.org/documents/1999/07/02/dces/`).

The Dublin Core Metadata Set is not an RDF application; RDF is just one of the ways to express this data. For instance, Dublin Core metadata can also be inserted without RDF in the metadata elements within the header of an HTML document. There is also an XML vocabulary for the Dublin Core elements that is independent of RDF.

The advantage of using RDF is, again, that the semantics of the language elements are clearly defined and that the data can be easily combined with other RDF data.

The URI of the namespace for the Dublin Core elements is `http://purl.org/dc/elements/1.1/`. In most cases, dc is used as the prefix for this namespace. As with all other namespace prefixes, it is just a convention; only the URI is crucial for the correct identification of the namespace.

The Dublin Core consists of 15 elements, namely, `title`, `creator`, `subject`, `description`, `publisher`, `contributor`, `date`, `type`, `format`, `identifier`, `source`, `language`, `relation`, `coverage`, and `rights`. I will use them in the following sections with the usual prefix, and will talk, for instance, about `dc:creator` and `dc:subject`. All these elements can be descendants of `channel`, `item`, `image`, and `textinput`. In the RDF data model, Dublin Core elements are predicates and properties. The respective subject is identified by a URI; with regard to RDF that means either by the URI of the channel or that of the feed, or by the URI of the described item, an image, or a text input field. The value of the property is either a literal, that is, a string, or—but only in future versions—a node of its own.

The elements of the Dublin Core act to hold metadata in the narrower sense. They don't have a structural function (like the RSS 1.0 elements) and they don't have a specific function in the publication process either.

The Dublin Core module doesn't provide the attributes of these elements. Today, the value of the `scheme` attribute can be used to indicate according to which rules the contents of one of the elements are formed, for example, whether it uses a specific controlled vocabulary.

In the specification of the module, the content of all elements is defined as #PCDATA; other XML elements are not allowed as descendants of the Dublin Core elements. The authors of the Dublin Core module have explicitly stated in the description of the data model about their expectation that in the course of its development, a richer semantics will replace the literals that are mostly used at present.

As an example, they employ a combination of the RSS taxonomy module with the specification of simple literals within the `rdf:value` element. Such a practice allows the processing software to determine which of the available data is to be used. Software that doesn't understand the specifications can work with the strings that appear as the content of the `rdf:value` element. The specification uses the following example:

```
<rdf:RDF
  xmlns:rdf="http://www.w3.org/1999/02/22-rdf-syntax-ns#"
  xmlns:dc="http://purl.org/dc/elements/1.1/"
  xmlns:taxo="http://purl.org/rss/1.0/modules/taxonomy/"
  xmlns="http://purl.org/rss/1.0/">
...
  <item rdf:about="http://c.moreover.com/click/here.pl?r123">
    <title>XML: A Disruptive Technology</title>
    <link>http://c.moreover.com/click/here.pl?r123</link>
    <dc:subject>
      <rdf:Description>
        <taxo:topic rdf:resource= "http://dmoz.org/Computers/
            Data_Formats/Markup_Languages/XML/" />
        <rdf:value>XML</rdf:value>
      </rdf:Description>
    </dc:subject>
    <dc:subject>
      <rdf:Description>
        <taxo:topic rdf:resource= "http://www.oreillynet.com/
            meerkat/?c=cat23" />
        <rdf:value>Data: XML</rdf:value>
      </rdf:Description>
    </dc:subject>
  </item>
...
```

The semantics of the elements of the Dublin Core module are independent of the objects described, whether they refer to `channels`, `items`, `images`, or `text input` fields. However, the metadata that refers to the `channel` element describes the channel or the feed itself, whereas the metadata of the individual data items refers to the information objects described in the channel. (There is a good summary of the meaning of the elements at `http://homepage.univie.ac.at/horst.prillinger/blog/archives/2005/01/000922.html`. Horst Prillinger describes primarily how they are to be used in relation to weblogs.)

The dc:title Element

The function of the `title` element is to hold the title of the subject described. This element is redundant within the module, because RSS 1.0, like the other RSS formats, has a `title` element of its own, which has the same function. The RSS 2.0 `title` element has the same function as well.

The dc:creator Element

The `creator` element refers, according to the specification, to "an entity primarily responsible for making the content of the resource". That could be, for instance, the author of an entry, or the editor in charge of a newsfeed. For a quoted entry or a link, the original author has to be mentioned.

In contrast to the `author` element in RSS 2.0, `dc:creator` requires not only the author's e-mail address, but also his or her name.

The dc:subject Element

The themes or topics discussed or displayed are the content of `dc:subject`. The `dc:subject` element is used to indicate the name of the category in weblog systems. The Dublin Core specification itself recommends using values from a controlled vocabulary or formal classification scheme here. (Such classification systems are offered, for instance, by the Library of Congress Online Catalogue, `http://catalog.loc.gov/webvoy.htm`; and the Dewey Decimal Classification System, `http://www.oclc.org/dewey/about/default.htm`.)

The dc:description Element

The Dublin Core `description` element, like the `description` element in other RSS formats, holds the description of an object. In RSS 1.0 too, HTML content is frequently used in the description, in which case markup has to be escaped.

The dc:publisher Element

The `publisher` element is the entity responsible for making a resource accessible. A publishing house or a website operator can be indicated within `dc:publisher`.

The dc:contributor Element

The `dc:contributor` element takes care of all other participants. They are not the original authors, but persons and other entities who support them.

The dc:date Element

The `dc:date` element is the container for the publication date. According to the description of the Dublin Core elements, it refers to the creation date or accessibility date (the date the resource was first accessible) of the resource. Thus the element corresponds to `pubdate` in RSS 2.0 as well as `lastBuildDate`. ISO 8601 is to be used as the date format according to the recommendations of the W3C in relation to date specifications (`http://www.w3.org/TR/NOTE-datetime`).

The dc:type Element

The dc:type element can be used to describe the type of object the described object is, for example, whether it is a book, an essay, or a weblog entry. The Dublin Core Initiative developed a vocabulary of its own for dc:type (http://dublincore.org/documents/dcmi-type-vocabulary/). Horst Prillinger suggests using "Text" for articles, "Sound" for audio blogs, "StillImage" for photo blogs, and "MovingImage" for video blogs.

The dc:format Element

The content of dc:format is a technical format specification. It is recommended to indicate the MIME type of online documents. In relation to a photo, for example, it could be explicitly indicated whether it is available as a JPEG, a GIF, or a PNG.

The dc:identifier Element

The dc:identifier element refers to an identifier of any kind, and it must be unique in the given context. This element's meaning corresponds to that of guid in RSS 2.0. The item and channel elements in an RSS 1.0 document already use the URI as an identifier.

The dc:source Element

The dc:source element allows explicit source references. This element corresponds to the element source in RSS 2.0. In dc:source a reference is inserted, or in the case of an online document, a link is inserted; however, in source, the name of the source is indicated.

The dc:language Element

Here, the language of the entry or the channel can be indicated according to the RFC 3066 specification (http://www.ietf.org/rfc/rfc3066.txt), which itself is based on ISO 639.2 (*Codes for the Representation of Names of Languages*, http://www.loc.gov/standards/iso639-2/langhome.html).

The dc:relation Element

The function of dc:relation is to indicate relationships with other objects. Prillinger suggests using this element for trackback URIs, for which previously, trackback:about was frequently used.

The dc:coverage Element

The content of dc:coverage is formed using specifications of time periods and geographical spaces. Here too, a controlled vocabulary should be used, for example, the Getty Thesaurus of Geographic Names (http://www.getty.edu/research/conducting_research/vocabularies/tgn/index.html).

The dc:rights Element

The `dc:rights` element includes specifications concerning copyright holders. Often `dc:rights` involves copyright notes.

3.5.2 Syndication Modules

The syndication module is the second of the RSS 1.0 standard modules. Its task is to inform aggregators and similar programs of the frequency of a feed update. Its function corresponds to that of `skipHours` and `skipDays` in RSS 2.0. The syndication module draws upon the Open Content Syndication format OCS (`http://internetalchemy.org/categories/ocs`), which was developed by Ivan Davis. The namespace of the module is identified by the URI `http://purl.org/rss/1.0/modules/syndication/`; the default prefix is `sy`. Its three elements are descendants of the `channel` element.

The sy:updatePeriod Element

This element describes the timescale with which a feed is updated. Possible values are `hourly`, `daily`, `weekly`, `monthly`, and `yearly`.

The sy:updateFrequency Element

This element gives an indication of how often a feed is updated in the specified update period, for instance if an update occurs twice a day. The value is a positive whole number. If this element is missing, it is assumed that the feed is updated once per indicated period.

The sy:updateBase Element

This element indicates the starting point from when the specifications in the other two elements apply, using the date formats recommended by the W3C (W3CDTF, `http://www.w3.org/TR/NOTE-datetime`).

3.5.3 Content Module

The Content module contains elements that can hold the actual content of websites. This element can be used to prevent having markup present in the `rss:description` element. However, it can be used for other content formats as well and therefore has a function similar to that of the `enclosure` element in RSS 2.0. The URI of the namespace is `http://purl.org/rss/1.0/modules/content/`; the default prefix is `content`.

The content:items Element

This element is a subelement, either of `item` or of `channel`. Its function is to contain an unordered list of `content:item` elements that include the actual content. This again requires an RDF container; in this case of the type `rdf:bag`. `rdf:bag` differs from the rdf:Seq element, already introduced, in the fact that the order of rdf:li elements that form its content is not specified. Further, within each of the elements of the type rdf:li is an element of the type content:item.

The content:item Element

This element contains the actual content. It is the descendant of an rdf:li element, which in turn is a descendant of the rdf:Bag element, which itself is a descendant of content:items. If the content is identifiable on the Web, this element has an rdf:about attribute with the appropriate URI. The content:item element has to contain a content:format element. In addition, if the content can't be retrieved through the URI in rdf:about, this element has to contain an element of the type rdf:value. Finally, an element of type content:encoding is optional.

The content:format Element

The content:format element contains the obligatory format specification for content:item. It has an attribute, rdf:resource, the value of which is the URI of the respective format. It is recommended to use the list of URIs that can be found under http://www.rddl.org/natures/ on the Resource Directory Description Language website. (RDDL is a language to describe information about vocabularies that are used on the Web. RDDL documents can be found under the namespace URIs and give advice on documentation material for the respective formats.)

The rdf:value Element

The rdf:value element includes the content of the content:item element, if the content is not simply referred to with a URI. If the content is XML that isn't encoded, the attribute rdf:parseType="literal" should be used, which we have already seen in the *RDF Compatibility of Extensions* section under section 3.4.

The content:encoding Element

This element indicates how the content is encoded. In this case, encoding means a method to embed the content in the element; the specification mentions, as an example, well-formed XML. With this element too, the identification occurs by indicating a URI as the value of the rdf:resource attribute. In the case of well-formed XML, this URI is http://www.w3.org/TR/REC-xml#dt-wellformed, that is, the URI of the XML specification (with an additional fragment identifier). If the content:encoding element is missing, it is to be assumed that the content is available in the form of character data (#PCDATA).

The content:encoded Element

Up to now, this element is just a suggestion. This element is supposed to hold a version of the content of an item element that is encoded through entity references or embedded in a CDATA section. Compared to the other elements, this would be a high degree of simplification.

3.5.4 Suggested Modules

The appendix gives detailed information about the numerous proposed modules (see section A.5). Of particular importance among them are mod_aggregation, which can aggregate feeds, and mod_dcterms, with which the qualified Dublin Core Metadata Vocabulary can be used to describe items. (See http://dublincore.org/documents/2000/07/11/dcmes-qualifiers/, latest version at http://dublincore.org/documents/dcmi-terms/.)

3.6 RSS 1.1

In January of 2005, Sean McGrath and Christopher Schmidt introduced the draft of a reformed RSS specification and called it RSS 1.1. RSS 1.1 is a reformulation of RSS 1.0. It corrects several mistakes—most importantly, it adjusts the outdated format to the current development status of RDF, RDF/XML, and XML.

```
<?xml version="1.0"?>
<Channel xmlns="http://purl.org/net/rss1.1#"
    xmlns:rdf="http://www.w3.org/1999/02/22-rdf-syntax-ns#"
    xmlns:dc="http://purl.org/dc/elements/1.1/"
    rdf:about="http://www.celawi.eu/webtrends/">
  <title>Webtrends</title>
  <link>http://www.celawi.eu/webtrends/</link>
  <description>News from the media business</description>
  <image rdf:parseType="Resource">
    <link>http://www.celawi.eu/webtrends/images/webtrends.png</link>
    <title>Logo</title>
    <url>http://www.celawi.eu/webtrends/</url>
  </image>
  <items rdf:parseType="Collection">
    <item rdf:about="http://www.celawi.eu/webtrends/">
      <title>Music downloads: Alliance of Microsoft and Nokia
          against Apple</title>
      <link>http://www.celawi.eu/webtrends/403</link>
      <dc:subject>Mobile</dc:subject>
      <description>Nokia and Microsoft allied. They want to break the
          dominance of the Apple group in the business of music
          downloads. In the future, Nokia is prepared to offer handys
          with software to play music and videos from its former rival
          Microsoft as well.
      </description>
      <dc:creator>Julia Preiner</dc:creator>
      <dc:date>2005/02/15 08:15:48.428 GMT+1</dc:date>
    </item>
```

```
<item rdf:about="http://www.celawi.eu/webtrends/">
  <title>BBC soon in first place in Digital TV business</title>
  <link>http://www.celawi.eu/webtrends/404</link>
  <dc:subject>Digital and Mobile</dc:subject>
  <description>For now, the station BSkyB is the leader on the
      British digital TV market. However,experts predict that the
      product Freeview of the public broadcast station BBC will
      soon take the top position. While BSkyB has been operating
      since the mid-1980s, Freeview started its business only in
      2002.  About 40 digital TV stations and 20 radio broadcasts
      can be received with the receiver box.
   </description>
  <dc:date>2005/02/15 08:18:06.206 GMT+1</dc:date>
  <dc:creator>Julia Preiner</dc:creator>
</item>
<item rdf:about="http://www.celawi.eu/webtrends/">
  <title>Mobilcom: Gain explosion thanks to Internet business
  </title>
  <link>http://www.celawi.eu/webtrends/405</link>
  <dc:subject>Provider</dc:subject>
  <description>Particularly the Internet- and fixed network
      business of their daughter company, Freenet, accounts for
      the downright gain explosion, that Mobilcom – Germany's
      second biggest mobile radio telephone service provider – can
      note.
  </description>
  <dc:creator>Martin Röller</dc:creator>
  <dc:date>2005/02/15 08:20:00.061 GMT+1</dc:date>
</item>
  </items>
</Channel>
```

The authors of RSS 1.1 only intended to correct the obvious mistakes of RSS 1.0. For the most part, RSS 1.1 is a new specification of the RSS 1.0 vocabulary that corresponds to the current status of RDF. In doing so, RSS 1.1 forgoes several of the syntactical features that were particular barriers to the further spread of RSS 1.0.

The extension modules of RSS 1.0 are integrated in a document with the help of the construct ANY. There is only one restriction here for the content: in an RDF graph, the root element in such a construct has to be a property by nature.

The following is a list of explicit differences to RSS 1.0:

- Elements from the RSS namespace can't appear within modules.

- The rdf:about attribute is no longer obligatory in the item element and doesn't occur in rss:image.

- RSS 1.1 feeds without items are possible.

- The input element, which was not being used in previous versions, was deleted.

- The internationalization is simplified by the xml:lang attribute, which can occur in many different locations within a document.

- The `rss:Image` element is used for images, because the old `rss:image` element was an instance of `rdf:Property` as well as of `rdf:Class`.

- The namespace URI is `http://purl.org/net/rss1.1`.

- The core is defined formally and for machine-readability by a Relax NG schema.

- All data types are defined as XML schema data types.

- There are several important rules for backward compatibility; here, attention was also paid to consider the backward compatibility to older versions of RSS 0.9x. All rules concerning backward compatibility are recommendations.

- Independent of their coding, all RSS 1.1 documents should begin with an XML prolog. Because no namespace definition is available for RSS 0.9x formats, RSS 1.1 documents shouldn't use a prefix at all for RSS elements, and ought to use the prefix `rdf` for all RDF names. It is also recommended to use the URI prefixes `http:`, `https:`, and `ftp:` only.

- In relation to images as well, the authors of RSS 1.1 feeds should restrict themselves to file formats like `.jpg`, `.gif`, and `.png`, which were commonly used in the older versions, and, if possible, also to maximum sizes of 144 x 400 or 88 x 31. It is recommended to use no more than 15 `item` elements.

- Finally, in the extension sections, elements of the same name are not to be repeated on the same level. For instance, `dc:subject` is not to be used more than once under an element. With that, allowance is made for situations where many RSS applications use the elements and their content to generate a hash table.

A Payload module should replace the older Content module. In contrast to its predecessor, content within Payload that contains markup is not encoded (that is, escaped). Rather, it has to be XHTML that is identifiable as such through the correct indication of the namespace. The use of the `rdf:parseType="Literal"` element within the root document makes sure that the content can be processed further correctly.

A simplification compared to RSS 1.0 is the fact that RSS 1.1, as well as Atom, are described by a Relax NG schema. This makes it easy to validate an RSS 1.1 document. There is also a Relax NG schema and an OWL ontology for extensions.

RSS 1.1 documents should be provided with the media type `application/rss+xml`; the media type `application/rdf+xml` is also allowed. Other values are not allowed.

3.6.1 Channel as Root Element

The root element of an RSS 1.1 document is called `Channel`. The namespace is defined by the URI `http://purl.org/net/rss1.1`. The most obvious difference in the structure of RSS 1.0 and RSS 1.1 documents is that RSS 1.1 doesn't use a document element of the type `rdf:RDF`. With that, RSS 1.1 is able to use RDF documents without `rdf:RDF` root elements. Externally, an RSS 1.1 document becomes an RDF document through the use of attributes from the RDF namespace like `rdf:about` and `rdf:parseType`; otherwise the syntax corresponds more to that of RSS 2.0 and its predecessors. Actually, RSS 1.1 is defined to be RDF compliant, so that a parser can construct the respective triples based on a schema or an ontology.

Like Atom, RSS 1.1 knows the attributes `xml:lang` and `xml:base`. The value of `xml:base` can be used to resolve relative URIs that are specified as the value of the `rdf:about` attribute or `rdf:resource` attribute, or as the content of elements or the value of other attributes. The language of an element is indicated by the value of `xml:lang`.

The rss:title Element

The `title` element doesn't differ from that of version 1.0. The specification explicitly states that it is synonymous with the `title` elements of the Dublin Core vocabulary and XHTML.

The rss:description Element

It is important for RSS 1.1 to explicitly prohibit that compliant software converts escaped markup within the `description` element into HTML markup. Rather, there is a separate Payload module, which takes the place of the RSS 1.0 mod_content module, for quoting HTML markup in an RSS 1.1 document.

Every `item` element of a channel is identifiable through a unique value of the `rdf:about` attribute. This attribute is not obligatory. Anyone who can't ensure that the values of this attribute are unique for the content they publish should forgo it. The specification explicitly eliminates the possibility of channels appearing within themselves.

Within a weblog, for instance, the value of `rdf:about` identifies the `item`; the `link` element refers to a potentially discussed resource. If the URI of an item is unique, for example, in the case of an entry in a weblog, it can form the content of the `link` element and the value of the `rdf:about` attribute at the same time.

The rss:items Element

The `rss:items` element doesn't play the role of a table of contents any more. Its descendants are now the `item` elements themselves. They belong to an RDF list, which the `parseType="Collection"` attribute takes care of.

The `items` element itself is a property element as in RSS 1.0; the value of this element is described differently syntactically, because the `item` elements are descendants of `items`. The `parseType` attribute with the value `collection` brings about, as with `rdf:seq`, that the value of `items` is a blank node. But this blank node is of the type `collection`. I won't discuss the specifics of this type at this juncture; above all, it differs from `rdf:seq` in that how many elements will follow every element in the collection is clearly determined. (In `rdf:seq`, how many other elements belong to the same sequence can't be identified.)

The rss:item Element

There are only small differences between the `item` element and its counterpart in RSS 1.0. These mostly concern the general differences between the formats. The only change specific to this element relates to the `rdf:about` attribute: it is no longer obligatory. The `rdf:about` attribute is to be used only if the author of an RSS document can ensure that the value is actually unique. If the attribute is missing, the parser again constructs a blank node for the resource that describes the `item` element.

Under no circumstances does `rdf:about` allow use of the URI of a weblog entry or any other resource that is discussed in the respective `item`. The attribute is to indicate the URI of the `item` it belongs to.

The rss:link Element

The definition of the `link` element differs from that in RSS 1.0 (see also section 3.3.2) only insofar as the data type is explicitly identified as any URI type of the XML schema data types. In addition, `link` is an optional descendant of the `image` element and no longer obligatory as it was in the previous version.

4

Atom

Atom is the most recent of the important syndication formats; it corresponds, in the range of its functionality, to RSS 2.0. The team that develops Atom set themselves the goal of providing a clean and clearly specified format for "periodically updated content".

4.1 Overview

Two motives in particular led to the development of Atom: the RSS specifications—except for RSS 1.0—are in many aspects vague and incomplete; in addition, there is a lack of a common protocol for the writing and editing of weblog-like publications. The Blogger API (`http://www.blogger.com/developers/api/1_docs/`) and the MetaWeblog API (`http://www.xmlrpc.com/metaWeblogApi`), which have been supported by many weblog systems up to now, are incomplete, unstable, and are based on a concept of web services that is frequently considered insufficient. On the one hand, Atom is supposed to eliminate the known imperfections of RSS as a specified format; on the other hand, it is meant to determine an open standard for the development of publishing tools that correspond to a modern, REST-oriented concept of web services.

It is not difficult to notice that the RSS 2.0 specification and its predecessors are incomplete and, above all, imprecise. Almost everywhere it is necessary to fall back on common practice in order to understand what the specification means. While presenting RSS 2.0, I referred repeatedly to the Atom specification to specify certain formulations.

Further Development? Or Alternative to RSS?

The Atom developers hold Dave Winer partly responsible for the fact that they haven't simply developed RSS 2.0 further, but instead defined a new format that is supposed to replace RSS and is not backward compatible. The RSS 2.0 specification itself determines that further developments of the format are to occur under a new name; Winer declared RSS 2.0 "frozen". The Atom developers refer to the fact that it would be confusing to keep the document element rss within a new format (for instance at `http://www.intertwingly.net/wiki/pie/Motivation`); considering that, backward compatibility with the existing RSS formats could no longer provided anyway.

Therefore, there is the chance to define the new format in such a way that it can fulfill all of today's relevant requirements.

Starting Points for the Development of Atom

Robin Cover summarized the key realizations that lie behind the development of Atom (*Atom as the New XML-Based Web Publishing and Syndication Format*, http://xml.coverpages.org/ni2003-10-22-a.html):

- Design Atom such that content is not treated as a second-class citizen.
- Insist upon a uniform mechanism for expressing the core concepts independent of the usage.
- Keep the format open and simple.

The criticism of Atom by RSS 2.0 advocates focuses on the point that a new standard isn't necessary, or might even be confusing and slow down the propagation of syndication technologies. (A search for the keyword "Atom" on Dave Winer's weblog is enlightening: http://archive.scripting.com/search/default?q=atom.) The arguments in regards to the content are barely addressed.

Standardizing Procedures and Specifications

A team of the Internet Engineering Task Force (IETF; http://www.ietf.org/) under the leadership of Paul Hoffman and Tim Bray is responsible for the standardizing of Atom.

"Atom" is a collective term for several protocols and specifications. The most important and stable specification defines the "Atom Publishing Format" or "Atom Syndication Format". The draft-ietf-atompub-format-11 was endorsed by the Internet Engineering Steering Group as a "proposed recommendation" and therefore an IETF standard in August 2005 (http://www.ietf.org/internet-drafts/draft-ietf-atompub-format-11.txt; HTML version under http://www.atomenabled.org/developers/syndication/atom-format-spec.php). The publication of Atom documents is described in the "Atom Publishing Protocol". Version 04 was published on May 9, 2005 (http://ietf.levkowetz.com/drafts/atompub/protocol/draft-ietf-atompub-protocol-04.txt); after that date important modifications were proposed and accepted by the developers of the protocol. A third document, "Atom Feed Discovery," determines how associated Atom feeds are found in a web document; as of now, version 01 (May 10, 2005) is the only one available (http://www.ietf.org/internet-drafts/draft-ietf-atompub-autodiscovery-01.txt).

All Atom specifications are Internet drafts that are submitted to the IETF. (The function and the status of these documents are described by *Internet Drafts*, http://www.ietf.org/ID.html.). If the specification process has advanced far enough, they are submitted to the Internet Engineering Steering Group (IESG; http://www.ietf.org/iesg.html). If the IESG accepts a document, it officially publishes it as "Request for Comments (RFC)".

The Atom Syndication Format will get an RFC Number in the near future and can be implemented as a stable specification.

The Atom Publishing Format is the format for Atom documents, that is, the counterpart to the formats RSS 2.0, RSS 1.0, and RSS 1.1, which I introduced in the previous chapters. For the development of the Atom specification there is a mailing list for the Atom syntax (http://www.imc.org/atom-syntax/index.html), a mailing list for the Atom protocol (http://www.imc.org/atom-protocol/index.html), and the Atom wiki (http://www.intertwingly.net/wiki/pie/FrontPage). The wiki documents problems and new suggestions in **paces**; the actual development of the specification takes place on the lists.

The Atom specification uses the terminology of the XML info set (http://www.w3.org/TR/xml-infoset/). The info set standard defines the different information items that are included in a document (that is, that can be extracted from the document by a parser). The specification does not explicitly talk about information items in regards to Atom elements and Atom attributes.

Sources of Information

The specifications, the mailing lists, and the wiki are the most important sources of information concerning Atom. A constantly updated overview is offered—as with most XML topics—by the "XML Cover Pages" (http://xml.coverpages.org/atom.html). Mark Pilgrim, Joe Gregorio, and other developers have discussed many aspects of Atom in articles at XML.com (http://www.xml.com/). Important resources in regards to Atom are the weblogs of the standard developers. Some of the most interesting and important minds within the XML scene participate in the discussion around Atom, among them

- Tim Bray (http://www.tbray.org/ongoing/),
- Sam Ruby (http://www.intertwingly.net/blog/),
- Mark Pilgrim (http://diveintomark.org/archives/), and
- Norman Walsh (http://norman.walsh.name/).

Differences Between Atom and the other Feed Formats

It is more difficult to describe the differences between Atom and RSS 2.0 in a few sentences than it is to set RSS 2.0 and RSS 1.0 apart. Atom wasn't designed as a competitor to RSS, but as a technically completely specified syndication format offering the same features as RSS 2.0. General differences are that in Atom, as in RSS 1.0, all elements belong to a defined namespace and they can all carry the attributes xml:base and xml:lang. In addition, Atom and RSS differ in numerous details, mostly concerning the definition of individual elements. Furthermore, the design principles of Atom result in differences that extend Atom's functionality compared to RSS 2.0 to such a degree that Atom itself can serve as a publication format for periodically updated information.

Extended Functionality

Extended functionality is present in at least four areas:

- **Content:** Atom allows for almost all kind of content that is possible on the Internet to be included in an entry—provided that it is clearly indicated which type of content is involved.

- **Links:** Atom has precise and, above all, extensible link semantics. The functions of links are clearly determined in an Atom document, and additional functions can be registered. The easiest way to extend the functionality of Atom is to define additional types of links.

- **Aggregation:** Atom entries can carry with them the metadata of the feed they belong to if they are incorporated in another feed. Thus it is possible to construct feeds with entries that are extracted from different feeds and continue having all relevant information (for instance, about their authors).

- **Publication:** Atom was defined as a format for the publication of content. Atom documents can contain information about the URIs that Atom clients need for publishing and editing. Atom documents with the entry document element serve to publish entries.

In all four cases, the new functionality results from the fact that the meaning of the elements is described more precisely than is the case with RSS 2.0. In RSS the extent to which the content of an element is data or metadata is left unspecified. The specification in Atom leads to a precise definition of exactly how content can be embedded in Atom documents. RSS also leaves unspecified whether the link element has to include the URI of the entry itself or the URI of a resource that is descibed in the entry. Atom makes it compulsory to declare the kind of link described in a link element; by doing so, it makes it possible to combine two or more kinds of links in one entry. In RSS 2.0 feeds, the same elements can occur on the level of the feed (channel) and on that of the entry (item), and the source element can hold only a little information. The specification in Atom provides for every entry under source to carry with it a container with the metadata of its original feed. The RSS 2.0 elements were also the starting point for the definition of publication interfaces like the MetaWeblog API. In Atom, the precise definition of the transport of documents through HTTP leads to a complete publication protocol as a subset of HTTP.

4.2 The Structure of an Atom Feed

4.2.1 Overview: Atom Elements

As in the chapters regarding the other feed formats, I would now like to introduce the Atom syntax step by step and show the functions that this syntax facilitates. Figure 4.1 shows the tree structure of an Atom feed with two entries. In this document, all Atom elements occur at least once.

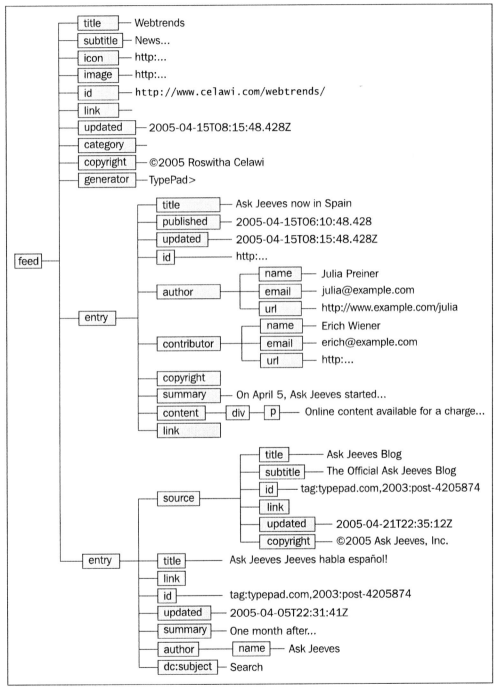

Figure 4.1 Structure of a Complex Atom Document

The document, whose structure you can see here, was only created to demonstrate Atom's possibilities. A realistic situation to apply this structure is not very likely.

The document skeleton shows several important characteristics of the Atom Publishing Format:

- The document element of an Atom feed is called feed. The news that belongs to this feed is contained in elements called entry.

- The functions of some RSS elements are divided up into several Atom elements. (Instead of the RSS image element, Atom has the elements icon and image; instead of the RSS description element, Atom has the three elements subtitle, summary, and content.)

- An entry in Atom can contain other content types than text. In the example, the first entry element includes a content element, which again has XHTML elements as descendants.

- An element of the type entry can contain metadata from a feed. The second entry element in the figure was extracted from another feed, and carries with it the metadata of that feed.

- The Atom elements entry and feed can contain several links with different tasks.

In the following sections I will start with the obligatory elements of an Atom feed—with its basic structure. Then we will learn about the metadata that the feed and entry elements in Atom can contain. After that we will see how different kinds of content can be incorporated into an Atom document. Another focus is the semantics of links in Atom.

4.2.2 The Basic Structure of an Atom Document

The following document contains all elements that have to occur in every Atom feed, provided that it contains entries at all:

```
<?xml version="1.0"?>
<feed xmlns="http://www.w3.org/2005/Atom">
  <title>Webtrends</title>
  <author>
     <name>Roswitha Celawi</name>
  </author>
  <updated>2005-04-15T08:15:48.428Z</updated>
  <id>http://www.celawi.com/webtrends/atom</id>
  <link rel="self" href="http://www.celawi.com/atom.xml"/>
  <link rel="alternate" href="http://www.celawi.com/webtrends.html"/>
  <entry>
    <title>Ask Jeeves now in Spain</title>
    <summary> On 5 April, Ask Jeeves started with the beta version of
      a new search service for Spain. It is the first of several
      starts planned in Europe this year.</summary>
    <updated>2005-04-15T08:15:48.428Z</updated>
    <id>http://www.celawi.com/webtrends/20040415_01.html</id>
    <link rel="alternate" href="http://www.celawi.com/webtrends
```

```
        /20040415_01.html"/>
    </entry>

    <entry>
        <title>Bitkom study: Paid content successful in Germany</title>
        <summary>Online content available for a charge becomes more and
            more accepted.
        </summary>
        <updated>2005-04-14T10:20:17.428Z</updated>
        <id>http://www.celawi.com/webtrends/20040414_01.html</id>
        <content type="xhtml">
            <div xmlns="http://www.w3.org/1999/xhtml">
                <p>Online content available for a charge becomes more and
                    more accepted: <q>The times of the free-of-charge culture
                    come to an end. At the same time the quality of the offers
                    increases," says the executive director of Bitkom,
                    Bernhard Rohleder.</q>
                </p>
            </div>
        </content>
    </entry>
</feed>
```

Listing 4.1 Simple Atom Document

The Atom Namespace and the xml:lang Attribute

Atom documents require the indication of an explicit namespace. In most cases atom is used as the prefix for that namespace. The namespace for Atom is identified by the URI http://www.w3.org/2005/Atom since the IETF has accepted Atom as a standard. (Please note that the older namespace-URIs used in drafts of the Atom specification are deprecated.)

Every Atom element can carry the xml:lang attribute, which is used as defined in the XML specification (http://www.w3.org/TR/REC-xml/#sec-lang-tag; RFC 3066 contains the language tags used to identify the languages: http://www.ietf.org/rfc/rfc3066.txt). Only in a few elements can this attribute influence the processing. The specification explicitly identifies these elements as language sensitive. In all other elements the language doesn't play a role; for instance, no language field has to be reserved in a relational database (http://www.intertwingly.net/wiki/pie/PaceLangSpecific).

Text, Person, and Date Constructs

For certain combinations of XML elements that can occur in different positions in an Atom document, so-called constructs are defined in the specification. Doing this shortens the specification. In addition, it ensures that the same language elements have the same meaning, independent of the context where they are used.

The most important and most complex of these constructs is called the **text construct**. You will learn about it in the sections about the content of Atom entries (see also section 4.2.3). There are also person and date constructs.

Person constructs describe not only persons, but also companies and other "legal entities". A person construct includes an obligatory name element, and optional elements for the e-mail address and a URI, usually the URI of a person's website. It can contain further elements for extensions (see also section A.7.3 in the appendix).

Date constructs are used to indicate points in time and calendar dates. The elements that use these constructs as content can have the attributes that are allowed for all Atom elements; their content corresponds with the XML Schema data type dateTime (http://www.w3.org/TR/xmlschema-2/#dateTime).

This type is compatible with ISO 8601 (International Organization for Standardization, *Data elements and interchange formats—information interchange representation of dates and times*, ISO Standard 8601, June 1988) and the recommendation of the W3C for dates and times (http://www.w3.org/TR/NOTE-datetime; see also section A.7.4 in the appendix).

feed and entry as Structuring Elements

The following figure shows the structure of the document.

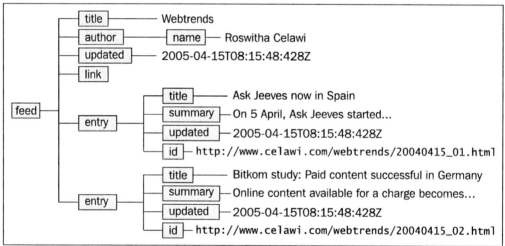

Figure 4.2 Structure of a Simple Atom Document

The hierarchy of an Atom document includes two levels. In this, Atom doesn't differ from the other important vocabularies for newsfeeds. feed is the document element of a—well—a feed. (In addition, Atom allows entry as a document element as well, but only if the Atom API is used to post an entry to a website or to change an entry.) feed represents the newsfeed as a whole. Together with the xmlns attribute, this element also indicates which vocabulary the document belongs to. (Thus it takes over the tasks of the RSS document elements rss or RDF and the following channel or Channel elements, respectively. The new names for the document elements indicate that compatibility with

RSS is no longer supported: Atom can only be used with software developed specifically for these formats—it is not another RSS format, but a deliberate new approach.) The URI of the namespace also indicates the version of Atom, and therefore, feed doesn't need a version attribute.

The feed element is a container for the data and metadata associated with a feed. The descendants of feed are elements that describe the newsfeed itself, and elements with the name entry. The entry elements represent entries that belong to the feed; thus they form the actual content. (The Atom specification accepts feeds without entries, but in practice they don't occur very often. On the other hand, a feed can include an unlimited number of entries.)

There are six elements with five different element names in the example that describe the whole feed, namely, title, author, updated, id and link. Their names describe their meaning:

- title contains the title of the newsfeed.
- author includes information about the author.
- updated indicates the latest update date.
- id contains a URI that uniquely identifies the feed.
- link refers to a different version of the content and to the URI of the Atom feed itself.

These elements are mandatory descendants of the feed element. If this information about the feed is missing, an Atom document is not valid.

title and updated are also required descendants of entry.

- In addition, entry contains the element summary with a summarizing text

The Atom specification doesn't determine the order of the elements that can be components of the elements entry and feed.

In its very basic structure, an Atom document doesn't deviate very much from documents in RSS formats. Most notably, the element names differ from each other: feed takes the place of channel, and entry takes the place of item. The name feed reflects the fact that newsfeeds have become a separate form of online publication.

Atom requires more metadata for every document compared to other feed formats. Behind this characteristic is the desire not to omit information that is necessary in almost every practical publication context and especially if information is syndicated and reused. Ben Hammersley talks in *Building Applications with RSS, Atom, and the Atom API* about a "principle of the conservation of metadata": "An Atom document explicitly states the minimum we can know about the resource and no less" (http://conferences. oreillynet.com/presentations/et2005/hammersley_ben.pdf). This allows a very high degree of flexibility in reusing content that is available online without losing essential features of its original context. Wherever the information appears on the Web, it has to carry the same identifier and its author is mentioned. The author element as a descendant of feed can only be omitted if an author is indicated for every single entry. In this connection, even institutions can be indicated. This rule distinguishes Atom from other syndication formats. The motivation is not technical, but social—it must be possible to identify a person responsible for every document. The rules every entry has to have an id element, which allows the message to be uniquely identified, along with the information about the last update, allow for deciding whether a message in a newsreader has already been displayed in its up-to-date form or not.

4.2.3 Content as a "First-Class Citizen"

Text in Atom Elements—HTML, XHTML, or Plain Text

The example shows two elements with text content—title and summary. The content of these elements is formed by pure text data. In regards to all elements with text content, Atom also offers the possibility of using HTML or XHTML, as the element content in the second entry of the example shows.

The Atom specification talks about "text constructs" as the content of the title, summary, and description elements. (The content element can include a text construct as well; I will elaborate on this characteristic in the next section.) In all elements that can hold text constructs, the type attribute can be used to indicate which kind of text they contain. Only three values are allowed for type: text, html, and xhtml:

- If the value is text, the content of the element is made up of plain text that doesn't include markup at all. (Since Atom is an XML format, the information items that a parser can extract are Unicode characters.)

- If the value is html, the content consists of text with escaped HTML markup. A section marked as HTML element em, for instance, would be reproduced like this: <em>...</em>. Also in this case, only Unicode characters occur in the XML infoset. However, the client can use the escaped markup for the presentation of the respective passage. An additional rule says that in a valid HTML document the content of the element has to be able to form element content of the type div. Thus randomly storing fragments of an HTML document in a text construct is not allowed. This ensures that the software that presents the fragment can process it according to the rules applicable to HTML.

- The third alternative is to indicate xhtml as the value of the type attribute and to use text along with XHTML markup as the content of the text construct. In the document tree of the Atom element, the XHTML elements are in this case descendants of the element that includes the text construct. Not only does the restriction that the HTML fragment must be able to be the content of a div element in a valid XHTML document apply here, but the HTML fragment also has to be actually embedded in an XHTML div. It is obligatory to indicate also the XHTML namespace. As in the case of HTML content, client software can interpret the XHTML markup to display the fragment. Unlike the case of HTML content, in this case escaped markup within the fragment can't be replaced by valid markup. In this way it is possible to quote markup in the content of an entry without any ambiguity how the escaped markup has to be interpreted: The escaped characters belong to the content, not the markup of the document.

If no value is indicated by using the attribute type, the content is interpreted as text. That means that if the content of one of these elements is to be processed as HTML or XML, a type attribute with an appropriate value must be used.

With these alternatives, the format lives up to the common practice of using HTML fragments as the content of RSS elements. Since the type attribute clearly indicates which format has been selected for the content, the element can be processed and rendered accordingly, without breaking the XML rules. Sam Ruby repeatedly referred to the fact (among others in the commentary http://blogs.law.harvard.edu/tech/comments?u=tech&p=648&link=http://blogs.law.harvard.edu/tech/2004/06/15#a648 - a676), that the common practice to use so-called "entity-coded" HTML as the content of an RSS document ignores the fact that there is no method to detect HTML in the content of an RSS document without ambiguity. Ben Trott points out (*Why we need Echo*, http://www.sixapart.com/about/news/2003/06/why_we_need_ech.html) that the representation of the content is the most important part of the feed. With RSS 2.0 it remains unclear when to use double-coded entities—a content:encoded element with a CDATA section—or the xhtml:body element. Another problem of entity-coded HTML is that it isn't clear how to deal with relative URIs, which are frequently included in it. Atom uses xml:base, so that it is clear how to interpret relative URIs. (Regarding this problem, see also section 2.2.3 *Text or HTML as the Content of title and description*.)

The following example shows how text constructs of the types text and html are used. In the summary element of the first entry, only the type attribute has been added. The content of the element is processed in the same way as the example at the beginning of the chapter, because the processing software has to assume that the content of the element is made up of text, as nothing else is indicated. The content of the second summary element could be presented by a newsreader as an HTML element of the type P with an internal quote (element type Q).

```
...
<entry>
  <title>Ask Jeeves now in Spain</title>
  <summary> On 5 April, Ask Jeeves started with the beta version of
    a new search service for Spain. It is the first of several
    starts planned in Europe this year.</summary>
  <updated>2005-04-15T08:15:48.428Z</updated>
```

```
   <id>http://www.celawi.com/webtrends/20040415_01.html</id>
   <link rel="alternate" href="http://www.celawi.com/webtrends/
      20040415_01.html"/>
</entry>

<entry>
   <title>Bitkom study: Paid content successful in Germany</title>
   <summary type="html">&lt;P&gt; Online content available for a
      charge becomes more and more accepted: &lt;Q&gt; The times of
      the free-of-charge culture come to an end. At the same time the
      quality of the offers increases &lt;/Q&gt;, says the executive
      director of Bitkom, Bernhard Rohleder. This year, the sales
      volume will increase by 137 percent - up to 484 million Euros.
      In 2004, a plus of 105 percent could be recorded.</summary>
   <updated>2005-04-14T10:20:17.428Z</updated>
   <id>http://www.celawi.com/webtrends/20040414_01.html</id>
   <content type="xhtml">
      <div xmlns="http://www.w3.org/1999/xhtml">
         <p>Online content available for a charge becomes more and
            more accepted: <q>The times of the free-of-charge culture
            come to an end. At the same time the quality of the offers
            increases," says the executive director of Bitkom, Bernhard
            Rohleder.</q>
         </p>
      </div>
   </content>
</entry>
```

Listing 4.2 Example for Text Constructs of the Types text and html

In the following example, XHTML is used for the content of the second element. Note that the namespace is indicated as specified, and that the XHTML content is embedded in an XHTML element of the type div!

```
<entry>
   <title> Bitkom study: Paid content successful in Germany </title>
   <summary type="xhtml">
      <div xmlns="http://www.w3.org/1999/xhtml">
      <p><q> The times of the free-of-charge culture come to an end. At
         the same time the quality of the offers increases </q>, says the
         executive director of Bitkom, Bernhard Rohleder. This year, the
         sales volume will increase by 137 percent - up to 484 million
         Euros. In 2004, a plus of 105 percent could be recorded.</p>
      </div>
   </summary>
   <updated>2005-04-15T08:15:48.428Z</updated>
   <id>http://www.celawi.com/webtrends/20040415_02.html</id>
   ...
</entry>
```

Listing 4.3 Example for a Text Construct of the Type xhtml

Only content that is clearly marked as XHTML is allowed to be parsed as XHTML. That makes it possible, among other things, to filter out potentially dangerous elements like JavaScript, for instance.

Escaping markup within XHTML fragments is not a problem. Therefore, the following construction is a feasible example:

```
<atom:title type="xhtml">
  <xhtml:div xmlns:xhtml="http://www.w3.org/1999/xhtml>"
  The element &lt;br/&gt;: mostly redundant!
  </xhtml:div>
</atom:title>
```

Listing 4.4 Escaped Markup in an XHTML Fragment within an Atom Element

An aggregator that interprets the content of the element as a fragment of a valid XHTML element can present it correctly as follows:

The element <br/>: mostly redundant!

If, however, the type of the text construct is HTML, it is up to the processing software how it uses escaped markup for presentation as HTML markup. Most RSS aggregators and newsreaders are likely to interpret escaped markup delimiters for the presentation as delimiters of HTML markup. The following fragment:

```
<atom:title type="html">
  The element &lt;br&gt;: mostly redundant!
</atom:title>
```

would be reproduced like this:

The element

: mostly redundant!

If the processing software converts escaped markup only once, it is possible to double-escape in order to quote markup. The following fragment shows one example:

```
<atom:title type="html">
  The element &amp;lt;br&amp;gt;: mostly redundant!
</atom:title>
```

Listing 4.5 Double-escaped Markup in an HTML Fragment

The atom:content Element—A Container for Content

In Atom the content is to have the rights of a "first-class citizen". For that reason, content is a container for any kind of content. It is not limited to contain the text constructs, which can also be the content of title, subtitle, and summary.

content is the most important element of many feeds. This element makes Atom a transfer format for different kinds of content. At the same time it might well be the most complex content model. The content:

- Can be within (inline) or outside a document (out-of-line)
- Can be textual or binary
- Can optionally be described additionally in a summary element

129

If one of these possibilities is chosen, it limits the choices in others. Out-of-line content, for instance, has to be described in a summary.

Embedded or Linked Content

Primarily, authors have to choose one of two alternatives to define the content of an entry:

- They can put the content directly between the start and the end content tags; the Atom specification talks in this case about inline content. Whenever the content is not plain text, the type attribute must be used to indicate which type of text it is.

- They can indicate a URI through which the content can be retrieved. The URI forms the value of the optional src attribute. In this case, the MIME media type of the content has to be indicated as the value of type. The specification calls this kind of content out-of-line content.

These two possibilities are mutually exclusive. The src attribute is allowed only if content is an empty element. Both possibilities are available for text as well as for binary content. However, as you will see in the following sections, important restrictions exist in connection with these two options.

The atom:content and atom:summary Elements

The description element in the different RSS standards has the task of holding a summary or synopsis of the content of an item. However, very often the complete content is actually stored in it.

These two ways of using description in RSS correspond to two different elements in Atom: summary and content. The summary element contains an overview and thus has the task that was originally intended for the description element in RSS. The content element doesn't hold descriptions, but holds the content itself, or contains a link to it.

Either summary or content *must* occur in an entry element. If an entry doesn't have content of its own, content has to be at least described (in this case, the link element usually indicates where the content is located). More than one element of these types isn't allowed; consequently, it is not permitted for an entry to contain or describe two or more items of content. Both element types can also exist together in one entry element. In such a case, the content of summary describes the content of content.

There are two cases where both summary and content have to be present:

- An entry element has to include a summary element whenever the content element has the src attribute and is therefore empty. Content that isn't located within the feed has to be described.

- summary is also required if the content of content is Base64-encoded. This is the case whenever it involves content in a MIME media type that doesn't start with text or end with xml.

These two requirements result from the principle of accessibility. If, for some reason (network problems, missing reproduction software, security issues, etc.), content can't be, or is not to be, loaded, at least a description has to be offered. Conversely, based on the description, users can decide how they want to deal with the content.

Text Content 1: Plain Text, HTML, and XHTML

As with the `title`, `subtitle`, and `summary` elements, `content` can also contain an Atom text construct, that is, plain text, HTML, or XHTML. In this instance, exactly as is the case with the other elements, the type of content involved is indicated by the `type` attribute, the value of which is `text`, `html`, or `xhtml`.

In the following example a complete message is stored in the `content` element and `summary` contains a summary in plain text:

```
...
<entry>
   <title>Bitkom study: Paid content successful in Germany</title>
   <summary type="text">A new study of the industry's association
      Bitkom says: Paid content is economically successful also in
      Germany by now.</summary>
   <content type="xhtml">
      <div xmlns="http://www.w3.org/1999/xhtml">
         <h2>Study: Online content available for a charge successful
            in Germany</h2>
          <div class="message_wrapper">
            <p>This year the sales volume of digital content through the
            Internet in this country will increase by 137 percent - up
            to 484 million Euros. That is the opinion of the industry's
            association <a href="http://www.bitkom.org"
            target="_blank">Bitkom</a>. After a plus of 105 percent
            in 2004, the growth would accelerate at a very high rate.
            Already in two years the market would reach a volume of much
            more than a billion Euros, the association continued to
            prophecy. Bitkom refers here to a current study of the
            European Information Technology Observatory (EITO).</p>
         </div>
      </div>
   </content>
   <updated>2005-04-15T08:15:48.428Z</updated>
   <id>http://www.celawi.com/webtrends/20040415_02.html</id>
</entry>
...
```

Listing 4.6 XHTML as Content of `content`

Text Content 2: Other Text Types and XML

In contrast to the rest of the Atom elements that can hold text constructs, `content` can also contain text in other formats, provided that it is a registered MIME media type. In the following example, which was extensively shortened, the message from the last example is transferred in rich text format:

```
<entry>
  <title>Bitkom study: Paid content successful in Germany </title>
  <summary type="text"> A new study of the industry's association
    Bitkom says: Paid content is also economically successful in
    Germany.</summary>
  <content type="text/rtf">
{\rtf1\mac\ansicpg10000\uc1\deff0\stshfdbch0\stshfloch0\stshfhich0\st
shfbi0\deflang1031\deflangfe1031{\upr{\fonttbl{\f0\fnil\fcharset256\f
prq2{\*\panose 00020206030504050203}Times New Roman;}
...
{\b\f178\fs48\insrsid873893\charrsid873893
        Study: Online content available for a charge successful
        in Germany
        \par
        \par }\pard \ql \li0\ri0\widctlpar\aspalpha\aspnum\faauto\
        adjustright\rin0\lin0\itap0 {\f179\fs32\insrsid873893\
        charrsid873893 This year the sales volume of digital content
        \u252\'9f
        through the Internet in this country will increase by 137
        percent - up to 484 million Euros... of the European
        Information Technology Observatory (EITO).}{\insrsid14698475
        \par }}
  </content>
  <updated>2005-04-15T08:15:48.428Z</updated>
  <id>http://www.celawi.com/webtrends/20040415_02.html</id>
</entry>
```

Listing 4.7 RTF Text as the Content of content

In practice, the ability to embed documents or fragments from other XML vocabularies in the content element is likely to be more interesting.

There are two possibilities for XML content:

- It can be directly embedded in the content element. In this case, the root element of the embedded XML is to be used as a descendant of content. XML elements should be directly embedded in content whenever the media type ends with +xml (for example, application/rdf+xml, image/svg+xml, or application/xhtml+xml), or starts with text (for instance, text/xml). The XML data can then be transferred at the client to a specialized application like an SVG viewer or an HTML browser.

- It can be retrieved through a URI that is indicated as the value of the src attribute. This procedure should only be used if the media type ends with /xml. In this case, the data can be downloaded if the respective software is available. (For more information about the media types see also RFC 3023, http://www.rfc-editor.org/rfc/rfc3023.txt, and *XHTML Media Types*, http://www.w3.org/TR/xhtml-media-types/. application/xml is a generic media type. For registered media types with +xml endings, for example, application/xhtml+xml, specialized applications are usually available.)

The following example shows how an SVG graphic can be included in an Atom entry.

```
...
<entry>
  <title>Example of a SVG graphic in an Atom Feed</title>
  <summary type="text">The graphic shows an ellipse.</summary>
  <content type="image/xml+svg">
    <svg xmlns="http://www.w3.org/2000/svg" width="12cm"
        height="12cm" viewBox="0 0 1000 1000">
      <path d="M 270,300 A 180, 90 0 0 0 630 300  A 180, 90 0
          0 0 270 300" stroke="red" fill="none"/>
    </svg>
  </content>
  <updated>2005-04-15T10:15:02.021Z</updated>
  <id>http://www.wittenbrink.net/streams/atom/07_02.html</id>
</entry>
...
```

Listing 4.8 XML Inline Content in an Atom Feed

This procedure opens a great many possibilities, because Atom can be used for the transfer of any kind of XML data. For example, it would be feasible for search results that are obtained in an OpenSearch fragment to be immediately processed (see also section 2.6.5).

Binary Content

For the sake of completeness, the following examples show how binary content can be inserted inline and out-of-line in an Atom entry. The first example uses a "spacer.gif". Since binary content is involved, it has to be described in the summary element.

```
...
<entry>
  <title>Example of a Base64-encoded GIF graphic in an
  Atom Feed</title>
  <summary type="text">The element content contains a transparent
  GIF file of the size of one pixel.</summary>
  <content type="image/gif">
    R0lGODlhAQABAJH/AP///wAAAMDAwAAAACH5BAEAAAIALAAAAAA
    BAAEAQAICVAEAOw==
  </content>
  <updated>2005-04-15T10:15:02.021Z</updated>
  <id>http://www.wittenbrink.net/streams/atom/07_03</id>
</entry>
...
```

Listing 4.9 Binary Inline Content in an Atom "entry"

In the following example a PDF file is incorporated out-of-line. Again, the summary element is mandatory.

```
...
<entry>
  <title>Almost one third of Americans who use MP3 players also
  use podcasts</title>
```

```
        <summary type="text">2 million US Americans have an MP3 player
        or an iPod. 29% of them have also used podcasts.</summary>
        <content type="application/pdf" src=" http://www.celawi.com/
              webtrends/20050415/pew.pdf"/>
        <updated>2005-04-15T10:15:02.021Z</updated>
        <id>http://www.wittenbrink.net/streams/atom/07_04</id>
      </entry>
      ...
```

Listing 4.10 PDF Document as Out-of-line Content in an Atom `entry`

This form of content of an `entry` allows distribution of data and documents of all kinds. However, in many cases it is easier to refer to such data through a link. The next section will discuss what kinds of possibilities links can offer in Atom documents.

The `enclosure` element, which has become famous due to the podcasting boom, obviously doesn't need Atom. Nevertheless, the Atom specification offers as a counterpart of the RSS `enclosure` element the possibility of using a `link` with `enclosure` as the value of the `rel` attribute. This possibility was added to the specification at a late stage to ensure feature equality with RSS.

4.2.4 The Use of Links in Atom

In the examples that you have seen so far, links occurred only as descendants of `feed`. The specification requires that a link should refer to an alternative presentation on the Web, at least on the level of the newsfeed as a whole. (It is possible, however, that this regulation will be replaced by a new one to make these references more obligatory. There are many cases where Atom feeds transfer content but don't inform about content that can be also received under other URIs.)

Links play an important role in the Atom vocabulary, even though there are Atom feeds where links don't (or hardly do) occur. They can have more functions than in the other XML applications for newsfeeds, and specific language tools, usually different values of the attributes of the `link` element, correspond to these functions. An Atom link always indicates what kind of relation there is between the link and the resource that it refers to.

In the newer versions of the Atom specification, links are defined through the `link` element, and no longer as a construct of their own.

In regards to links the authors of the Atom specification also tried to replace the ambiguities and obscurities of the RSS specification with clear descriptions of the element semantics. In RSS documents the `link` element can be used either to refer to related information (this practice is described in the Netscape specification of RSS 0.91 as well), or to indicate the URI of the respective `item` (or its HTML version). Today, they often incorporate so-called permalinks (for which the element `guid` was introduced). The attributes in Atom indicate where a link refers to; they were adopted from HTML, so the `link` element can have the attributes `href`, `type`, and `title` in Atom as well.

The Structure of an Atom Link

Links describe the relationship between the Atom element and a resource on the Web. In Atom the URI of the resource for which a link is established is always the value of the `href` attribute of a link. It doesn't form the content of the `link` element, as is the case in RSS.

Like the HTML `link` element, `link` in Atom also has a `rel` attribute, the value of which indicates the type of the relationship. An important additional aspect is the fact that the meaning of this attribute is extensible. The Atom specification only specifies a minimum. In the future, the values that `rel` can have are to be registered with the IANA (Internet Assigned Numbers Authority; `http://www.iana.org`). If a name is indicated as the value of `rel`, it is to be interpreted as one of the names of the (still to be established) IANA Registry of Link Relations. It can then be turned into a URI by attaching it to the string `http://www.iana.org/assignments/relation/`.

However, some values are valid right from the start and are defined in the Atom specification. They refer to the URI that is indicated as the value of `href`, and they describe the relation of the resource that the URI identifies to the feed or entry the `link` belongs to, as follows:

- `alternate`: The URI identifies an alternative representation of the resource.
- `related`: The URI identifies a resource that is related to the resource that the respective link belongs to.
- `self`: The URI identifies the resource that includes the `link`.
- `enclosure`: The URI identifies a resource that is related to the resource that includes the respective `link`. It is possibly extensible and asks for specific requirements in the processing software.
- `via`: The URI identifies a source for the information in the feed or entry that the link belongs to.

The `rel` attribute can be missing. In this case, the `link` element has to be processed as if the value of `rel` was `alternate`.

The Atom Publishing Protocol defines several other values of `rel` that will be registered soon with the IANA. These values describe the relations toward URIs that—according to the REST concept for websites—are used for the posting and editing of resources. A URI that can be used to start a new resource with the POST request is indicated in a `link` by a `rel` attribute that has the value `resource.post`. Another URI, the `EditURI`, is used to edit a resource by using the HTTP PUT method, or to delete with the HTTP DELETE method. The value of `rel` in this case is `service.edit`.

In addition, links can be marked with the optional attributes `hreflang`, `title`, `type`, and `length`.

The value of the optional `hreflang` attribute is the language of the resource that is referred to; the language is labeled according to RFC 3066. If the value of `rel` is alternate, the resource is interpreted as the translation of the entry that was referred from. The optional title attribute of the link element is also taken from HTML.

The value of the ref attribute is formed by a URI reference according to the latest specification of URIs RFC2396 bis (http://gbiv.com/protocols/uri/rev-2002/rfc2396bis.html). It can be a URI fragment that is resolved by appending to the value in xml:base. If the type of a link is defined as alternate, an alternative representation of the resource that is described in the parent element of link is to be found under the indicated URI, such as an HTML document, for instance. The value related indicates that there is a relation with the resource the indicated URI refers to. Entries or feeds referring to Google can, for example, contain the element <link rel="related" href="http://www.google.com">.

The type attribute of the link element holds the media type or data type of the document's representation that is to be expected from the server if link is updated; it has to be a registered MIME media type. In this way, it is possible, for example, to indicate within a link that the link leads to a PDF document.

A human-readable title of a link is used as the value for the title attribute. As length, the size of the resource that is referred to can also be indicated (its value being the number of bytes). Here, the values of length and type can't ensure that a document that can be reached through this link actually has the indicated length and media type.

atom:link as a Descendant of atom:feed

In all cases a feed element has to contain exactly one element of the type title and one element of the type link with the attribute value rel='alternate'. It is possible that this regulation will be revised before the publication of version 1.0 of the Atom syndication format. If this link refers to an HTML element, that is, if the value of the type attribute of the link element is html, the respective HTML element should also contain a link to the feed. It should allow the discovery of the Atom feed with the autodiscovery mechanism that is included in the Atom specification. Other link elements are possible, but they have to refer to data of different types.

Thus, an Atom document can be defined as an alternative for a different document more explicitly than documents in the other feed formats.

Feed Autodiscovery in Atom

The Atom specification—as a counterpart to the regulation above—also requires that an Atom feed called for by an HTML element can be automatically recognized. That is the function of the autodiscovery mechanism (http://www.ietf.org/internet-drafts/draft-ietf-atompub-autodiscovery-01.txt), which uses the HTML link element. The value of rel in the HTML link for the autodiscovery is in this case alternate; the value of type is atom+xml. (In HTML, attribute values can be written in either upper or lower case—unlike in the XML-based Atom.)

It is also possible to indicate several links to different Atom feeds in an HTML document; for instance, one to a feed for a weblog, one for an associated linkblog, and a third feed with commentaries. In this case, the value of the `title` attribute that contains a human-readable identification should clarify what kind of content is included in the different feeds. If feeds are automatically subscribed to from a site, the first of the link elements is used for clarification of the content. Therefore, the author of the HTML element should make sure that the most important feed is the first reference. (For more information about the `link` element see section A.7.17 in the appendix.)

4.2.5 Other Metadata

Feed Characterization with atom:subtitle, atom:icon, and atom:image

Unlike RSS documents, in which an element of the type `description` is mandatory within `channel`, an Atom document doesn't necessarily have to contain a `subtitle` element that corresponds in function with `description`.

The content of `subtitle` includes a short characterization of the feed. `subtitle` is an element that can occur only as an immediate descendant of feed, not within `entry`. Here, the `summary` element occurs instead, but it has other functions, though. In an Atom document, elements have the same name only if they have the same meaning and the same content.

In addition, the elements `image` and `icon` can indicate an image and a small icon. Their role is to visually characterize a feed, for instance, by displaying the image in a newsreader. The content of both elements is a URI. The specification recommends that the images referred to by the URIs in `image` have a width/height ratio of 2:1 and those specified in `icon` have an aspect ratio of 1:1; however, this is not mandatory. In this regard, `icon` refers to an image that corresponds in size and function with the *favicon* of an HTML page.

The following document fragment shows how the beginning of the Atom example looks if the elements `subtitle`, `icon`, and `image` are added:

```
<?xml version="1.0"?>
<feed xmlns="http://purl.org/atom/ns#draft-ietf-atompub-format-07">
  <title>Webtrends</title>
  <subtitle>News about commercial websites and online
  advertising</subtitle>
  <icon>http://www.celawi.com/webtrends/images/feed_icon.png</icon>
  <image>http://www.celawi.com/webtrends/images/feed_icon.png</image>
```

atom:author and atom:contributor

The Atom specification makes it mandatory to indicate the author of an entry. For this purpose, the `author` element is used, which can be a sub-element of feed and `entry`. Both feed and `entry` can only have one author each. The author identification can only be omitted if the author indicated for a feed is the author of all entries. (For more information about the `author` element see also section A.7.5 in the appendix.)

The content of this element is one of the person constructs (see also section A.7.3), which are typical for Atom. Person constructs include a name, an optional e-mail address, a URI, as well as the indication of extension elements. The specification of the name is dependent on the language.

Although an entry or a feed can only have one author, the number of other persons who were involved in its creation is unlimited. They are listed within the contributor element, which also contains a person construct. (For more information about the contributor element see also section A.7.8 in the appendix.)

Identification with atom:id

id is one of the elements that are obligatory for every feed and every entry. This element is defined in a way that—if used correctly—makes sure that the resource it refers to is uniquely and unmistakably identifiable. The value of the element is a URI (more correctly, an IRI), which has to be generated in such a way that its uniqueness is guaranteed.

Relative URIs are not allowed. In order to decide whether two URIs are identical, it doesn't matter whether they lead to the same resource when they are dereferenced. The only thing that counts is whether they are identical in regards to their characters. The specification contains (as example URIs among others) http://www.example.org/thing and http://www.example.org/Thing, which differ as identifiers from each other even though their processing presently leads to the same resource.

In order to prevent a confusion of URIs that lead to the same resource when dereferenced but differ in their character value, the specification lists a set of rules, for instance, as a matter of principle to indicate the rule, the schema, and the host in lower case.

Copyright Specification with atom:copyright

The Atom copyright element only contains a human-readable copyright specification; machine-readable rights information has to be stored in extension elements. If an entry doesn't have a copyright specification, the specification for the feed—if available—is applicable. (For more information about the copyright element see section A.7.9 in the appendix.)

Publication Dates with atom:updated and atom:published

The updated element refers to the latest date on which an entry was changed in a way that the publishing individual or institution considers relevant. The date doesn't change with every change of an entry, or if the feed is regenerated. The content of this element is a date construct. (For more information about the updated element see section A.7.25 in the appendix.)

The published element, on the other hand, indicates—roughly speaking—the date on which an entry was published for the first time. The specification talks a little flowerily about "an instant in time associated with an event early in the life cycle of the entry". (For more information about the published element see section A.7.19 in the appendix.)

Metadata about Sources: atom:source

The publication options, which in Atom exceed by far those of the rest of the feed formats, include that an entry from one feed can be taken over by another feed, and, in doing so, can carry with it the metadata of the original feed in a source element of its own. The source element in Atom doesn't only include the name and the URI of the original feed as in RSS 2.0. It can hold as descendants all the elements—except for the entry elements—that were descendants of the feed element in the original feed.

The specification recommends at least copying the author, category, copyright, and contributor elements from the original feed to the target feed, provided that these elements exist. Again, Atom follows the principle of keeping at least a minimum of metadata.

By providing the possibility to transfer metadata from one feed into another, Atom facilitates aggregated feeds, that is, feeds that, according to certain criteria, collate entries from a number of feeds into a new feed. In the coming years, such aggregated feeds are likely to become more and more important in regards to organizing current information from heterogeneous resources. In this way, a feed about a topic can be generated from different weblogs; a weblog like Planet RDF (http://planetrdf.com/) could be produced as a synthesized feed. The feeds of "prospective search engines" like PubSub (http://www.pubsub.com/) will make use of this possibility too. (For more information about the source element see also section A.7.21 in the appendix.)

Classification of Content with atom:category

Even in categorizing content, Atom is more precise than RSS 2.0. category in Atom is an empty element with three attributes: term, scheme, and label. The term attribute is obligatory; it identifies the category that an entry or a feed is assigned to. scheme defines the schema that the categorization follows. It is optional, as is the language-sensitive label attribute, which can incorporate a human-readable identification of the category. The identifier of the category in this schema is not identical to the identifier for a reader. Thus it is possible, for instance, to follow the English category system of the Open Directory Project (http://dmoz.org/), but to give the respective category a German name. (For more information about the category element see section A.7.6.)

Identification of the Creator Software with atom:generator

The generator element fulfills the same function in Atom as in RSS. It indicates the software that created a feed; if bugs occur in a software program, its producers can be informed. The URI and the version of the software are indicated. (For more information about the generator element see section A.7.13 in the appendix.)

4.3 Extensibility

Atom, like RSS 2.0 and RSS 1.0, is an extensible format. Atom doesn't have modules of its own yet, but many of the modules that were developed for RSS formats can likely be used with Atom as well. In contrast to the RSS 2.0 specification, the Atom specification describes minimal syntactical requirements for extensions. But unlike the RSS 1.0 specification, it doesn't determine how language elements of Atom extensions are to be interpreted semantically. (RSS 1.0 modules have to be defined in a way that RDF triples can be extracted from them. XML that isn't RDF compliant has to be marked with the attribute `rdf:parsetype='literal'` in a way that it can be interpreted by an RDF parser.)

The Atom specification defines an extension construct of its own for extensions. Extension constructs can occur in an Atom element at the following positions: within person constructs, feeds, and entries. If "foreign" markup appears, software can leave the respective passages unprocessed.

If the foreign markup appears within text constructs or in the content of the Atom `content` element, the software should leave it unprocessed. All descendants of `feed` and `entry` elements as well as of person constructs are treated as metadata that describe these elements. The interpretation of "foreign markup" in other positions is not regulated in the specification. The specification distinguishes between simple and complex extensions. Simple extensions are elements without attributes except the `xmlns` attribute. Extensions of this type are to be understood as name/value pairs, which refer to the feed, the entry, or the person they belong to. The URI of the namespace and the local name of the element form the name; the content of the element makes up the value.

The Atom specification doesn't say anything about how "foreign" language tools are to be understood in complex extensions. Elements that belong to complex extensions have attributes and/or other elements as descendants; they are always language-sensitive.

4.4 Publishing with the Atom Publishing Protocol

As the counterpart of the Atom Syndication Format, the **Atom Publishing Protocol (APP)** (`http://www.ietf.org/internet-drafts/draft-ietf-atompub-protocol-04.txt`) describes a standardized way to edit the content of regularly updated websites. The protocol defines rules for the communication of clients and servers in a publishing environment. APP clients will work in a similar way as today's blogging tools like ecto or MarsEdit. The server side is represented today by services as Radio UserLand Typepad and blogger.com or by blogging software as Movable Type or WordPress. Since the Atom Feed Format is not limited to weblogs or to weblog-like content, the Atom Publishing Format will support other content types as well. Wherever a publication consists of a collection of items of a defined type, the Atom Publishing Protocol can be used to edit the items—they may be text documents, bank account data, or whatsoever. This functionality distinguishes the APP from existing APIs used to update weblogs (Blogger API, MetaWeblogAPI).

The specification of the Atom Publishing Protocol isn't completed yet; unlike the Atom Syndication Format, there will probably be further extensive changes and additions. The following section addresses the main features of the protocol. Please regard the document types and XML elements described in this section as illustrations of the underlying principles; they represent the current results of the discussion of the Atom Protocol Working Group, and may change soon.

4.4.1 Design Principles

The goals of the Atom Publishing Protocol, which is often also called the Atom API, overlap with the goals of the syndication format (Mark Pilgrim: *The Atom API*, `http://diveintomark.org/public/2003/11/atomapi.pdf`). The protocol is to be completely provider neutral and easy for anyone to implement; furthermore, it is actually to be implemented by every provider that comes into question. Consequently, it has to also work on hosted accounts and be accessible for users who can't change a `.htaccess` file. Access is to be made possible through pure CGI functionality. In addition to that, the protocol has to be arbitrarily and freely extensible. Like the Syndication Format, it is to be completely and cleanly specified. Also, it shouldn't show any security holes.

The Atom Publishing Protocol is a REST API and doesn't use SOAP for several important reasons. Pilgrim lists these: No additional wrapper is needed, because the Atom format itself already defines a wrapper around content in a different format. For the existing providers the authentication mechanisms that HTTP offers are sufficient; none of them is interested in a stronger or more exotic procedure. In addition, the existing providers also don't need a procedure that is independent of the HTTP transport mechanism.

The question comes to mind, why shouldn't the already existing and thoroughly specified WEBDAV protocol be used for updating of websites? In order to answer this question, Pilgrim refers to the specific conditions under which the Atom Publishing Protocol is to be used. It is designed to work on periodical websites, and not on any documents on a server. It is supposed to facilitate the communication with different user-specific back ends through a common API, not more. Furthermore, it has to function through CGI, so that it's also possible to work with it on hosted sites that don't allow access to a `.htaccess` file.

The Atom API will offer even more functions beyond editing. Among them will be the posting of commentaries as well as the managing of users, user preferences, site templates, and categories.

It is still open at present, above all, how the Publishing Protocol wants to treat collections of entries (see also *Getting ready for protocol discussion*, `http://www.imc.org/atom-protocol/mail-archive/msg00464.html`).

The architecture of the API includes these aspects:

- It is to work with literals that represent the document, and not use Remote Procedure Calls. This requirement coincides with the requirement for the Atom Syndication Format to work as an authoring and a publication format at the same time.

- It should be a slim and well-defined format that doesn't fail by defining too many features for too many different requirements. In particular, it is not to be a new form of the WEBDAV protocol.

- Furthermore, the format is to use the possibilities of existing web architecture, that is, it is supposed to utilize all possibilities that are offered by HTTP and XML. The specification says that in the core, the Atom Publishing Protocol describes the transfer of representations in the Atom format over the HTTP protocol.

- Finally, as a result of security requirements, passwords are not to be transferred in plaintext when using the Atom API.

- In contrast to other APIs, the Atom API is also to have a standardized procedure for the discovery of APIs. The existing APIs leave it to the user to find the API of the service. Some functions aren't fully documented.

The discovery of the Atom API only requires that a user knows the URI of an HTML web document through which the API can be reached. A `link` element as a descendant of `feed` points to a `service.feed` or introspection file. This introspection file contains a list of the supported functions and extensions. The introspection document is a simple and well-formed XML document. Every provider can extend the format of this document by using the XML namespace mechanism.

Interaction via HTTP

The Atom Publishing Protocol is usually used to manipulate collections of resources. The HTTP protocol defines the methods regarding the treatment of every resource that are represented in these four important HTTP verbs:

- GET is used to retrieve a representation of the resource or to search for resources with a read-only enquiry.

- PUT is used to update a known resource.

- POST is used to create new dynamically named resources.

- DELETE is used to delete a resource.

This procedure is considerably simpler and more transparent than the procedures of the older weblog APIs. There, the processing method was passed as the value of a parameter of its own (LiveJournal), was transferred as a function name in the body of an XML remote procedure call (Manila API, Blogger API, and MetaWeblog API), or was indicated through a function name within a SOAP body. For that purpose, it also has to appear in the SOAP Action header.

The APP elaborates on the HTTP transfer of Atom-formatted representations. It deals with the data formats and the communication of client and server during this transfer, but not with the URIs themselves. Which URIs are used is up to the server or those who control the related URI space.

Members, Collections, and Workspaces

The APP describes an API for regularly updated sets of items. These items are not necessarily Atom entries but can be represented by such entries. In the APP Atom entries serve to exchange information about items in order to publish or to edit them on a web server. In addition to feeds and entries, the APP speaks of "collections" and "members".

Collections are sets of items that have already been published or will be published in the future. Member is the name for an item that belongs to such a collection and therefore shares certain features with other members. The APP compares collections with the directories or folders of file systems. Whereas it was relatively easy to describe how members are handled in the APP up to now, there are still a lot of open questions regarding the management of collections.

Many weblogs consist of more than one collection. Imagine a blog with longer, descriptive entries in a main column and a sidebar with a linkblog and a photoblog! The APP is intended to allow a common editing interface for the three collections. For this reason the specification introduces the term **workspace** for a group of related collections on a server.

The basic forms of interaction in the APP are similar for members and collections. They are realized via HTTP requests with the common HTTP verbs GET, POST, PUT, and DELETE. A service supporting the APP offers specific URIs for the manipulation of collection and member resources.

The Publication Service as URI Space

As a REST protocol, the Publishing Protocol works with URIs. Again and again, URIs are mentioned that are used for sending and processing entries. In its current state (October 1 2005) the APP describes client server interaction via the URIs in the following table:

URI	Request (HTTP-Verb)	Server-response	Function
Editable Resource URI	HEAD or GET	200 OK; representation of the resource	Reading of a member resource
	PUT + updated representation	200 OK; representation of the updated resource (optional)	Updating of a member resource
	DELETE	200 OK	Deleting of a member resource
Collection Resource URI	GET	collection document with description of the capabilities of the collection	Information about the capabilities of a collection resource
	POST	201 created; location header with the URI of the newly created resource	Creation of a new member resource
Search Resource URI	GET	Atom Feed Document with entries matching the search criteria	Listing of member resources matching specified criteria
Service Description Resource	GET	Introspection Document	Description of the service

The URIs are mapped to different representations. These representations are XML documents, but the types or schemes of these documents are not yet fully specified. In the case of the Editable Resource URI it is clear that the representation is an Atom entry element. The representation of the Collection Resource URI will be an XML document describing the properties of the collection; it is pretty clear at the actual point of the discussion on the mailing list that a specific new document type is needed in order to fulfill this function. Whether this document will also contain a complete or partial listing of the members of a collection is not agreed; probably it will only communicate to the client how it can request for such a listing.

4.4.2 Entry Documents and Publishing Extensions

Contrary to the various RSS versions, Atom includes a document type of its own for the editing of articles. The document element in this case is called entry; an entry document can be considered as a fragment of an Atom feed. It follows the same grammar as the feed documents. Every entry describes a web resource of its own with metadata, and if necessary, also with a text representation.

4.4.3 Functions of the Atom APIs

Finding Entries

The first basic function of the API is to find individual entries or groups of entries. A respective URI is indicated in the introspection document. Through this URI it is possible to find documents that describe collections of entries.

Processing Entries

Every entry has a specific URI by which it can be processed: the EditURI. This URI is also included in lists of entries; it is returned after the creation of a new entry. It is up to the server software to decide how it is named. The introspection document informs the client of this URI.

Processing a Group of Entries by Using the FeedURI

The FeedURI, which is used for processing, serves to download an Atom feed that differs from a "common" feed through having links that lead from each entry to the previous and following entries, and simplify the processing. In addition, the feed can contain a link element with rel="service.post" by which new entries can be sent to the server. Every individual entry should contain a link with rel="service.edit", the URIs of which are EditURIs.

The service.feed is an introspection file in which the server's range of functionality is published. The different facets the server offers are found through link elements. The value of the rel attribute in these links starts with the service character string, and is followed by the name of the respective service. Also, there is no search service any more, but only links pointing to other feeds that either have rel="service.feed" and different titles, or simply refer to previous or following feeds with rel="prev" or rel="next".

Posting of other Data with ResourcePostURI

The ResourcePostURI sends non-entry resources to the server. This URI, again, is found through links. These links either belong to the header of an HTML document, or they are children of an atom:feed or atom:entry element. The link has a rel="resource.post" attribute. The HTTP request that is sent to the server includes a content type and a content length header. The server answers with the standard response codes.

4.4.4 Format of Documents in the Communication Between Client and Server

The Atom Publishing Protocol uses the Atom Format as a format for the documents that are exchanged between client and server; consequently, the message content is not extracted from the XML representation and wrapped-up in parameters of a remote procedure call, as is the case with older weblog APIs.

By using the Atom Publishing Protocol, the documents have to fulfill several additional conditions apart from the requirements of the format. Documents that are received through the FeedURI and the EditURI have to have the element `atom:id`; the same applies for documents that are sent through the EditURI to the server. If, on the other hand, a document is sent through the PostURI to the sender for the first time, the `atom:id` can still be missing; in this case, the server will add it. If FeedURI and EditURI are used to communicate, the `atom:link` element is also obligatory.

If PostURI is used, it can be employed to determine the URI of the resource that is created on the server. The `title` element is always necessary, but can be empty—not every entry has to have a title. The server should not create titles. There are no specific rules for the `summary`, `content`, `author`, and `contributor` elements. A publication date has to be indicated in every case; if the PostURI is used, a modification date can't be indicated under any circumstances. If the PostURI is used, the design of the protocol specification arranges for the `generator` element to be available in all cases; it then indicates the codebase that is employed to create a request. Also mandatory in this case is the indication of a version number as the value of the `version` attribute.

4.4.5 How to Support Specific Functionality of Publishing Systems?

New weblog authoring systems do much more than simply posting and updating entries on a server. They allow, for instance, to store drafts. Many weblog clients can inform the publishing system that trackbacks to an entry are accepted. Brent Simmons has summarized the most important shared features of weblog publishing systems. Simmons has proposed that these features be supported by future similar systems in a standardized manner in order to allow clients to communicate with all of them in the same way. (`http://inessential.com/2004/11/18.php`). The developers of the Atom Publishing Protocol decided to comply with this requirement. The extension mechanism of the Atom Format makes it easy to incorporate information that the server needs in the document itself.

In the months after the publication of draft-04, the participants of the mailing list reached consensus to reserve a namespace for such additions (see `http://www.intertwingly.net/`

wiki/pie/PacePubControl). The provisional URI of this namespace is
http://example.net/appns/; generally the prefix pub is used for its elements.

A publishing extension of an entry element is always included in an element of the type
pub:control. This element has several attributes and one optional child element of the
type pub:draft. Extension elements are allowed. pub:control may appear only once in
an entry that is published or updated.

One child element of pub:control will be part of the APP specification itself; its name is
pub:draft. pub:draft informs the server that the entry containing the control element is
a draft that may not be made publicly available. pub:draft can appear once in a
document; the only allow values of this element are yes and no. The respective pace of
the Wiki (http://www.intertwingly.net/wiki/pie/PacePubControl) gives the
following example:

```
<entry>
 <title>Lorem Ipsum</title>
 <link href="http://example.org/lorem" />
 <updated>2003-12-13T18:30:02Z</updated>
 <summary>Lorem ipsum dolor sit amet, consectetur adipisicing
elit...</summary>
 <control xmlns="http://example.net/appns/">
  <draft>yes</draft>
 </control>
</entry>
```

Further publishing extensions can be developed as extension elements to be used in
pub:control. With these extensions it will be possible to use the Atom Publishing
Protocol in a flexible manner for editing different kinds of content. J. Snell and E. Torres
have proposed blog-specific extension elements in an Internet draft
(http://www.ietf.org/internet-drafts/draft-snell-atompub-app-blogcontrol-
00.txt). They use the namespace URI http://purl.org/atompub/blogcontrols/1.0;
in the draft it is bound to the prefix blog. The elements are:

- blog:private: To indicate that the audience of an entry is limited; possible
  values are yes and no.

- blog:notify: To name services that have to be informed about updates; the
  services are mentioned with their child element blog:endpoint.

- blog:enable: To state which features of the blogging system (e.g.
  comments) should be used; children elements used for this purpose are
  blog:Comments , blog:Trackbacks, blog:Pingbacks, blog:Plugin,
  blog:CommentsNotify, blog:TrackbacksNotify, blog:PingbacksNotify,
  blog:TextEncoding.

The draft contains the following example:

```
<entry xmlns="http://www.w3.org/2005/Atom"
          xmlns:pub="..."
          xmlns:blog="...">
     <id>tag:example.com,2005:/entries/1234</id>
```

```
            <title>A simple blog entry</title>
            <updated>2005-10-10T00:00:00Z</updated>
            <content>This is a simple blog entry</content>
            <pub:control>
              <blog:private>no</blog:private>
              <blog:notify>
                <blog:endpoint
                  type="http://www.movabletype.org/trackback/"> \
                  http://www.example.com/entry1.tb</blog:endpoint>
                <blog:endpoint
                  type="http://www.technorati.com/developers/ping/"> \
                  http://www.technorati.com/ping/</blog:endpoint>
              </blog:notify>
              <blog:enable>
                <blog:comments
                  until="2005-12-12T00:00:00Z">moderated</blog:comments>
                <blog:trackbacks
                  until="2005-12-12T00:00:00Z">moderated</blog:trackbacks>
              </blog:enable>
              <blog:scheduled>2005-11-11T00:00:00Z</blog:scheduled>
            </pub:control>
          </entry>
```

Security Aspects

Unlike its predecessors, the Atom Publishing Protocol is to comply with high security requirements. Particularly, the transfer of passwords in plain text, which is typical for the XML-RPC-based APIs, is to be avoided.

It has to be ensured that only authorized users can create and change entries. HTTP Digest Authentication and, as an alternative, a CGI authentication (as of May 20, 2005) are used as authentication procedures. Furthermore, Atom servers and clients can encode messages according to the LS Protocol [RFC2246].

It is also possible to forgo the authentication, for example, in regards to wikis, which are open for everybody to edit, and commentaries. The alternative, CGI authentication, was included in the protocol to allow the use of Atom servers and clients that don't support HTTP Digest Authentication, but allow the users to create HTTP headers of their own, and to set up a CGI program for the authentication of entries.

The specification mentions the risks involved in HTTP Digest Authentication and CGI authentication. Both are not fully protected against dictionary-based attacks.

4.4.6 Communication through SOAP

Several times I have pointed out the fact that the Atom Publishing Protocol is a typical REST web service. The client tells the server through HTTP messages how the status on the server is to be changed. Because there are clients that have only limited ability to communicate via HTTP, it is also possible for Atom servers and clients to communicate through SOAP. It is not mandatory that Atom servers support SOAP. However, the specification lays down requirements if they do use SOAP. A SOAP client has to be able to assume that an Atom server fulfills these requirements, if it supports SOAP at all.

As mentioned before, SOAP defines envelopes for messages that are independent of the protocol used to exchange messages. If possible, Atom clients should use the correct HTTP methods as described. If not, they should use the POST method and send a SOAP Action HTTP header that is specified as follows:

The action is indicated as the value of the header in a URI that begins with `http://schemas.xmlsoap.org/wsdl/http/`; attached to it is the name of the desired HTTP method. If the XML document that was sent to the server is provided with a SOAP envelope, it has to correspond exactly with the HTTP method.

A SOAP-supporting server has to be able to process well-formed XML. However, it is not necessary that it can process processing instructions or DTDs. In addition, the server has to accept content wrapped in a SOAP envelope. The server has to send its answers as the content of a SOAP envelope to the client, or create a SOAP error.

4.4.7 Extensions of the Publishing Protocol

Extensions should fulfill the following requirements:

- They have to support a mechanism of autodiscovery, so that the client can find them without users having to deal with technical details.

- They have to inform the client of possibilities they provide if these are not already included in the service itself.

- The data exchange with the server should not be more difficult than in the core Atom functionality.

- Other functionalities are not to be broken by the extensions.

The Atom Publishing Protocol employs the same mechanisms for extensions as for its core functionalities: the communication with the server works through URIs and HTTP methods. The client can discover the offered methods in a file that the server provides, and can receive information from the server. Resources on the server are to be changed by XML documents in the body of the HTTP requests and responses. Syntactically, namespaces are used to extend existing document formats if needed.

Appendix

A.1 Reference: XML Namespaces

The namespace mechanism is considered complicated, but wrongly so, because it is based on a simple principle to clearly allocate names that are used in a XML document to a particular XML vocabulary. This vocabulary forms the "namespace," which includes the names that refer to it.

In an XML document, names are used for elements and attributes. The name of an element is placed between the angle brackets of the tags; the attribute name is placed within the tags in front of an equal sign. Consider the following example:

```
<?xml version="1.0"?>
<feed version="0.4>
<head></head>
</feed>
```

Here, feed and channel are the names of two elements. (It is not correct to talk about a feed or head tag, if the whole element as a container is meant.) It is also possible to say: an element has the name feed, or an element is of the type feed. The character string version within the start tag of the element feed is an attribute name.

These element and attribute names are so-called local names. The names as such don't reveal which vocabulary they belong to. An application that this document is transferred to can't decide whether it is, for instance, an Atom document or not.

In order to clearly express how the names feed and head are to be understood, they have to be "qualified." This qualification can be achieved by referring element identifiers explicitly to the namespace they belong to. This allocation is carried out by the xmlns attribute. The value of this attribute is a URI. In the following example, the xmlns attribute is used for the declaration of the namespace:

```
<?xml version="1.0"?>
<feed  version="0.4"
       xmlns="http://purl.org/atom/ns#draft-ietf-atompub-format-04">
<head></head>
</feed>
```

feed and head are considered to be qualified names, because the declared namespace applies for the element in which the declaration takes place, as well as for all elements that are included inside that element (unless, as we will see in a moment, one of the descendants is assigned its own namespace).

Globally Clear Identifier

In order to clarify this qualification, we can also write the element identifiers in their expanded form as follows (in this connection, it is not valid XML, but only a didactic clarification; it follows http://www.jclark.com/xml/xmlns.htm):

```
<?xml version="1.0"?>
<{http://purl.org/atom/ns#draft-ietf-atompub-format-04}feed
    {http://purl.org/atom/ns#draft-ietf-atompub-format-04}
    version="0.4"
  <{http://purl.org/atom/ns#draft-ietf-atompub-format-04}head>
  </{http://purl.org/atom/ns#draft-ietf-atompub-format-04}head>
</{http://purl.org/atom/ns#draft-ietf-atompub-format-04}feed>
```

These qualified names are no longer local names, but globally clear names.

The reason for that is simple: a URI, like in our case, http://purl.org/atom/ns#draft-ietf-atompub-format-08, is globally **clear**; it has the same meaning in any document. For this, it isn't even necessary to actually have a document at the address that is used here as a URI. The rules for the allocation of names on the Net make *sure* that this identifier isn't used with different meanings.

Avoiding Name Conflicts

We can insert an element from a different namespace in our document. In order to do this, we use an element from the XML version of the Dublin Core,[1] which we have come across several times already in this book. For our example we choose the element named author, which belongs to this vocabulary, and insert it for now in our document without identifying the namespace:

```
<?xml version="1.0"?>
<feed  version="0.4"
       xmlns="http://purl.org/atom/ns#draft-ietf-atompub-format-04">
<head>
<author>James Clark</author>
</head>
</feed>
```

---

[1] Librarians developed the Dublin Core metadata set for bibliographical references on the Net. It can be combined with all syndication vocabularies that are introduced in this book.

Written like this, the element is not identifiable as a Dublin Core element for an application that processes Atom data. Atom includes an element with the name author as well; however, the contents of this element have to be formed by further elements, among them an element with the name name, like in the following example:

```
<?xml version="1.0"?>
<feed  version="0.4"
       xmlns="http://purl.org/atom/ns#draft-ietf-atompub-format-04">
<head>
<author>
<name>James Clark</name>
</author>
</head>
</feed>
```

To determine that we want to use the element author from the Dublin Core instead of the one from Atom, we have to allocate it to the namespace of that vocabulary as in the following listing:

```
<?xml version="1.0"?>
<feed   version="0.4"
        xmlns="http://purl.org/atom/ns#draft-ietf-atompub-format-04">
<head>
<author xmlns="http://purl.org/dc/elements/1.1/">James Clark</author>
</head>
</feed>
```

In our didactic notation with the prefixed URIs, this document would look like this:

```
<?xml version="1.0"?>
<{http://purl.org/atom/ns#draft-ietf-atompub-format-04}feed
    {http://purl.org/atom/ns#draft-ietf-atompub-format-04}
    version="0.4">
  <{http://purl.org/atom/ns#draft-ietf-atompub-format-04}head>
    <{http://purl.org/dc/elements/1.1/}author>James Clark
    </{http://purl.org/dc/elements/1.1/}author>
  </{http://purl.org/atom/ns#draft-ietf-atompub-format-04}head>
</{http://purl.org/atom/ns#draft-ietf-atompub-format-04}feed>
```

Now, the element author is also qualified, so it can't be confused with the element author from the Atom vocabulary. Both elements have the same local name, but not the same qualified name. They can even be combined like in the following example:

```
<?xml version="1.0"?>
<feed  version="0.4"
       xmlns="http://purl.org/atom/ns#draft-ietf-atompub-format-04">
<head>
  <author>
    <name>James Clark</name>
  </author>
  <author xmlns="http://purl.org/dc/elements/1.1/">
          James Clark</author>
</head>
</feed>
```

An application that only understands Atom elements can ignore the Dublin Core element author in this document. However, an application compatible with Dublin Core can recognize that the name of an author is indicated here according to this standard.

That is (almost) everything! We have presented the basics of the namespace mechanism. Problems for many users as well as application developers arise from the fact that the allocation of namespaces can also be done with abbreviations. In order to not have to repeat the xmlns attribute with a URI as a value, it is possible to define that a certain character string represents this attribute together with one of its values. In the following version of our example we use such abbreviations for both namespaces:

```
<?xml version="1.0"?>
<atom:feed version="0.4"
  xmlns:atom="http://purl.org/atom/ns#draft-ietf-atompub-format-04">
  xmlns:dc="http://purl.org/dc/elements/1.1/">
<atom:head>
<atom:author>
  <atom:name>James Clark</atom:name>
</atom:author>
  <dc:author>James Clark</dc:author>
</atom:head>
</atom:feed>
```

This notation is mostly used for XML documents in which elements and attributes from different namespaces occur. The names consist of a prefix, a colon, and then the local name. It is also possible to specify a default namespace in the document element of an element with the xmlns attribute; this namespace is then valid for all elements that don't include a prefix. We can rewrite the document from the last example as follows:

```
feed version="0.4"
  <xmlns="http://purl.org/atom/ns#draft-ietf-atompub-format-04">
    xmlns:dc="http://purl.org/dc/elements/1.1/">
  <head>
  <author>
   <name>James Clark</name>
  </author>
  <dc:author>James Clark</dc:author>
  <head>
<feed>
```

For an XML parser, that is, an application that extracts processing information from an XML document, these versions are the same. In other words: they have the same info set. The information that can be extracted from them is identical. They only differ in the **serialization**, the presentation of the information in consecutive characters.

The basis of a namespace prefix is the fact that it connects a local name with a URI. The choice of the prefix is arbitrary and is left to the author of a document. The following example represents the same info set as the last one, even though it uses different character strings as prefixes:

```
<atom:feed version="0.4"
  xmlns:syndication="http://purl.org/atom/
        ns#draft-ietf-atompub-format-04">
  xmlns:metadata="http://purl.org/dc/elements/1.1/">
 <syndication:head>
  <syndication:author>
    <syndication:name>James Clark</syndication:name>
  </syndication:author>
  <metadata:author>James Clark</metadata:author>
 </syndication:head>
</syndication:feed>
```

To repeat once more: These prefixes have no other meaning for a parser than to allocate the local names to a URI; it is the task of this URI to identify the valid namespace. However, in practice, certain prefixes have established themselves: for instance, dc for the Dublin Core, or xsl for XSLT stylesheets.

Unfortunately, it can't be assumed that every RSS or Atom document is processed by an application that has a complete XML parser. Often, documents are not parsed in a way that the info set is completely represented and transferred. Many RSS applications only recognize a fixed vocabulary and interpret qualified names as local names. So, some RSS standards determine namespace prefixes, for example, in regards to the modules through which RSS 1.0 is extensible. In either case it is advantageous for authors and developers to use the introduced namespace prefixes, even though it wouldn't be necessary from the XML perspective.

The formats that are introduced at length in this book all use the XML namespace mechanism. RSS 2.0 was defined without a namespace of its own, though. The older syndication formats (RSS 0.9x) don't use this technology. XML namespaces are the most important precondition for extending XML vocabularies.

A.2 Outline Processor Markup Language

The Outline Processor Markup Language is an exchange format for lists of newsfeeds. It is used above all to export (or import) the addresses of a number of newsfeed from aggregators. Contrary to the feed formats that this book introduced you to, OPML allows hierarchies of any depth. This way, users can combine newsfeeds in groups, which can be grouped again, and so on.

The following sample document was created by an export from NetNewsWire (a feed reader). (The document is slightly shortened.)

```
<?xml version="1.0" encoding="ISO-8859-1"?>
<opml version="1.1">
  <head>
    <title>mySubscriptions</title>
  </head>
  <body>
    <outline text="Web" title="Web">
      <outline text="Technik" title="Technik">
```

```
      <outline text="Ars Technica" description="Ars Technica:..."
          title="Ars Technica" type="rss" version="RSS"
          htmlUrl="http://arstechnica.com"
          xmlUrl="http://arstechnica.com/etc/rdf/ars.rdf"/>
      <outline text="Apache Week" description="Apache Week:..."
          title="Apache Week" type="rss" version="RSS"
          htmlUrl="http://www.apacheweek.com/"
          xmlUrl="http://www.apacheweek.com/issues/
              apacheweek-headlines.xml"/>
    </outline>
    <outline text="Design" title="Design">
      <outline text="Digital Web Magazine - What's New"
          description="Digital Web Magazine - What's New:
              http://www.digital-web.com/"
          title="Digital Web Magazine - What's New"
          type="rss" version="RSS"
          htmlUrl="http://www.digital-web.com/"
          xmlUrl="http://www.digital-web.com/new/rss.php"/>
      <outline text="A List Apart"
          description="A List Apart: Web design news, info, and
              insights since 1995..."
          title="A List Apart" type="rss" version="RSS"
          htmlUrl="http://www.alistapart.com/"
          xmlUrl="http://www.alistapart.com/articles.rdf"/>
    </outline>
  </outline>
  <outline text="Politics" title="Politics">
    <outline text="NETZEITUNG.DE"
          description="NETZEITUNG.DE: Principally faster"
          title="NETZEITUNG.DE" type="rss" version="RSS"
          htmlUrl="http://www.netzeitung.de"
          xmlUrl="http://www.netzeitung.de/export/news/
              rss/titlepage.xml"/>
    <outline text="news.ORF.at"
          description="news.ORF.at:..."
          title="news.ORF.at" type="rss" version="RSS"
          htmlUrl="http://news.orf.at"
          xmlUrl="http://rss.orf.at/news.xml"/>
  </outline>
  </body>
</opml>
```

Listing A.1 Example of an OPML Document

The following graphic shows the structure of this document:

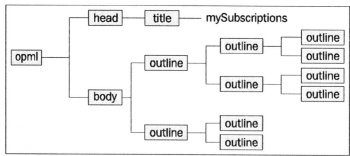

Figure A.1 Structure of an OPML Document

The opml document element has two descendants, head and body. The descendants of body are called outline. An outline element can be located in an element with the same name. In this way, an outline element can be imbedded in elements of the same name at any depth: it can be used recursively.

The outline elements are characterized by attributes. The following figure shows the structure of one of the elements from the example:

Figure A.2 Attributes of the Element "outline" in an OPML Document

Dave Winer describes OPML in the OPML 1.0 specification http://www.opml.org/spec of 2000. OPML documents can describe outlines of any kind. In connection with newsfeeds, the head element doesn't play an important role. body is only the container for elements of the type outline.

outline has several attributes that are defined in the specification; among these, type has the function of indicating the nature of the content. Another attribute defined in the specification is text (you can also find it in the example), whose value is a string displayed when the document is reproduced with outliner software, or is edited.

The really interesting thing about it, however, is that further attributes can be used in addition to these defined attributes. How these attributes are called and which values they are allowed to have depends on the respective application area. In our example, they are the description, htmlUrl, xmlurl, and version attributes.

A.3 Overview: RSS 2.0 Elements

A.3.1 The rss Element

Meaning
Root element of every RSS document.

Ancestors
None

Descendants/Content

Obligatory: `channel`

Attributes

Name	Value	Meaning	Obligatory
`version`	0.91, 0.92, 1.0, 2.0	Indicates the RSS version	Yes

Example

```
<rss version="2.0">
  <channel> ... </channel>
</rss>
```

Remarks

The indication of a namespace for the root element is not included in RSS 2.0 so as to maintain compatibility with previous versions.

Language Version

RSS 0.91, 0.92, 2.0

Equivalences

RSS 1.0	RSS 1.1	Atom
`rss:RDF`	–	–

A.3.2 The channel Element

Meaning

Gathers information about the described resource as a whole; it can include any number of elements of the type `item`, which contain information about the individual information objects that belong to the described resource.

Ancestor

`rss`

Descendants/Content

Obligatory: `title`, `link`, `description`
Optional: `item`, `language`, `copyright`, `managingEditor`, `webMaster`, `pubDate`, `lastBuildDate`, `category`, `generator`, `docs`, `cloud`, `ttl`, `image`, `rating`, `textInput`, `skipHours`, `skipDays`

Attributes

None

Example

```
<channel>
    <link>http://www.example.com/astronomy_news<link>
    <title>Astronomy-News</title>
    <description> Daily up-to-date news on astronomy</description>
    <item...</item>
    <item...</item>
</channel>
```

Remarks

None

Language Version

RSS 0.91, 0.92, 0.93, 2.0

Equivalences

RSS 1.0	RSS 1.1	Atom
rss:channel	rss:Channel	atom:feed

A.3.3 The title Element

Meaning

Title of a feed, an entry, or the logo of the feed. The title of a channel indicates the entire information channel, and should be identical to the title of the HTML document that is referred to in the link element.

The title of an image is to be reproduced as the value of the alt attribute if it is converted to HTML.

Ancestors

channel, item, image

Descendants/Content

Text

Attributes

Standard attributes (see also section A.4)

Example

```
<rss version="2.0">
  <channel>
    <title>Webtrends</title>
    ...
    <image>
      <title>Webtrends Logo</title>
      ...
    </image>
    <item>
      <title>Music Downloads: Alliance of Microsoft
             and Nokia against Apple</title>
      ...
    </item>
  </channel>
</rss>
```

Remarks

The RSS specification leaves open the question of whether escaped markup is allowed in the content of this element. Nevertheless, it should be omitted.

Language Version

RSS 0.91, 0.92, 0.93, 2.0

Equivalences

RSS 1.0	RSS 1.1	Atom
rss:title	rss:title	atom:title (in atom:entry and atom:feed)

A.3.4 The item Element

Meaning

An information object within a feed; it represents in most cases a message or a history.

Ancestor

channel

Descendants/Content

Optional: title, link, description, item, language, copyright, author, pubDate, and category

Attributes

None

Example

```
<channel>
  <item>
    <guid isPermaLink="true">http://www.celawi.eu/
        webtrends/403</guid>
    <title>Music Downloads: Alliance of Microsoft
        and Nokia against Apple</title>
    <link>http://www.celawi.eu/webtrends/403</link>
    <category>Mobil</category>
    <description>Nokia and Microsoft allied.... </description>
    <author>Julia Preiner</author>
    <pubDate>Tu, 2 Feb 2005 08:15:48 GMT+1</pubDate>
  </item>
</channel>
```

Remarks

All elements within item are optional.

Language Version

RSS 0.91, 0.92, 0.93, 2.0

Equivalences

RSS 1.0	RSS 1.1	Atom
rss:item	rss:channel	atom:entry

A.3.5 The link Element

Meaning

In channel: Address of the HTML document the channel corresponds with.

In item: URI of the item.

In image: URI of the site; when reproduced in HTML, the image functions as the link to this site.

Ancestors

channel, item, link

Descendants/Content

URI

Attributes

None

Example

```
<channel>
  <link>http://www.celawi.eu/webtrends/</link>
  ...
  <image>
    <link>http://www.celawi.eu/webtrends/</link>
    ...
  </image>
  <item>
    <link>http://www.celawi.eu/webtrends/403</link>
  </item>
</channel>
```

Remarks

With regards to images, the URI indicated here is the URI of the feed, and not that of the image file!

Language Versions

RSS 0.91, 0.92, 0.93, 2.0

Equivalences

RSS 1.0	RSS 1.1	Atom
rss:link	rss:link	atom:link (in atom:entry and atom:feed)

A.3.6 The description Element

Meaning

In channel: Description of the feed.

In item: Description or reproduction of the content.

In image: Text description; when converted to HTML, it is the content of the attribute title of the generated link.

Ancestors

item, channel, image

Descendants/Content

Text (markup has to be escaped)

Attributes

None

Example 1

```
<channel>
  <description>News fron the media business</description>
  ...
  <item>
    <description>Nokia and Microsoft have allied. They want to break
        the dominance of the Californian Apple group in the
        music downloads business...</description>
  </item>
</channel>
```

Example 2

```
<channel>
  <description>News from the media business</description>
  ...
  <item>
    <description>&lt;a href="http://www.nokia.com">Nokia&lt;/a> and
        &lt;a href="http://www.microsoft.com">Microsoft&lt;/a> have
        allied. They want to break the dominance of the Californian
        &lt;a href="http://www.apple.com">Apple>&lt;/a> group
        in the business of music downloads ...  </description>
  </item>
</channel>
```

Remarks

Escaped HTML markup is explicitly allowed in the content of description within the item element (see *Example 2* above).

Language Version

RSS 0.91, 0.92, 0.93

Equivalences

RSS 1.0	RSS 1.1	Atom
description	description	For a feed: atom:tagline
(Attention: not intended to reproduce content, but only to describe or summarize it; mod_content has the function of reproducing content.)	(Attention: not intended to reproduce content, but only to describe or summarize it; the Payload module has the function of reproducing content.)	For an entry: atom:summary (for descriptions and summaries) atom:content (for the reproduction of content.)

A.3.7 The language Element

Meaning

Language of a feed.

Ancestor

`channel`

Descendants/Content

Language codes; values need to conform to RFC 1766 (`http://www.ietf.org/rfc/rfc1766.txt`) or to the list under `http://blogs.law.harvard.edu/tech/stories/storyReader$15` (initially defined by Netscape).

Attributes

None

Example

```
<channel>
  <language>de-DE</language>
</channel>
```

Remarks

None

Language Version

RSS 0.91, 0.92, 0.93, 2.0

Equivalences

RSS 1.0	RSS 1.1	Atom
dc:language	xml:lang	xml:lang
	(Attention: an attribute, not an element; also possible with other elements)	(Attention: an attribute, not an element; possible with all elements in an Atom document)

A.3.8 The copyright Element

Meaning

Copyright note for the content of the feed.

Ancestor

`channel`

Descendants/Content

Text

Attributes

None

Example

```
<channel>
  <copyright>©2004 Austria Press Agency</copyright>
</channel>
```

Remarks

None

Language Version

RSS 0.91, 0.92, 0.93, 2.0

Equivalences

RSS 1.0	RSS 1.1	Atom
dc:rights	dc:rights	atom:rights

A.3.9 The managingEditor Element

Meaning

E-mail address of the person who is responsible for the content of the feed.

Ancestor

channel

Descendants/Content

E-mail address

Attributes

None

Examples

```
<channel>
  <managingEditor>heimo@apag.at</managingEditor>
  ...
</channel>
```

Remarks

None

Language Version

RSS 0.91, 0.92, 0.93, 2.0

Equivalences

RSS 1.0	RSS 1.1	Atom
rss091:managingEditor	rss091:managingEditor	atom:author
dc:publisher	dc:publisher	(Attention: not identical in meaning!)
dc:creator	dc:creator	
(Attention: the Dublin Core elements do not have the same meaning; mod_rss091 is supported only by a few applications.)	(Attention: the Dublin Core elements do not have the same meaning; mod_rss091 is supported only by a few applications.)	

A.3.10 The webMaster Element

Meaning

E-mail address of the person who is responsible for all technical questions connected with the feed.

Ancestor

channel

Descendants/Content

E-mail address

Attributes

Standard attributes (see section A.4)

Example

```
<channel>
  <webMaster>webmaster@apag.at</webMaster>
  ...
</channel>
```

Remarks

None

Language Version

RSS 0.91, 0.92, 0.93, 2.0

Equivalences

RSS 1.0	RSS 1.1	Atom
dc:publisher	dc:publisher	-
rss091:webmaster	rss091:webmaster	
(Attention: dc:publisher is only distantly related in its meaning; mod_rss091 is supported only by a few applications.)	(Attention: dc:publisher is only distantly related in its meaning; mod_rss091 is supported only by a few applications.)	

A.3.11 The pubDate Element

Meaning

Publication date.

Ancestors

channel, item

Descendants/Content

Date and time according to RFC 822 (http://asg.web.cmu.edu/rfc/rfc822.html); either two or four digits can be used here for the date. The difference compared to GMT can be indicated with four digits (for hours and minutes).

Attributes

None

Example

```
<channel>
<pubDate>Tu, 2 Feb 2005 08:15:48 +0100</pubDate>
  ...
  <item>
    <pubDate>Tu, 2 Feb 2005 07:15:48 GMT</pubDate>
    ...
  </item>
</channel>
```

Remarks

The RSS 2.0 specification suggests that aggregators don't show an entry if the indicated publication date lies in the future. Existing programs don't comply with this rule.

Language Version

RSS 0.93, 2.0

Equivalences

RSS 1.0	RSS 1.1	Atom
dcterms:available	dcterms:available	atom:published

A.3.12 The lastBuildDate Element

Meaning

Point of time of the last content change.

Ancestor

channel

Descendants/Content

Date and time according to RFC 822 (http://asg.web.cmu.edu/rfc/rfc822.html); either two or four digits can be used here for the date. The difference compared to GMT can be indicated with four digits (for hours and minutes).

Attributes

Standard attributes (see section A.4)

Example

```
<channel>
  ...
  <pubDate>Tu, 2 Feb 2005 08:15:48 +0100</pubDate>
  <lastBuildDate>Tu, 2 Feb 2005 10:45:48 +0100</lastBuildDate>
</channel>
```

Remarks

None

Language Version

RSS 0.91, 0.92, 0.93, 2.0

Equivalences

RSS 1.0	RSS 1.1	Atom
dcterms:modified	dcterms:modified	atom:updated

A.3.13 The category Element

Meaning

Indicates one or several categories for the feed or entry.

Ancestors

channel, item

Descendants/Content

Names of categories

Attributes

Standard attributes (see section A.4)

Name	Value	Meaning	Obligatory?
domain	Text or URI	Indicates a category system	Yes

Example

```
<channel>
  <category domain="http://www.dmoz.org/">
      News/Media/Industry_News/</category>
  <category domain="http://www.dmoz.org">
        Business/Information_Technology/News_and_Media/
        Internet/</category>
  <category domain="http://www.dmoz.org/">
        Business/Telecommunications/Equipment/Telephones/
        Wireless_Phones/</category>
  <item>
    <link>http://www.celawi.eu/webtrends/403</link>
    <category domain="http://www.dmoz.org/">
        News/Media/Industry_News/</category>
    <category domain="http://www.dmoz.org">
        Business/Information_Technology/News_and_Media/
        Internet/</category>
    <category domain="http://www.dmoz.org/">
        Business/Telecommunications/Equipment/Telephones/
        Wireless_Phones/</category>
  </item>
</channel>
```

Remarks

None

Language Version

RSS 0.92, 0.93, 2.0

Equivalences

RSS 1.0	RSS 1.1	Atom
dc:subject	dc:subject	atom:category

A.3.14 The generator Element

Meaning

Indicates the program that generated the feed.

Ancestor

channel

Descendants/Content

Text

Attributes

None

Example

```
<channel>
  <generator>CoreBlog v. 2.0</generator>
  ...
</channel>
```

Remarks

None

Language Version

RSS 0.91, 0.92, 0.93, 2.0

Equivalences

RSS 1.0	RSS 1.1	Atom
`admin:generator`	`admin:generator`	`atom:generator`

A.3.15 The docs Element

Meaning

Reference to the documentation of the format.

Ancestors

None

Descendants/Content

None

Attributes

None

Example

```
<channel>
  <docs>http://blogs.law.harvard.edu/tech/rss</docs>
</channel>
```

Remarks

None

Language Version

RSS 0.91, 0.92, 0.93, 2.0

Equivalences

RSS 1.0	RSS 1.1	Atom
Indication of namespace	Indication of namespace	Indication of namespace

A.3.16 The cloud Element

Meaning

Indication of a possibility to subscribe the feed.

Ancestor

`channel`

Descendants/Content

None

Attributes

Standard attributes (see section A.4)

Name	Value	Meaning	Obligatory?
`domain`	Name of the host	Name of the host	Yes
`port`	Number	Port number by which the service can be reached	Yes
`path`	File path	Path of the service at the indicated host	Yes
`registerProcedure`	String	Name of the registration procedure	Yes
`protocol`	xml-rap or soap	-	Yes

Example 1

```
<channel>
  <cloud domain="triest.fh-joanneum.at"
         port="9673"
         path="/RPC2"
         registerProcedure="pingMe"
         protocol="soap"/>
  ...
</channel>
```

Example 2

```
<cloud domain="http://www.oreilly.com" port="80" path="/RPC2"
       registerProcedure="pleaseNotify" protocol="XML-RPC"/>
```

Remarks

Documentation under SOAP meets RSS,
`http://blogs.law.harvard.edu/tech/soapMeetsRss`.

Language Version

RSS 0.92, 0.93, 2.0

Equivalences

RSS 1.0	RSS 1.1	Atom
cp:server	p:server	Atom uses the Atom Notification Protocol to inform of updates.

A.3.17 The ttl Element

Meaning

Indicates how long the content of the feed stays unaltered, so that the dates can be cached during this time.

Ancestor

channel

Descendants/Content

Number (number of minutes)

Attributes

None

Example

```
<channel>
  <ttl>120</ttl>
</channel>
```

Remarks

The specification defines that this element allows spreading of feeds through file-sharing networks like Gnutella.

Language Version

RSS 0.91, 0.92, 0.93, 2.0

Equivalences

None

A.3.18 The image Element

Meaning

Indicates an image that can be used as a logo or an item.

Ancestors

None

Descendants/Content

Obligatory: url, title, link

Optional: width, height, description

Example

```
<channel>
  <image>
    <url>http://www.celawi.eu/webtrends/images/webtrends.png</url>
    <title>Logo Webtrends</title>
    <link>http://www.celawi.eu/webtrends/</link>
    <width>88</width>
    <height>144</height>
    <description>Logo</description>
  </image>
</channel>
```

Remarks

None

Language Version

RSS 0.91, 0.92, 0.93, 2.0

Equivalences

RSS 1.0	RSS 1.1	Atom
image	image	link rel="image"

A.3.19 The rating Element

Meaning

PICS rating according to http://www.w3.org/PICS/.

Ancestor

channel

Descendants/Content

None

Attributes

None

Example

```
<channel>
  <rating>(PICS-1.1 "http://www.classify.org/safesurf/" l r
        (SS--000 1))</rating>
  ...
</channel>
```

Remarks

None

Language Version

RSS 0.91, 0.92, 0.93, 2.0

Equivalences

rss091:rating

(Attention: rarely supported!)

A.3.20 The textInput Element

Meaning

Generates a text input field.

Ancestor

channel

Descendants/Content

title, description, name, link

Attributes

None

Example

None

Remarks

Isn't practically used any more, and is kept only for backward compatibility with older versions. link refers to a CGI script; name corresponds with the HTML attribute of the same name; description contains an explanation; title includes the label of the submit button.

Language Version

RSS 0.91, 0.92, 0.93, 2.0

Equivalences

RSS 1.0	RSS 1.1	Atom
textinput	-	-

A.3.21 The skipHours and hour Elements

Meaning

Tells software during which hours it is not to check a feed for updates.

Ancestor

channel

Descendants/Content

hour (1-24fold), each time with a number from 1 to 23

Attributes

None

Example

```
<channel>
  <skipHours>
    <hour>2</hour>
    <hour>3</hour>
    <hour>4</hour>
    <hour>5</hour>
    <hour>6</hour>
  </skipHours>
  ...
```

Remarks

None

Language Version

RSS 0.91, 0.92, 0.93, 2.0

Equivalences

RSS 1.0	RSS 1.1	Atom
rss091:skipHours (Attention: rarely supported!)	rss091:skipHours (Attention: rarely supported!)	-

A.3.22 The skipDays and day Elements

Meaning

Tells software on which days it is not to check a feed for updates.

Ancestors

None

Descendants/Content

None

Attributes

None

Example

```
<channel>
  <skipDays>
    <day>Saturday</day>
    <day>Sunday</day>
  </skipDays>
  ...
</channel>
```

Remarks

None

Language Version

RSS 0.91, 0.92, 0.93, 2.0

Equivalences

RSS 1.0	RSS 1.1	Atom
rss091:skipDays (Attention: rarely supported!)	rss091:skipDays (Attention: rarely supported!)	-

A.3.23 The author Element

Meaning

Author of the document.

Ancestor

item

Descendants/Content

E-mail address, possibly with the name of the author in brackets

Attributes

None

Example

```
<item>
  <author>martin.roeller@apag.at (Martin Röller)</author>
  ...
</item>
```

Remarks

When weblogs are created by just one author, the element can be omitted because the author is also indicated by managingEditor.

Language Version

RSS 0.91, 0.92, 0.93, 2.0

Equivalences

RSS 1.0	RSS 1.1	Atom
dc:creator	dc:creator	atom:author

A.3.24 The comments Element

Meaning
Address of comments on an entry.

Ancestor
`item`

Descendants/Content
URI

Attributes
None

Example
```
<item>
  <comments>http://www.celawi.eu/webtrends/405#comments</comments>
  ...
</item>
```

Remarks
None

Language Version
RSS 0.91, 0.92, 0.93, 2.0

Equivalences

RSS 1.0	RSS 1.1	Atom
annotate:reference	annotate:reference	link rel="comments"

A.3.25 The enclosure Element

Meaning
Reference to binary data; `enclosure` is the basis for podcasting.

Ancestor
`item`

Descendants/Content

None

Attributes

Name	Value	Meaning	Obligatory
url	URI	Address of the attachment	Yes
length	Number	Size of the attachment in byte	Yes
type	Name of a registered media type	Type of the attachment	Yes

Example

```
<item>
   <enclosure url="http://triest.fh-joanneum.at/SDR25FEB.mp3"
              length="1024"
              type="audio/mpeg"/>
   ...
</item>
```

Remarks

It was suggested to admit more than one element of this type per item.

Language Version

RSS 0.92, 0.93, 2.0

Equivalences

RSS 1.0	RSS 1.1	Atom
enc:Enclosure (Attention: rarely supported!)	enc:Enclosure (Attention: rarely supported!)	Link rel="enclosure"

A.3.26 The guid Element

Meaning

Clear identifier of an entry.

Ancestor

item

Descendants/Content

String

Attributes

Standard attributes (see section A.4)

Name	Value	Meaning	Obligatory?
IsPermaLink	True, false	Specifies whether the indicated string is a permanently valid URI of the entry.	No

Example

```
<item>
  <guid isPermaLink="true">http://www.celawi.eu/webtrends/405</guid>
  ...
</item>
```

Remarks

The attribute is optional; its default value is true. If the attribute is missing, the application can assume that the content of the element is a permalink.

Language Version

RSS 0.91, 0.92, 0.93, 2.0

Equivalences

RSS 1.0	RSS 1.1	Atom
rdf:about (Attribute of the elements channel and entry)	rdf:about (Attribute of the elements channel and entry)	atom:id

A.3.27 The source Element

Meaning

If an entry was transferred from another feed, this element indicates where the entry derives from.

Ancestor

item

Descendants/Content

Name of the feed the entry derives from

Attributes

Standard attributes (see section A.4)

Name	Value	Meaning	Obligatory?
url	URI	Address of the original feed	Yes

Example

```
<item>
  <source url="http://derstandard.at/etat/feed.xml">
        Der Standard:    Etat</source>
  ...
</item>
```

Remarks

None

Language Version

RSS 0.92, 0.93, 2.0

Equivalences

RSS 1.0	RSS 1.1	Atom
-	-	atom:source

A.4 Overview: RSS 1.0 Elements

A.4.1 Preliminary Notes

The RSS namespace is defined by the URI `http://purl.org/rss/1.0/` as well. The address of the RDF validators is `http://www.w3.org/RDF/Validator/`. John Reagle created the Relax NG schema, which is used to explain the elements. The URI is `http://www.w3.org/2002/09/rss-rng/`. It was transferred with Trang in the complete Relax NG syntax, and was revised slightly.

As protocol schemas for URIs, RSS 1.0 only allows `http:`, `https:`, `ftp:`, and `mailto:` within text-input fields.

Concerning the MIME type, the specification talks about `application/xml`.

A certain data extension is not necessary; `.xml` and—preferably—`.rdf` are recommended.

A.4.2 rdf:RDF

Meaning

Document element of an RSS 1.0 element.

Schema

```
element rdf:RDF { RDFContent }
RDFContent =
    element channel { channelContent }
  & element image { imageContent }?
  & element item { itemContent }+
```

Ancestors

None

Descendants/Content

Obligatory: channel, item (obligatory, once or several times)

Optional: image

Attributes

Name	Values	Meaning	Obligatory?
xmlns (Also in the xmlns:rdf, xmlns:rss, xmlns:dc, type forms)	http://www.w3.org/1999/ 02/22-rdf-syntax-ns# (URI of the RDF namespace), http://purl.org/rss/1.0/ (URI of the RSS namespace)	Indication of namespace URIs according to the *XML Namespaces* recommendation	Obligatory is the indication of the namespace for the element rdf:RDF; other namespaces can be indicated in subsequent elements.

Example

```
<rdf:RDF  xmlns="http://purl.org/rss/1.0/"
      xmlns:rdf="http://www.w3.org/1999/02/22-rdf-syntax-ns#">
    <channel rdf:about="http://www.celawi.eu/webtrends">
    ...
    </channel>
    <item rdf:about="http://www.celawi.eu/webtrends/20040415_01">
    ...
    </item>
</rdf:RDF>
```

Remarks

None

Equivalences

RSS 1.1	RSS 2.0	Atom
-	-	-

A.4.3 rdf:li

Meaning

Represents an item in the table of contents.

Schema

```
element rdf:li {
      attribute resource { xsd:anyURI }
      | attribute rdf:resource { xsd:anyURI }
}
```

Ancestor

rdf:Seq

Descendants/Content

None

Attributes

Name	Values	Meaning	Obligatory?
rdf:resource	URI	URI of an item	Yes

Example

```
<rdf:Seq>
  <rdf:li rdf:resource="http://www.celawi.eu/
        webtrends/20040415_01"/>
  <rdf:li rdf:resource="http://www.celawi.eu/
        webtrends/20040415_02"/>
</rdf:Seq>
```

Remarks

None

Equivalences

RSS 1.1	RSS 2.0	Atom
-	-	-

A.4.4 rdf:Seq

Meaning

Represents a collection of items.

Schema

```
element rdf:Seq {
    element rdf:li {
        attribute resource { xsd:anyURI }
        | attribute rdf:resource { xsd:anyURI }
    }+
}
```

Ancestor

rss:items

Descendants/Content

rdf:li (obligatory for every item element that is included in the document)

Attributes

None

Example

```
<items>
    <rdf:Seq>
    ...
    </rdf:Seq>
</items>
</item>
```

Remarks

None

Equivalences

RSS 1.1	RSS 2.0	Atom
-	-	-

A.4.5 rdf:channel

Meaning

Gathers the metadata for a feed.

Schema

```
element channel { channelContent }
  & element image { imageContent }?
  & element item { itemContent }+
channelContent &=
  element title { xsd:string }
  & element link { xsd:anyURI }
  & element description { xsd:string }
  & element image {
      attribute rdf:resource { xsd:anyURI }
  }?
  & element items { itemsContent }
  & attribute rdf:about { xsd:anyURI }
```

Ancestor

rdf:RDF

Descendants/Content

items, title, link, description (obligatory); image (optional)

Attributes

Name	Values	Meaning	Obligatory?
rdf:about	URI	Indicates the URI of the feed	Yes

Example

```
<rdf:RDF xmlns="http://purl.org/rss/1.0/"
    xmlns:rdf="http://www.w3.org/1999/02/22-rdf-syntax-ns#">
  <channel rdf:about="http://www.celawi.eu/webtrends">
    <title>Webtrends</title>
    <link>http://www.celawi.eu/webtrends.html</link>
    <description>News about...</description>
    <items>
    ...
    </items>
  </channel>
</rdf:RDF>
```

Remarks

None

Equivalences

RSS 1.1	RSS 2.0	Atom
rss:Channel	channel	Atom:feed

A.4.6 rdf:item

Meaning

Represents an entry within a feed.

Schema

```
element item { itemContent }
itemContent =
  element title { xsd:string }
  & element link { xsd:anyURI }
  & element description { xsd:string }?
  & anyThing
  & attribute rdf:about { xsd:anyURI }
anyThing =
  (text
  | element * - ns1:* {
      anyThing,
      attribute * { text }*
    })*
```

Ancestor

rdf:RDF

Descendants/Content

Obligatory: rss:title, rss:link, rss:description

Further elements from other namespaces optional

Attributes

Name	Values	Meaning	Obligatory?
rdf:about	URI	URI of the item	Yes

Example

```
<rdf:RDF xmlns="http://purl.org/rss/1.0/"
    xmlns:rdf="http://www.w3.org/1999/02/22-rdf-syntax-ns#">
    ...
  <item rdf:about="http://www.celawi.eu/webtrends/20040415_01">
    <title>Ask Jeeves now in Spain</title>
    <link>http://www.celawi.eu/webtrends/20040415_01.html</link>
    <description>Ask Jeeves...</description>
  </item>
</rdf:RDF>
```

Remarks

None

Equivalences

RSS 1.1	RSS 2.0	Atom
rss:item	item	atom:entry

A.4.7 rdf:items

Meaning

Represents the items in the table of contents of a channel.

Schema

```
element items { itemsContent }
itemsContent =
  element rdf:Seq {
    element rdf:li {
      attribute resource { xsd:anyURI }
      | attribute rdf:resource { xsd:anyURI }
    }+
  }
```

Ancestor

rss:channel

Descendants/Content

rdf:Seq

Attributes

None

Example

```
<channel rdf:about="http://www.celawi.eu/webtrends">
  ...
  <items>
    <rdf:Seq>
    ...
    </rdf:Seq>
  </items>
</channel>
```

Remarks

None

Equivalences

RSS 1.1	RSS 2.0	Atom
-	-	-

A.4.8 rdf:title

Meaning

Title of a channel, item, or image.

Schema

```
element title { xsd:string }
```

Ancestors

rss:channel, rss:item, rss:image

Descendants/Content

Text (obligatory)

Attributes

None

Example

```
<channel rdf:about="http://www.celawi.eu/webtrends">
  <title>Webtrends</title>
  ...
</channel>
<item rdf:about="http://www.celawi.eu/webtrends/20040415_01">
  <title>Ask Jeeves now in Spain</title>
  ...
</item>
<image rdf:about="http://www.celawi.eu/logo.gif">
  <title>Webtrends-Logo</title>
  ...
</image>
```

Remarks

None

Equivalences

RSS 1.1	RSS 2.0	Atom
rss:title	title	atom:title

A.4.9 rdf:link

Meaning

Contains the target of a reference.

Schema

```
element link { xsd:anyURI }
```

Ancestors

rss:channel, rss:item, rss:image

Descendants/Content

URI

Attributes

None

Example

```
<channel rdf:about="http://www.celawi.eu/webtrends">
  <link>http://www.celawi.eu/webtrends.html</link>
  ...
</channel>
<item rdf:about="http://www.celawi.eu/webtrends/20040415_01">
  <link>http://www.celawi.eu/webtrends/20040415_01.html</link>
  ...
</item>
<image rdf:about="http://www.celawi.eu/logo.gif">
  <link> http://www.celawi.eu/webtrends.html</link>
  ...
</image>
```

Remarks

None

Equivalences

RSS 1.1	RSS 2.0	Atom
rss:link	link	atom:link (In Atom the semantics of this element are more multifaceted.)

A.4.10 rdf:description

Meaning
Description of a channel or an item.

Schema
```
element description { xsd:string }
```

Ancestors
rss:channel, rss:item

Descendants/Content
Text

Attributes
None

Example
```
<channel rdf:about="http://www.celawi.eu/webtrends">
  ...
  <description>News about...</description>
</channel>
<item rdf:about="http://www.celawi.eu/webtrends/20040415_01">
  ...
  <description>Ask Jeeves...</description>
</item>
```

Remarks
Text is the only content allowed in this element.

Equivalences

RSS 1.1	RSS 2.0	Atom
rss:description	description	atom:subtitle atom:summary atom:content

A.4.11 rdf:url

Meaning
Address of an image.

Schema

```
element url { xsd:anyURI }
```

Ancestor

`rss:image`

Descendants/Content

URI

Attributes

None

Example

```
<image rdf:about="http://www.celawi.eu/logo.gif">
  <url>http://www.celawi.eu/logo.gif</url>
</image>
```

Remarks

None

Equivalences

RSS 1.1	RSS 2.0	Atom
rss:url	url	atom:uri

A.4.12 rdf:image

Meaning

Represents an image that illustrates a feed; has to occur on the top level below `rdf:RDF` as well as within `rss:channel`.

Schema 1

```
element image { imageContent }
imageContent =
  element title { xsd:string }
  & element link { xsd:anyURI }
  & element url { xsd:anyURI }
  & attribute rdf:about { xsd:anyURI }
```

Schema 2

```
element image {
  attribute rdf:resource { xsd:anyURI }
}?
```

Ancestors

`rss:channel`, `rdf:RDF`

Descendants/Content

`rss:link`, `rss:title`, `rss:url` if the element is a descendant of `rdf:RDF`; if the element is a descendant of `rss:channel`, it remains empty—the reference of the resource is then indicated as the value of the `rdf:resource` attribute.

Attributes

Name	Value	Meaning	Obligatory
`rdf:resource`	URI	URI of the image	Obligatory as the descendant of `rss:channel` if an image is indicated
`rdf:about`	URI	URI of the image	Obligatory, if `rss:image` is the descendant of `rdf:RDF`

Example

```
<rdf:RDF xmlns="http://purl.org/rss/1.0/"
    xmlns:rdf="http://www.w3.org/1999/02/22-rdf-syntax-ns#">
    <channel rdf:about="http://www.celawi.eu/webtrends">
        <image rdf:resource=" http://www.celawi.eu/logo.gif"/>
    </channel>
...
    <image rdf:about="http://www.celawi.eu/logo.gif">
        <url>http://www.celawi.eu/logo.gif</url>
        <link>http://www.celawi.eu/webtrends.html</link>
        <title>Webtrebds-Logo</title>
    </image>
<rdf:RDF>
```

Remarks

The element has different content models depending on whether it occurs in the table of contents of a channel, or whether it is the container for the characteristics of the image.

Equivalences

RSS 1.1	RSS 2.0	Atom
`rss:image`	`image`	`atom:image`, `atom:icon`

A.5 RSS 1.0 Modules

Because of the great number of suggested RSS 1.0 modules, the elements are explained in table form. The element name forms the respective table heading.

A.5.1 mod_admin

The administration module gives details about the owners of a feed, and about the tool kit used to create it. It is supposed to help the owners synchronize with their provider and allow the community to recognize errors in RSS feeds that can be retraced to the use of certain software. It has a function similar to the `webMaster` and `generator` elements in RSS 2.0.

Specification

```
http://groups.yahoo.com/group/rss-dev/files/Modules/Proposed/
mod_admin.html
```

Namespace

```
xmlns:admin="http://webns.net/mvcb"
```

admin:errorReportsTo

Parent Element	Content	Meaning
channel	Empty element; URI mostly mailto URI as the value of the rdf:Resource attribute.	Indicates the administrator of the feed who can be notified if errors occur.

admin:generatorAgent

Parent Element	Content	Meaning
channel	Empty element; URI as the value of the rdf:Resource attribute.	Indicates the homepage of the software used to create the feed. If possible, it should be the URI of a certain version, in which case the employed URI should give information about the version.

A.5.2 mod_aggregation

Purpose

Information added by the aggregator concerning the original resource of an entry.

Specification

```
http://groups.yahoo.com/group/rss-dev/files/Modules/
Proposed/mod_aggregation.html
```

Namespace

```
xmlns:ag=http://purl.org/rss/modules/aggregation/
```

ag:source

Parent Element	Content	Meaning
item	(#PCDATA)	Name of the original feed

ag:sourceURL

Parent Element	Content	Meaning
item	(#PCDATA)	URI of the original feed

ag:timestamp

Parent Element	Content	Meaning
item	(#PCDATA) (According to ISO 8601)	Publication date

A.5.3 mod_annotation

Purpose

Refers to the resource that is annotated for entries that are annotations for other resources.

Specification

```
http://purl.org/rss/1.0/modules/annotation/
```

Namespace

```
xmlns:annotate=http://purl.org/rss/1.0/modules/annotate/
```

annotate:reference

Parent Element	Content	Meaning
item	URI as the value of the rdf:resource attribute.	URI of the resource that is referred to.

A.5.4 mod_audio

Purpose

Syndicating audio data based on ID3 tags (http://www.id3.org/).

Specification

```
http://web.resource.org/rss/1.0/modules/audio/
```

Namespace

```
xmlns:audio=http://media.tangent.org/rss/1.0/
```

audio:songname

Parent Element	Content	Meaning
item	(#PCDATA)	Name of the title

audio:artist

Parent Element	Content	Meaning
item	(#PCDATA)	Artist

audio:album

Parent Element	Content	Meaning
item	(#PCDATA)	Album

audio:year

Parent Element	Content	Meaning
item	(#PCDATA)	Year date

audio:comment

Parent Element	Content	Meaning
item	(#PCDATA)	Comment

audio:genre

Parent Element	Content	Meaning
item	(#PCDATA)	Genre

audio:recording_time

Parent Element	Content	Meaning
item	(#PCDATA)	Recording time

audio:bitrate

Parent Element	Content	Meaning
item	(#PCDATA)	Bitrate

audio:track

Parent Element	Content	Meaning
item	Positive whole number	Track number

audio:genre_id

Parent Element	Content	Meaning
item	Positive whole number	ID of the genre

audio:price

Parent Element	Content	Meaning
item	(#PCDATA)	Price

A.5.5 mod_cc

Purpose

Information about Creative Commons licenses.

Specification

http://web.resource.org/rss/1.0/modules/cc/

Namespace

xmlns:cc="http://web.resource.org/cc/"

cc:license

Parent Element	Content	Meaning
item, channel, image	URI as the value of the rdf:resource attribute	URI of the used license

cc:License

Parent Element	Content	Meaning
rdf:RDF	URI as the value of the rdf:about attribute	URI of a license other elements refer to

cc:permits

Parent Element	Content	Meaning

`cc:License rdf:about=""`	`<cc:permits rdf:resource="http://web.resource.org/cc/Reproduction"/>`
	
	`<cc:permits rdf:resource="http://web.resource.org/cc/Distribution"/>`
	
	`<cc:permits rdf:resource="http://web.resource.org/cc/DerivativeWorks"/>`
		Indication of the use covered by the license

cc:requires

Parent Element	Content	Meaning

`cc:License rdf:about=""`	`<cc:permits rdf:resource="http://web.resource.org/cc/Notice"/>`
	
	`<cc:permits rdf:resource="http://web.resource.org/cc/Attribution"/>`
	
	`<cc:permits rdf:resource="http://web.resource.org/cc/ShareAlike"/>`
		Indication of the behavior that the license requires from users

cc:prohibits

Parent Element	Content	Meaning
`cc:License rdf:about=""`	`<cc:permits rdf:resource="http://web.resource.org/cc/CommercialUse"/>`	Prohibition of commercial use

A.5.6 mod_changedpage

Purpose

Subscribing information about changes on a page.

Specification

`http://purl.org/rss/1.0/modules/changedpage/`

Namespace

```
xmlns:cp=http://my.theinfo.org/changed/1.0/rss/
```

cp:server

Parent Element	Content	Meaning
item	URI as the value of the rdf:resource attribute	URI of the server that provides information about updates

A.5.7 mod_company

Purpose

Indicates company data in connection with ticker symbols.

Specification

```
http://groups.yahoo.com/group/rss-dev/files/Modules/
Proposed/mod_company.html
```

Namespace

```
xmlns:company="http://purl.org/rss/1.0/modules/company"
```

company:name

Parent Element	Content	Meaning
item	(#PCDATA)	Company name

company:symbol

Parent Element	Content	Meaning
item	(#PCDATA)	Company symbol

company:market

Parent Element	Content	Meaning
item	(#PCDATA)	Stock market where the company is noted

company:category

Parent Element	Content	Meaning
item	taxo:topic (See also: section A.5.21)	Category the company belongs to

A.5.8 mod_context

Purpose

Contains contextual information about the origin of a feed, its subscribers, etc.

Specification

```
http://nurture.nature.com/tony/rss/modules/mod_context.html
```

Namespace

```
xmlns:ctx="http://www.openurl.info/registry/fmt/xml/rss10/ctx"
```

For more information on the details of this very complex module please see Tony Hammond's specification.

A.5.9 mod_dcterms

Purpose

Description of metadata with the qualified Dublin Core elements.

Specification

```
http://web.resource.org/rss/1.0/modules/dcterms/
```

Namespace

```
xmlns:dcterms=http://purl.org/dc/terms/
```

dcterms:alternative

Parent Element	Content	Meaning
channel, item, image, textinput	(#PCDATA)	Alternative to the official title

dcterms:abstract

Parent Element	Content	Meaning
channel, item, image, textinput	(#PCDATA)	Summary

dcterms:tableOfContents

Parent Element	Content	Meaning
channel, item, image, textinput	URI	URI of a table of contents

dcterms:created

Parent Element	Content	Meaning
channel, item, image, textinput	Date according to http://www.w3.org/TR/NOTE-datetime	Creation date

dcterms:valid

Parent Element	Content	Meaning
channel, item, image, textinput	Period of time according to http://dublincore.org/documents/dcmi-period/	Validity period of a resource

dcterms:available

Parent Element	Content	Meaning
channel, item, image, textinput	Period of time according to http://dublincore.org/documents/dcmi-period/	Duration of the availability of a resource

dcterms:issued

Parent Element	Content	Meaning
channel, item, image, textinput	Date according to http://www.w3.org/TR/NOTE-datetime	Official publication date

dcterms:modified

Parent Element	Content	Meaning
channel, item, image, textinput	Date according to http://www.w3.org/TR/NOTE-datetime	Date of modification of a resource

dcterms:dateAccepted

Parent Element	Content	Meaning
channel, item, image, textinput	Date according to http://www.w3.org/TR/NOTE-datetime	Date of the official approval or acceptance of a resource

dcterms:dateCopyrighted

Parent Element	Content	Meaning
channel, item, image, textinput	Date according to http://www.w3.org/TR/NOTE-datetime	Date of the copyright statement

dcterms:dateSubmitted

Parent Element	Content	Meaning
channel, item, image, textinput	Date according to http://www.w3.org/TR/NOTE-datetime	Date when the resource was suggested or submitted

dcterms:extent

Parent Element	Content	Meaning
channel, item, image, textinput	(#PCDATA)	Extension or duration

dcterms:medium

Parent Element	Content	Meaning
channel, item, image, textinput	(#PCDATA)	Material or physical medium

dcterms:isVersionof

Parent Element	Content	Meaning
channel, item, image, textinput	URI	URI of a resource, the version of which is the just described resource

dcterms:hasVersion

Parent Element	Content	Meaning
channel, item, image, textinput	URI	URI of a version of the described resource

dcterms:isReplacedBy

Parent Element	Content	Meaning
channel, item, image, textinput	URI	URI of a resource that replaces the just described resource

dcterms:replaces

Parent Element	Content	Meaning
channel, item, image, textinput	URI	URI of a resource that is replaced by the just described resource

dcterms:isRequiredBy

Parent Element	Content	Meaning
channel, item, image, textinput	URI	URI of a resource that takes the described resource physically or logically for granted

dcterms:requires

Parent Element	Content	Meaning
channel, item, image, textinput	URI	URI of a resource the described resource takes for granted

dcterms:isPartof

Parent Element	Content	Meaning
channel, item, image, textinput	URI	URI of a resource the described resource is part of

dcterms:hasPart

Parent Element	Content	Meaning
channel, item, image, textinput	URI	URI of a part of the described resource

dcterms:isReferencedBy

Parent Element	Content	Meaning
channel, item, image, textinput	URI	URI of a resource that refers to the described resource

dcterms:references

Parent Element	Content	Meaning
channel, item, image, textinput	URI	URI of a resource that refers to the described resource

dcterms:isFormatOf

Parent Element	Content	Meaning
channel, item, image, textinput	URI	URI of a resource that is represented by the described resource in a different format

dcterms:hasFormat

Parent Element	Content	Meaning
channel, item, image, textinput	URI	URI of a resource that is represented by the described resource in a different format

dcterms:conformsTo

Parent Element	Content	Meaning
channel, item, image, textinput	URI	URI of a specification

dcterms:spatial

Parent Element	Content	Meaning
channel, item, image, textinput	(#PCDATA)	Space characterization

dcterms:temporal

Parent Element	Content	Meaning
channel, item, image, textinput	Period of time according to http://dublincore.org/ documents/dcmi-period/	Time characterization

dcterms:audience

Parent Element	Content	Meaning
channel, item, image, textinput	(#PCDATA)	Target audience

dcterms:mediator

Parent Element	Content	Meaning
channel, item, image, textinput	(#PCDATA)	Mediator or instance that controls the access to a resource

A.5.10 mod_email

Purpose

Representation of e-mail headers.

Specification

```
http://purl.org/rss/1.0/modules/email/
```

Namespace

`xmlns:email=http://purl.org/rss/1.0/modules/email/`

email:from

Parent Element	Content	Meaning
item	(#PCDATA)	Content of the from header

email:to

Parent Element	Content	Meaning
item	(#PCDATA)	Content of the to header

email:subject

Parent Element	Content	Meaning
item	(#PCDATA)	Content of the subject header

email:date

Parent Element	Content	Meaning
item	(#PCDATA)	Content of the date header

email:message-id

Parent Element	Content	Meaning
item	(#PCDATA)	Content of the message-id header

email:sender

Parent Element	Content	Meaning
item	(#PCDATA)	Content of the sender header

email:reply-to

Parent Element	Content	Meaning
item	(#PCDATA)	Content of the reply-to header

email:in-reply-to

Parent Element	Content	Meaning
item	(#PCDATA)	Content of the in-reply-to header

email:references

Parent Element	Content	Meaning
item	(#PCDATA)	Content of the references header

email:content-type

Parent Element	Content	Meaning
item	(#PCDATA)	Content of the content-type header

email:content-disposition

Parent Element	Content	Meaning
item	(#PCDATA)	Content of the content-disposition header

email:mime-version

Parent Element	Content	Meaning
item	(#PCDATA)	Content of the mime-version header

email:user-agent

Parent Element	Content	Meaning
item	(#PCDATA)	Content of the user-agent header

A.5.11 mod_event

Purpose
Description of characteristics of events.

Specification
http://purl.org/rss/1.0/modules/event/

Namespace
xmlns:ev=http://purl.org/rss/1.0/modules/event/

ev:startdate

Parent Element	Content	Meaning
item	Date according to http://www.w3.org/TR/NOTE-datetime	Start date of an event

ev:enddate

Parent Element	Content	Meaning
item	Date according to http://www.w3.org/TR/NOTE-datetime	End date of an event

ev:location

Parent Element	Content	Meaning
item	(#PCDATA)	Location of the event

ev:organizer

Parent Element	Content	Meaning
item	(#PCDATA)	Name of the person who organizes the event

ev:type

Parent Element	Content	Meaning
item	(#PCDATA)	Type of the event; for example, conference, project meeting.

A.5.12 mod_link

Purpose

An extensible link mechanism; based on the functionality of HTML links.

Specification

http://purl.org/rss/1.0/modules/link/

Namespace

xmlns:l="http://purl.org/rss/1.0/modules/link/"

l:link

Parent Element	Content	Meaning
item, channel	(#PCDATA)	Link to a resource

Attributes	Value	Meaning
rdf:resource	URL	URL of the link target
l:type	MIME Media type	Media type of the link target
l:title	String	Title of the usable link

Attributes	Value	Meaning

`1:rel`	`http://purl.org/rss /1.0/modules/propos ed/link/#print`
	
	`http://purl.org/rss /1.0/modules/propos ed/link/#permalink`
	
	`http://purl.org/rss /1.0/modules/propos ed/link/#service`
	
	`http://purl.org/rss /1.0/modules/propos ed/link/#source`
	
	`http://purl.org/rss /1.0/modules/propos ed/link/#topic`
	
	`http://purl.org/rss /1.0/modules/propos ed/link/#alternate`
		Nature of the resource that is referred to: print version, permaLink, service, resource, topic, or alternative representation

`1:lang`	Language identification	Language of the link target
`1:charset`	Indication of the code	Code of the link target

A.5.13 mod_prism

Purpose

Description of content according to the industry standard PRISM (Publishing Requirements for Industry Standard Metadata). For more detailed information, please see the specification as well. PRISM is especially used by magazine publishers.

Specification

`http://www.prismstandard.org/resources/mod_prism.html`

Namespace

`xmlns:prism="http://prismstandard.org/namespaces/1.2/basic/"`

prism:byteCount

Parent Element	Content	Meaning
`channel`, `item`, `image`, `textinput`	Positive whole number	Size of the described resource in bytes

prism:category

Parent Element	Content	Meaning
channel, item, image, textinput	(#PCDATA) or the value of an rdf:resource attribute.	Category or genre of the content

prism:complianceProfile

Parent Element	Content	Meaning
channel, item, image, textinput	(#PCDATA)	PRISM specification compliance profile that the resource corresponds to

prism:copyright

Parent Element	Content	Meaning
channel, item, image, textinput	(#PCDATA)	Copyright statement

prism:corporateEntity

Parent Element	Content	Meaning
channel, item, image, textinput	(#PCDATA)	Organization the resource is connected with; for example, a publisher

prism:coverDate

Parent Element	Content	Meaning
channel, item, image, textinput	Date according to http://www.w3.org/TR/NOTE-datetime	Date on the cover of a magazine

prism:coverDisplayDate

Parent Element	Content	Meaning
channel, item, image, textinput	(#PCDATA)	Date on the cover as a string

prism:creationDate

Parent Element	Content	Meaning
channel, item, image, textinput	Date according to http://www.w3.org/TR/NOTE-datetime	Creation date; mostly for in-house use

prism:distributor

Parent Element	Content	Meaning
channel, item, image, textinput	(#PCDATA) or the value of an rdf:resource attribute	Distribution partner: for example, the owner of a syndication service

prism:edition

Parent Element	Content	Meaning
channel, item, image, textinput	(#PCDATA)	Identifier for one of several issues

prism:elssn

Parent Element	Content	Meaning
channel, item, image, textinput	(#PCDATA)	ELSSN number (only in regards to electronic publications)

prism:embargoDate

Parent Element	Content	Meaning
channel, item, image, textinput	Date according to http://www.w3.org/TR/NOTE-datetime	Earliest time for using the resourcez

prism:endingPage

Parent Element	Content	Meaning
channel, item, image, textinput	(#PCDATA)	Last page of the described resource in a print version

prism:event

Parent Element	Content	Meaning
channel, item, image, textinput	(#PCDATA) or the value of an rdf:resource attribute	Event that has a reference to the resource

prism:expirationDate

Parent Element	Content	Meaning
channel, item, image, textinput	Date according to http://www.w3.org/TR/NOTE-datetime	When the resource can be used till

prism:hasAlternative

Parent Element	Content	Meaning
channel, item, image, textinput	(#PCDATA) or the value of an rdf:resource attribute	Alternative resource, if the described resource cannot be used for legal or other reasons

prism:hasCorrection

Parent Element	Content	Meaning
channel, item, image, textinput	(#PCDATA) or the value of an rdf:resource attribute	Identifies known corrections of the resource

prism:hasFormat

Parent Element	Content	Meaning
channel, item, image, textinput	(#PCDATA) or the value of an rdf:resource attribute	Identifies the same content in a different format

prism:hasPart

Parent Element	Content	Meaning
channel, item, image, textinput	(#PCDATA) or the value of an rdf:resource attribute	Identifies a resource that is part of the described resource

prism:hasPreviousVersion

Parent Element	Content	Meaning
channel, item, image, textinput	(#PCDATA) or the value of an rdf:resource attribute	Identifies an older version of the described resource

prism:hasTranslation

Parent Element	Content	Meaning
channel, item, image, textinput	(#PCDATA) or the value of an rdf:resource attribute	Identifies a translation

prism:industry

Parent Element	Content	Meaning
channel, item, image, textinput	(#PCDATA) or the value of an rdf:resource attribute	Industry sector that is indicated as the topic of the described resource

prism:isCorrectionOf

Parent Element	Content	Meaning
channel, item, image, textinput	(#PCDATA) or the value of an rdf:resource attribute	The described resource is a corrected version of the resource indicated here.

prism:isFormatOf

Parent Element	Content	Meaning
channel, item, image, textinput	(#PCDATA) or the value of an rdf:resource attribute	The described resource has the same content as the resource indicated here, but in a different format.

prism:isPartOf

Parent Element	Content	Meaning
channel, item, image, textinput	(#PCDATA) or the value of an rdf:resource attribute	The described resource is a physical or logical part of the resource indicated here.

prism:isReferencedBy

Parent Element	Content	Meaning
channel, item, image, textinput	(#PCDATA) or the value of an rdf:resource attribute	The resource indicated here refers to the described resource.

prism:isRequiredBy

Parent Element	Content	Meaning
channel, item, image, textinput	(#PCDATA) or the value of an rdf:resource attribute	The resource indicated here takes the described resource physically or logically for granted.

prism:issn

Parent Element	Content	Meaning
channel, item, image, textinput	(#PCDATA)	ISSN number

prism:issueIdentifier

Parent Element	Content	Meaning
channel, item, image, textinput	(#PCDATA)	Identifier of a certain issue of a magazine, or similar

prism:issueName

Parent Element	Content	Meaning
`channel`, `item`, `image`, `textinput`	(#PCDATA)	Name for special issues, or similar

prism:isTranslationOf

Parent Element	Content	Meaning
`channel`, `item`, `image`, `textinput`	(#PCDATA) or the value of an `rdf:resource` attribute	The described resource is a translation of the resource indicated here.

prism:isVersionOf

Parent Element	Content	Meaning
`channel`, `item`, `image`, `textinput`	(#PCDATA) or the value of an `rdf:resource` attribute	The described resource is a version of the resource indicated here.

prism:location

Parent Element	Content	Meaning
`channel`, `item`, `image`, `textinput`	(#PCDATA) or the value of an `rdf:resource` attribute	Location indicated as a topic for a resource

prism:modificationDate

Parent Element	Content	Meaning
`channel`, `item`, `image`, `textinput`	Date according to `http://www.w3.org/TR/NOTE-datetime`	When the last change occurred

prism:number

Parent Element	Content	Meaning
`channel`, `item`, `image`, `textinput`	(#PCDATA)	Number of the described issue

prism:objectTitle

Parent Element	Content	Meaning
`channel`, `item`, `image`, `textinput`	(#PCDATA) or the value of an `rdf:resource` attribute	Object indicated as the topic for a resource

prism:organization

Parent Element	Content	Meaning
channel, item, image, textinput	(#PCDATA) or the value of an rdf:resource attribute	Organization indicated as the topic for a resource

prism:person

Parent Element	Content	Meaning
channel, item, image, textinput	(#PCDATA) or the value of an rdf:resource attribute	Person indicated as the topic for a resource

prism:publicationDate

Parent Element	Content	Meaning
channel, item, image, textinput	Date according to http://www.w3.org/TR/NOTE-datetime	Publication date

prism:publicationName

Parent Element	Content	Meaning
channel, item, image, textinput	(#PCDATA)	Title of the publication in which the resource was published

prism:references

Parent Element	Content	Meaning
channel, item, image, textinput	(#PCDATA) or the value of an rdf:resource attribute	The described resource refers to the resource indicated here.

prism:requires

Parent Element	Content	Meaning
channel, item, image, textinput	(#PCDATA) or the value of an rdf:resource attribute	The described resource needs the resource indicated here to be complete in regards to the content.

prism:rightsAgent

Parent Element	Content	Meaning
channel, item, image, textinput	(#PCDATA)	Name of the person responsible for dealing with copyrights

prism:section

Parent Element	Content	Meaning
channel, item, image, textinput	(#PCDATA)	Name of the section (for instance, of a magazine) in which the described resource appears

prism:startingPage

Parent Element	Content	Meaning
channel, item, image, textinput	(#PCDATA)	First page number of the described resource

prism:subsection1

Parent Element	Content	Meaning
channel, item, image, textinput	(#PCDATA)	Name of the first-order subsection in which the described resource is printed

prism:subsection2

Parent Element	Content	Meaning
channel, item, image, textinput	(#PCDATA)	Name of the second-order subsection in which the described resource is printed

prism:teaser

Parent Element	Content	Meaning
channel, item, image, textinput	(#PCDATA)	Teaser text

prism:volume

Parent Element	Content	Meaning
channel, item, image, textinput	(#PCDATA)	Identifier of a volume in which the described resource appears

prism:wordCount

Parent Element	Content	Meaning
channel, item, image, textinput	(#PCDATA)	Approximate number of words in the described resource

A.5.14 mod_richequiv

Purpose

Equivalences for the title and description properties of RSS 1.0, these also allow using XML elements as content.

Specification

    http://purl.org/rss/1.0/modules/richequiv/

Namespace

    xmlns:reqv=http://purl.org/rss/1.0/modules/richequiv/

reqv:title

Parent Element	Content	Meaning
channel, item, textinput	(#PCDATA)	Container for any kind of XML elements

reqv:description

Parent Element	Content	Meaning
channel, item, textinput	(#PCDATA)	Container for any kind of XML elements

A.5.15 mod_rss091

Purpose

Equivalences for the elements of RSS 0.91.

Specification

    http://purl.org/rss/1.0/modules/rss091/

Namespace

    xmlns:rss091=http://purl.org/rss/1.0/modules/rss091#

rss091:language

Parent Element	Content	Meaning
channel	(#PCDATA)	Corresponds with the language element in RSS 0.91

rss091:rating

Parent Element	Content	Meaning
channel	(#PCDATA)	Corresponds with the rating element in RSS 0.91

rss091:managingEditor

Parent Element	Content	Meaning
channel	(#PCDATA)	Corresponds with the managingEditor element in RSS 0.91

rss091:webMaster

Parent Element	Content	Meaning
channel	(#PCDATA)	Corresponds with the webMaster element in RSS 0.91

rss091:pubDate

Parent Element	Content	Meaning
channel	(#PCDATA)	Corresponds with the pubDate element in RSS 0.91

rss091:lastBuildDate

Parent Element	Content	Meaning
channel	(#PCDATA)	Corresponds with the lastBuildDate element in RSS 0.91

rss091:copyright

Parent Element	Content	Meaning
item	(#PCDATA)	Corresponds with the copyright element in RSS 0.91

rss091:skipHours

Parent Element	Content	Meaning
channel	(#PCDATA)	Corresponds with the skipHours element in RSS 0.91

rss091:hour

Parent Element	Content	Meaning
rss091:skipHours	0, 1, 2,...	Corresponds with the hour element in RSS 0.91

rss091:skipDays

Parent Element	Content	Meaning
channel	(#PCDATA)	Corresponds with the skipDays element in RSS 0.91

rss091:day

Parent Element	Content	Meaning
rss091:skipDays	(#PCDATA)	Corresponds with the day element in RSS 0.91

rss091:width

Parent Element	Content	Meaning
image	(#PCDATA)	Corresponds with the width element in RSS 0.91

rss091:height

Parent Element	Content	Meaning
image	(#PCDATA)	Corresponds with the height element in RSS 0.91

rss091:description

Parent Element	Content	Meaning
item	(#PCDATA)	Corresponds with the description element in RSS 0.91

A.5.16 mod_search

Purpose

Additional specifics about objects that are search results.

Specification

```
http://purl.org/rss/1.0/modules/search/
```

Namespace

```
xmlns:search="http://purl.org/rss/1.0/modules/search/"
```

search:relevance

Parent Element	Content	Meaning
item	(#PCDATA)	Meaning of the result in terms of the enquiry, for example, indicated as a number

search:scope

Parent Element	Content	Meaning
item	(#PCDATA)	Reference to the topic of the enquiry

A.5.17 mod_servicestatus

Purpose

Allows indicating the status and the availability of servers and services.

Specification

```
http://purl.org/rss/1.0/modules/servicestatus/
```

Namespace

```
xmlns:ss="http://purl.org/rss/1.0/modules/servicestatus/"
```

ss:aboutStats

Parent Element	Content	Meaning
channel	rdf:resource	URI of the service

ss:responding

Parent Element	Content	Meaning
item	true/false	Whether the service responded when it was last tested

ss:lastChecked

Parent Element	Content	Meaning
item	Date according to http://www.w3.org/TR/NOTE-datetime	When the service was last tested

ss:lastSeen

Parent Element	Content	Meaning
item	Date according to http://www.w3.org/TR/NOTE-datetime	Last time that the service answered

ss:availability

Parent Element	Content	Meaning
item	Whole number	Statistical indication of the availability in percent

ss:averageResponseTime

Parent Element	Content	Meaning
item	Float	Average latency in seconds

ss:statusMessage

Parent Element	Content	Meaning
item	(#PCDATA)	Allows messages concerning the status of the service and its availability

A.5.18 mod_slash

Purpose

Allows metadata that are specific to sites that use Slash (http://www.slashcode.com/) as an engine.

Specification

```
http://www.egroups.com/files/rss-dev/Modules/Proposed/mod_slash.html
```

Namespace

```
xmlns:slash="http://purl.org/rss/1.0/modules/slash/"
```

slash:section

Parent Element	Content	Meaning
item	(#PCDATA)	Corresponds with the section on sites that use Slash

slash:department

Parent Element	Content	Meaning
item	(#PCDATA)	Corresponds with the department on sites that use Slash

slash:comments

Parent Element	Content	Meaning
item	Positive whole number	Number of comments on sites that use Slash

slash:hit_parade

Parent Element	Content	Meaning
item	Positive whole number separated by commas	Indication of popularity on sites that use Slash

A.5.19 mod_streaming

Purpose

Allows describing the characteristics of the media that are streamed.

Specification

    http://hacks.benhammersley.com/rss/streaming/

Namespace

    xmlns:str="http://hacks.benhammersley.com/rss/streaming/"

str:type

Parent Element	Content	Meaning
channel, item	audio / video / both	Type of the streamed data

str:associatedApplication

Parent Element	Content	Meaning
channel, item	(#PCDATA)	Application to play the data

str:associatedApplication.version

Parent Element	Content	Meaning
channel, item	(#PCDATA)	Version of the application to play the data

str:associatedApplication.downloadUri

Parent Element	Content	Meaning
channel, item	(#PCDATA)	URI to download the application to play the data

str:codec

Parent Element	Content	Meaning
channel, item	(#PCDATA)	Codec

str:codec.name

Parent Element	Content	Meaning
channel, item	(#PCDATA)	Name of the codec

str:codec.version

Parent Element	Content	Meaning
channel, item	(#PCDATA)	Version of the codec

str:codec.url

Parent Element	Content	Meaning
channel, item	(#PCDATA)	URI to identify codec

str:codec.downloadURI

Parent Element	Content	Meaning
channel, item	(#PCDATA)	URI to download codec

str:codec.sampleRate

Parent Element	Content	Meaning
channel, item	(#PCDATA)	Sampling rate of the media in kHz

str:codec.stereo

Parent Element	Content	Meaning
channel, item	stereo / mono	Corresponds with the section on sites that use Slash

str:codec.ResolutionX

Parent Element	Content	Meaning
channel, item	(#PCDATA)	Length in pixels of the x-axis

str:codec.ResolutionY

Parent Element	Content	Meaning
channel, item	(#PCDATA)	Length in pixels of the y-axis

str:duration

Parent Element	Content	Meaning
channel, item	HH-MM-SS	Duration in hours, minutes, and seconds

str:live

Parent Element	Content	Meaning
channel, item	live / recorded	Specifies whether live or not

str:live.scheduledStartTime

Parent Element	Content	Meaning
channel, item	Date according to http://www.w3.org/TR/NOTE-datetime	Intended start

str:live.scheduledEndTime

Parent Element	Content	Meaning
channel, item	Date according to http://www.w3.org/TR/NOTE-datetime	Intended end

str:live.location

Parent Element	Content	Meaning
channel, item	(#PCDATA)	Location, especially in regards to live events

str:live.contactURI

Parent Element	Content	Meaning
channel, item	(#PCDATA)	URI of a contact person

A.5.20 mod_subscription

Purpose

Simplifies the syndication of RSS 1.0 feeds; for more details please see the specification. The content requires attributes.

Specification

```
http://www.purl.org/rss/1.0/modules/subscription/
```

Namespace

```
xmlns:sub="http://purl.org/rss/1.0/modules/subscription/"
```

sub:channel

Parent Element	Content	Meaning
channel	(#PCDATA)	Local title for a channel

sub:vendor

Parent Element	Content	Meaning
sub:channel	(#PCDATA)	Provider-specific URI for subscribing

sub:site

Parent Element	Content	Meaning
sub:site	(#PCDATA)	Indicates an alternative URI for a channel

A.5.21 mod_taxonomy

Purpose

Indicates taxonomies.

Specification

```
http://purl.org/rss/1.0/modules/taxonomy/
```

Namespace

```
xmlns:taxo="http://purl.org/rss/1.0/modules/taxonomy/"
```

taxo:topic

Parent Element	Content	Meaning
channel	All elements that are possible within rss:channel	Description of a topic, the URI of which contains the rdf:about attribute

taxo:topics

Parent Element	Content	Meaning
channel, item, taxo:topic	rdf:Bag with a list of topics	List of topics

A.5.22 mod_threading

Purpose

Indicates parent-child relationships; for example, for the description of components of an aggregated feed.

Specification

    http://purl.org/rss/1.0/modules/threading/

Namespace

    xmlns:thr=http://purl.org/rss/1.0/modules/threading/

thr:children

Parent Element	Content	Meaning
item	rdf:Seq	Marks the item as the parent element of a sequence of resources

A.5.23 mod_wiki

Purpose

Description of metadata typical for wikis.

Specification

    http://www.usemod.com/cgi-bin/mb.pl?ModWiki

Namespace

    xmlns:wiki="http://purl.org/rss/1.0/modules/wiki/"

wiki:interwiki

Parent Element	Content	Meaning
channel	(#PCDATA)	Abbreviation of Meatball:InterWiki

wiki:host

Parent Element	Content	Meaning
item	IP address or host name	Host on which the wiki page is edited

wiki:version

Parent Element	Content	Meaning
item	(#PCDATA)	Version of the page

wiki:status

Parent Element	Content	Meaning
item	new / update / deleted	Status of the page

wiki:importance

Parent Element	Content	Meaning
item	major / minor	Importance of a change to the page

wiki:diff

Parent Element	Content	Meaning
item	URI	URIs through which the differences compared to older versions are published

wiki:history

Parent Element	Content	Meaning
item	(#PCDATA)	Corresponds with the section on sites that use Slash

A.6 Overview: RSS 1.1 Elements

A.6.1 rss:Channel

Meaning

Gathers the metadata for a feed.

Schema

```
start = Channel
Channel = element Channel { Channel.content }
Channel.content = (
    AttrXMLLang?, AttrXMLBase?, AttrRDFAbout,
    (title & link & description & image? & Any* & items)
)
```

```
Any = element * - ( rss:* ) { Any.content }
Any.content = (
    attribute * - ( rss:* | NoNS:* ) { text }*,
    mixed { Any* }
)

AttrXMLLang = attribute xml:lang { xsd:language }
AttrXMLBase = attribute xml:base { xsd:anyURI }
AttrRDFAbout = attribute rdf:about { xsd:anyURI }
```

Ancestors

None

Descendants/Content

Obligatory: items, title, link, description

Optional: image

Attributes

Name	Values	Meaning	Obligatory?
rdf:about	URI	Indicates the URI of the feed	Yes

Example

```
<Channel xmlns="http://purl.org/net/rss1.1#"
    xmlns:rdf="http://www.w3.org/1999/02/22-rdf-syntax-ns#"
    xmlns:dc="http://purl.org/dc/elements/1.1/"
    rdf:about="http://www.celawi.eu/webtrends/">
</Channel>
```

Remarks

None

Equivalences

RSS 1.1	RSS 2.0	Atom
rss:Channel	channel	atom:feed

A.6.2 rss:title

Meaning

Title of a channel, item, or image.

Schema

```
title = element title { title.content }
title.content = (
    AttrXMLLang?, text
)

AttrXMLLang = attribute xml:lang { xsd:language }
```

Ancestors

rss:channel, rss:item, rss:image

Descendants/Content

Text (obligatory)

Attributes

None

Example

```
<title>Webtrends</title>
```

Remarks

None

Equivalences

RSS 1.1	RSS 2.0	Atom
rss:title	title	atom:title

A.6.3 rss:link

Meaning

Contains the target of a reference.

Schema

```
link = element link { link.content }

link.content = ( xsd:anyURI )
```

Ancestors

rss:channel, rss:item, rss:image

Descendants/Content

URI

Attributes

None

Example

```
<link>http://www.celawi.eu/webtrends/</link>
```

Remarks

None

Equivalences

RSS 1.1	RSS 2.0	Atom
rss:link	link	atom:link (In Atom the semantics of this element are more multifaceted.)

A.6.4 rss:description

Meaning

Description of a channel or an item.

Schema

```
description = element description { description.content }
description.content = (
    AttrXMLLang?, text
)

AttrXMLLang = attribute xml:lang { xsd:language }
```

Ancestors

rss:channel, rss:item

Descendants/Content

Text

Attributes

None

Example

```
<description>News from the media business</description>
```

Remarks

The content can be text only!

Equivalences

RSS 1.1	RSS 2.0	Atom
rss:description	description	atom:subtitle, atom:summary, atom:content.

A.6.5 rss:image

Meaning

Represents an image that illustrates a feed; has to occur on the top level below rdf:RDF as well as within rss:channel.

Schema

```
image = element image { image.content }
image.content = (
    AttrXMLLang?, AttrRDFResource,
    (title & link? & url & Any*)
)

Any = element * - ( rss:* ) { Any.content }
Any.content = (
    attribute * - ( rss:* | NoNS:* ) { text }*,
    mixed { Any* }
)

AttrXMLLang = attribute xml:lang { xsd:language }
AttrRDFResource = attribute rdf:parseType { "Resource" }
```

Ancestors

rss:channel, rdf:RDF

Descendants/Content

rss:link, rss:title, rss:url (if the element is a descendant of rdf:RDF or rss:channel)

Attributes

Attribute

Name	Values	Meaning	Obligatory?
rdf:resource	URI	URI of the image	Obligatory as the descendant of rss:channel, if an image is indicated
rdf:about	URI	URI of the image	Obligatory if rss:image is the descendant of rdf:RDF

Example

```
<rdf:RDF xmlns="http://purl.org/rss/1.0/"
    xmlns:rdf="http://www.w3.org/1999/02/22-rdf-syntax-ns#">
    <channel rdf:about="http://www.celawi.eu/webtrends">
        <image rdf:resource=" http://www.celawi.eu/logo.gif"/>
    </channel>
    ...
    <image rdf:about="http://www.celawi.eu/logo.gif">
        <url>http://www.celawi.eu/logo.gif</url>
        <link>http://www.celawi.eu/webtrends.html</link>
        <title>Webtrends-Logo</title>
    </image>
<rdf:RDF>
```

Remarks

The element has different content models dependent on whether it appears in the table of contents of a channel, or whether it is the container for the characteristics of the image.

Equivalences

RSS 1.1	RSS 2.0	Atom
rss:image	image	atom:image, atom:icon

A.6.6 rss:url

Meaning

Address of an image.

Schema

```
url = element url { url.content }

url.content = ( xsd:anyURI )
```

Ancestors

rss:image

Descendants/Content

URI

Attributes

None

Example

```
<image rdf:about="http://www.celawi.eu/logo.gif">
    <url>http://www.celawi.eu/logo.gif</url>
</image>
```

Remarks

None

Equivalences

RSS 1.1	RSS 2.0	Atom
rss:url	url	atom:uri

A.6.7 rss:items

Meaning

Represents the items in the table of contents of a channel.

Schema

```
items = element items { items.content }
items.content = (
    AttrXMLLang?, AttrRDFCollection,
    item*
)

AttrXMLLang = attribute xml:lang { xsd:language }
AttrRDFCollection = attribute rdf:parseType { "Collection" }
```

Ancestors

rss:Channel

Descendants/Content

rdf:item

Attributes

None

Example

```
<Channel rdf:about="http://www.celawi.eu/webtrends">
  ...
  <items>
    <item>
      ...
    </item>
  </items>
</Channel>
```

Remarks

None

Equivalences

RSS 1.1	RSS 2.0	Atom
rss:item	-	-

A.6.8 rss:item

Meaning

Represents an entry within a feed.

Schema

```
item = element item { item.content }
item.content = (
    AttrXMLLang?, AttrRDFAbout,
    (title & link & description? & image? & Any*)
)

Any = element * - ( rss:* ) { Any.content }
Any.content = (
    attribute * - ( rss:* | NoNS:* ) { text }*,
    mixed { Any* }
)

AttrXMLLang = attribute xml:lang { xsd:language }
AttrRDFAbout = attribute rdf:about { xsd:anyURI }
```

Ancestors

rss:item

Descendants/Content

Obligatory: `rss:title`, `rss:link`, `rss:description`

Optional: further elements from other namespaces

Attributes

Name	Values	Meaning	Obligatory?
rdf:about	URI	URI of the item	Yes

Example

```
<item rdf:about="http:// www.celawi.eu/webtrends/"
    <title>Music Downloads: Alliance of Microsoft and Nokia
        against Apple</title>
    <link>http://www.celawi.eu/webtrends/403</link>
    <dc:subject>Mobil</dc:subject>
    <description>Nokia and Microsoft allied. They want to break
        the dominance of the Apple group in the business of music
        downloads. In the future, Nokia is prepared to offer
        handys with software to play music and videos from its
        former rival Microsoft as well.</description>
    <dc:creator>Julia Preiner</dc:creator>
    <dc:date>2005/02/15 08:15:48.428 GMT+1</dc:date>
</item>
```

Remarks

None

Equivalences

RSS 1.1	RSS 2.0	Atom
rss:item	item	atom:entry

A.6.9 Any

```
Any = element * - ( rss:* ) { Any.content }
Any.content = (
    attribute * - ( rss:* | NoNS:* ) { text }*,
    mixed { Any* }
)
```

A.7 Overview: Atom Elements

A.7.1 Atom Standard Attributes

xml:base—Possible in every Atom element; its function is to solve relative URI references.

xml:lang—Possible in every Atom element; its function is to indicate the language of the element content according to RFC 3066.

A.7.2 Atom Text Construct

Meaning

For the inclusion of plain text, HTML text, or XHTML text.

Schema

```
atomPlainTextConstruct =
      atomCommonAttributes,
      attribute type { "text" | "html" }?,
      text

atomXHTMLTextConstruct =
      atomCommonAttributes,
      attribute type { "xhtml" },
      xhtmlDiv

atomTextConstruct = atomPlainTextConstruct | atomXHTMLTextConstruct
```

A.7.3 Atom Person Construct

Meaning

For persons and institutions.

Schema

```
atomPersonConstruct =
      atomCommonAttributes,
      (element atom:name { text }
      & element atom:uri { atomUri }?
      & element atom:email { atomemailAddress }?
      & extensionElement*)
```

A.7.4 Atom Date Construct

Meaning

For dates

Schema

```
atomDateConstruct =
        atomCommonAttributes,
        xsd:dateTime
```

A.7.5 atom:author

Meaning

Document element of a feed document (of a document that represents a newsfeed); container for all data and metadata of the newsfeed.

Schema

```
atomAuthor =
    element atom:author { atomPersonConstruct }
```

Ancestors

feed, entry

Descendants/Content

Obligatory: name

Optional: E-Mail, uri

Attributes

Standard attributes (see section A.7.1)

Example

```
<atom:author xml:lang="de">
    <atom:name>Julia Preiner</atom:name>
    <atom:E-Mail>j.preiner@celawi.eu</atom:E-Mail>
    <atom:uri>http://www.celawi.eu/julia</atom:uri>
</atom:author>
```

Remarks

The author of an entry has to be indicated either within the element itself, or within the element feed for all entries together.

Equivalences

RSS 2.0	RSS 1.0	RSS 1.1
author managingEditor	dc:creator	dc:creator

A.7.6 atom:category

Meaning

Indicates the categories for the content.

Schema

```
atomCategory =
        element atom:category {
            atomCommonAttributes,
            attribute term { text },
            attribute scheme { atomUri }?,
            attribute label { text }?,
            undefinedContent
        }
```

Ancestors

feed, entry

Descendants/Content

Allowed but not defined by the specification

Attributes

Standard attributes (see section A.7.1)

Name	Value
scheme	URI of a categorizing schema
term	Identifier of the category
label	Characterization of the category

Example

```
<atom:category scheme="http://technorati.com/tag/" term="technology"
label="Technology"/>
```

Remarks

Any number of categories can be indicated for feed as well as for entry.

Equivalences

RSS 2.0	RSS 1.0	RSS 1.1
category	dc:subject	dc:subject

A.7.7 atom:content

Meaning

Container for the content of an entry, or a link to the content.

Schema

```
atomInlineTextContent =
    element atom:content {
        atomCommonAttributes,
        attribute type { "text" | "html" }?,
        (text)*
    }

atomInlineXHTMLContent =
    element atom:content {
        atomCommonAttributes,
        attribute type { "xhtml" },
        xhtmlDiv
    }

atomInlineOtherContent =
    element atom:content {
        atomCommonAttributes,
        attribute type { atomMediaType }?
        {text | anyElement}*

    }

atomOutOfLineContent =
    element atom:content {
        atomCommonAttributes,
        attribute type { atomMediaType }?,
        attribute src { atomUri },
        empty
    }

atomContent = atomInlineTextContent
    | atomInlineXHTMLContent
    | atomInlineOtherContent
    | atomOutOfLineContent
```

Ancestors

entry

Descendants/Content

Textual or binary content (see section 4.2.3, *Content as a "First-Class Citizen"*)

Attributes

Standard attributes (see section A.7.1)

Name	Value
type	text, html, xhtml, or a registered MIME media type (RFC 2045) with a discrete top-level type (RFC 2045, section 5)
src	IRI-reference (RFC 3987)

Example

See: chapter 4, section 4.2.3

Remarks

If the attribute type is not indicated, it has to be assumed that its value is text. The src attribute has to be used if the content isn't included inline. Binary content has to be Base64-encoded. Text content (including XML) should be provided inline.

Equivalences

RSS 2.0	RSS 1.0	RSS 1.1
item	rss:item	rss:item

A.7.8 atom:contributor

Meaning

Person (or any other entity) who contributed to an entry.

Schema

```
atomContributor = element atom:contributor { atomPersonConstruct }
```

Ancestors

feed, entry

Descendants/Content

Obligatory: name

Optional: E-Mail, uri

Attributes

Standard attributes (see section A.7.1)

Example

```
<atom:name>Harry Schwitzer</atom:name>
  <atom:E-Mail>h.schwitzer@celawi.eu</atom:E-Mail>
  <atom:uri>http://www.celawi.eu/harry</atom:uri>
</atom:contributor>
```

Remarks

Can occur on the levels of feed and entry any number of times.

Equivalences

RSS 2.0	RSS 1.0	RSS 1.1
None	dc:contributor	dc:contributor

A.7.9 atom:rights

Meaning

Indicates the rights holders in a form readable by people.

Schema

```
atomRights = element atom:Rights { atomTextConstruct }
```

Ancestors

feed, entry

Descendants/Content

Atom text construct

Attributes

Standard attributes (see section A.7.1)

Example

```
<rights>©2005 Ask Jeeves, Inc.</rights>
```

Remarks

In feed, the indication can be done either for all entries together or for each entry individually.

Equivalences

RSS 2.0	RSS 1.0	RSS 1.1
copyright	dc:rights	dc:rights

A.7.10 atom:email

Meaning

Indicates the e-mail address in a person construct.

Schema

```
element atom:email { atomEmailAddress }
```

Ancestors

author, contributor

Descendants/Content

E-mail address (according to RFC2822, http://www.faqs.org/rfcs/rfc2822.html)

Attributes

Standard attributes (see section A.7.1)

Example

```
<email>erich@example.com</email>
```

Remarks

Within person constructs, it is only allowed to indicate one e-mail address.

Equivalences

RSS 2.0	RSS 1.0	RSS 1.1
-	-	-

A.7.11 atom:entry

Meaning

Container for all content and data that belong to an entry in an Atom feed; document element of an entry document that can be used for posting or editing an entry.

Schema

```
atomEntry = element atom:entry {
      atomCommonAttributes,
      (atomAuthor*
       & atomCategory*
       & atomContent?
       & atomContributor*
       & atomId
       & atomLink*
       & atomPublished?
       & atomRights?
       & atomSource?
       & atomSummary?
       & atomTitle
       & atomUpdated
       & extensionElement*)
}
```

Ancestors

feed

Descendants/Content

id, title, updated (obligatory); content, summary (one of these two elements has to exist); author (obligatory if not indicated in feed); category, contributor (optional, and can appear several times); rights, link, published, source (optional); optional extensions

Attributes

Standard attributes (see section A.7.1)

Example

```
<atom:entry>
  <atom:id>http://www.celawi.eu/webtrends/405</atom:id>
  <atom:title>Mobilcom: Gain explosion thanks to Internet
        business </atom:title>
  <atom:link href="http://www.celawi.eu/webtrends/405"/>
  <category term="Provider"/>
  <atom:content type="text">Particularly the Internet and fixed
        network business of their daughter company, Freenet, accounts
        for the downright explosion that Mobilcom – Germany's
        second biggest mobile radio telephone service provider – can
        note. </atom:content>
  <atom:contributor>
    <atom:name>Harry Schwitzer</atom:name>
    <atom:email>h.schwitzer@celawi.eu</atom:email>
    <atom:uri>http://www.celawi.eu/harry</atom:uri>
  </atom:contributor>
  <atom:author>
```

```
    <atom:name>Martin Röller</atom:name>
  </atom:author>
  <atom:updated>2005-02-15T08:20:00Z</atom:updated>
</atom:entry>
```

Remarks

The order of the elements that make up the content is not specified.

Equivalences

RSS 2.0	RSS 1.0	RSS 1.1
item	rss:item	rss:item

A.7.12 atom:feed

Meaning

Document element of a feed document (a document that represents a newsfeed);
container for all data and metadata of the newsfeed.

Schema

```
atomFeed = element atom:feed {
      atomCommonAttributes,
      (atomAuthor?
       & atomCategory*
       & atomContributor*
       & atomGenerator?
       & atomIcon?
       & atomId
       & atomLink*
       & atomLogo?
       & atomRights?
       & atomSubtitle?
       & atomTitle
       & atomUpdated
       & extensionElement*),
     & atomEntry*
}
```

Ancestors

None

Descendants/Content

author, link, title, updated, id (obligatory); category, contributor, entry (optional,
can appear several times); rights, generator, icon, icon, logo, link, subtitle
(optional)

Attributes

Standard attributes (see section A.7.1)

Example

See section 4.2.2, *The Basic Structure of an Atom Document.*

Remarks

None

Equivalences

RSS 2.0	RSS 1.0	RSS 1.1
rss, channel	rdf:RDF, rss:Channel	rss:Channel

A.7.13 atom:generator

Meaning

Identifies the software that created the feed; primarily used for debugging.

Schema

```
atomGenerator = element atom:generator {
    atomCommonAttributes,
    attribute uri { atomUri }?,
    attribute version { text }?,
    text
}
```

Ancestors

feed

Descendants/Content

Text (optional)

Attributes

Standard attributes (see section A.7.1)

Name	Value
uri	IRI reference according to RFC3987 (optional)
version	Indicates the version (optional)

Example

```
<generator url="http://www.movabletype.org/" version="4.3">Movable
Type</generator>
```

Remarks

None

Equivalences

RSS 2.0	RSS 1.0	RSS 1.1
generator	-	-

A.7.14 atom:icon

Meaning

Reference to an image that can be used as the icon for a feed.

Schema

```
atomIcon = element atom:icon {
    atomCommonAttributes,
    (atomUri)
}
```

Ancestors

feed

Descendants/Content

None

Attributes

Standard attributes (see section A.7.1 on page 271)

Example

```
<icon>/images/logo.gif...</icon>
```

Remarks

None

Equivalences

RSS 2.0	RSS 1.0	RSS 1.1
image	rss:image	rss:image

A.7.15 atom:id

Meaning

Identifies a feed or an entry permanently and clearly.

Schema

```
atomId = element atom:id {
    atomCommonAttributes,
    (atomUri)
}
```

Ancestors

feed, entry

Descendants/Content

IRI (Internationalized Resource Identifier), as defined in RFC3987 (ftp://ftp.rfc-editor.org/in-notes/rfc3987.txt)

Attributes

Standard attributes (see section A.7.1)

Example

```
<id>tag:typepad.com,2003:post-4205874</id>
```

Remarks

Relative URIs are not allowed to make up the content.

When checking whether two IRIs are identical, the two character strings are compared character by character. It is not relevant whether dereferencing the IRIs leads to the same resource.

Equivalences

RSS 2.0	RSS 1.0	RSS 1.1
guid	rdf:about	rdf:about

A.7.16 atom:logo

Meaning

Reference to an image that can be used to visually identify a feed.

Schema

```
atomLogo = element atom:logo {
        atomCommonAttributes,
        (atomUri)
}
```

Ancestors

feed

Descendants/Content

IRI reference according to RFC3987 (ftp://ftp.rfc-editor.org/in-notes/rfc3987.txt)

Attributes

Standard attributes (see section A.7.1)

Example

```
<image>images/channel.png</image>
```

Remarks

The width/height ratio should be 2:1.

Equivalences

RSS 2.0	RSS 1.0	RSS 1.1
image	rss:image	rss:image

A.7.17 atom:link

Meaning

Reference to a resource on the Web.

Schema

```
atomLink = element atom:link {
        atomCommonAttributes,
        attribute href { atomUri },
        attribute rel { atomNCName | atomUri }?,
        attribute type { atomMediaType }?,
        attribute hreflang { atomLanguageTag }?,
        attribute title { text }?,
        attribute length { text }?,
        undefinedContent
}
```

Ancestors

feed, entry

Descendants/Content

None

Attributes

Standard attributes (see section A.7.1)

Name	Value
href	IRI reference according to RFC3987 (ftp://ftp.rfc-editor.org/in-notes/rfc3987.txt) (obligatory)
rel1	Indication of the kind of relationship with the resource that is referred to. At present, possible values are alternate, related, self, enclosure, and via. Further values can be registered with the IANA. (optional; if the attribute is not explicitly indicated, it is assumed that the value is alternate; see also section 4.2.4, *The Use of Links in Atom*.)
type	Valid MIME media type of the representation of the resource that is referred to (optional)
hreflang	Indication of the language of the target resource with a language label according to RFC3066 (http://www.faqs.org/rfcs/rfc3066.html) (optional)
title	Information about the link that is readable by people (optional)

Example

```
<link rel="alternate" href="http://www.celawi.com/webtrends.html"/>
<link rel="via" type="text/html"
href="http://blog.ask.com/2005/04/jeeves_habla_es.html" />
```

Remarks

None

Equivalences

RSS 2.0	RSS 1.0	RSS 1.1
link	rss:link	rss:link

A.7.18 atom:name

Meaning

Contains the name of a person; also used with collectives, for example, institutions and companies.

Schema

```
element atom:name { text }
```

Ancestors

author, contributor

Descendants/Content

Text

Attributes

Standard attributes (see section A.7.1)

Example

```
<name>Julia Preiner</name>
```

Remarks

The author and contributor elements have to include the indication of a name.

Equivalences

RSS 2.0	RSS 1.0	RSS 1.1
-	-	-

A.7.19 atom:published

Meaning

Indicates the publication date or date of a similar event.

Schema

```
atomPublished = element atom:published { atomDateConstruct }
```

Ancestors

```
entry
```

Descendants/Content

Date construct

Attributes

Standard attributes (see section A.7.1)

Example

```
<published>2005-04-15T06:10:48.428</published>
```

Remarks

None

Equivalences

RSS 2.0	RSS 1.0	RSS 1.1
pubDate	dc:date	dc:date

A.7.20 atom:subtitle

Meaning

Short characterization of a feed.

Schema

```
atomSubtitle = element atom:subtitle { atomTextConstruct }
```

Ancestors

```
feed
```

Descendants/Content

Text

Attributes

Standard attributes (see section A.7.1)

Example

```
<subtitle>Up-to-date information about viral marketing</subtitle>
```

Remarks

None

Equivalences

RSS 2.0	RSS 1.0	RSS 1.1
description	description	description

A.7.21 atom:source

Meaning

Meta-information of a feed from which an entry was copied into the current feed.

Schema

```
atomSource = element atom:source {
          atomCommonAttributes,
          (atomAuthor*
          & atomCategory*
          & atomContributor*
          & atomGenerator?
          & atomIcon?
          & atomId?
          & atomLink*
          & atomLogo?
          & atomRights
          & atomSubtitle?
          & atomTitle?
          & atomUpdated
          & extensionElement*)
   }
```

Ancestors

entry

Descendants/Content

title, updated, link (obligatory); category, contributor (optional, can appear several times); copyright, generator, icon, id, image, subtitle (optional); extension elements

Attributes

Standard attributes (see section A.7.1)

Example

```
<entry>
  <source>
    <title>Ask Jeeves Blog</title>
    <subtitle>The Official Ask Jeeves Blog</subtitle>
    <id>tag:typepad.com,2003:weblog-103453</id>
    <link rel="alternate" type="text/html"
        href="http://blog.ask.com/" />
    <updated>2005-04-21T22:35:12Z</updated>
    <copyright>©2005 Ask Jeeves, Inc.</copyright>
  </source>
  <title>Ask Jeeves speaks Spanish!</title>
...
</entry>
```

Remarks

None

Equivalences

RSS 2.0	RSS 1.0	RSS 1.1
-	-	-

A.7.22 atom:summary

Meaning

Summary of the content of an entry.

Schema

```
atomSummary = element atom:summary { atomTextConstruct }
```

Ancestors

entry

Descendants/Content

Text

Attributes

Standard attributes (see section A.7.1)

Example

```
<summary>Nokia and Microsoft allied. They want to break the dominance
of the Apple group in the business of music downloads.</summary>
```

Remarks

None

Equivalences

RSS 2.0	RSS 1.0	RSS 1.1
description	rss:description	rss:description

A.7.23 atom:title

Meaning

Title of an entry or a document that is usable for people.

Schema

```
atomTitle = element atom:title { atomTextConstruct }
```

Ancestors

feed, entry

Descendants/Content

author, link, title, updated (obligatory); category, contributor, entry
(optional, can appear several times); copyright, generdator, icon, id, image, link,
subtitle (optional)

Attributes

Standard attributes (see section A.7.1)

Example

```
<title>Music Downloads: Alliance of Microsoft and Nokia against
Apple<title>
```

Remarks

None

Equivalences

RSS 2.0	RSS 1.0	RSS 1.1
title	rss:title	rss:title

A.7.24 atom:uri

Meaning

Indicates an IRI associated with a person in a person construct.

Schema

```
element atom:uri { atomUri }
```

Ancestors

atom:author, atom:contributor

Descendants/Content

IRI reference according to RFC 3987 (ftp://ftp.rfc-editor.org/in-notes/rfc3987.txt)

Attributes

Standard attributes (see section A.7.1)

Example

```
<author xml:lang="de">
...
    <uri>http://www.celawi.eu/julia</atom:uri>
</author>
```

Remarks

None

Equivalences

RSS 2.0	RSS 1.0	RSS 1.1
-	-	-

A.7.25 atom:updated

Meaning

Time of the last relevant change of an entry or a feed.

Schema

```
atomUpdated = element atom:updated { atomDateConstruct }
```

Ancestors

feed, entry

Descendants/Content

Date construct

Attributes

Standard attributes (see section A.7.1)

Example

```
<updated>2005-04-05T22:31:41Z</updated>
```

Remarks

None

Equivalences

RSS 2.0	RSS 1.0	RSS 1.1
lastBuildDate	None	None

A.8 Bibliography

Ben Hammersley: *Developing Feeds with RSS and Atom*. Beijing, Cambridge, Sebastopol i.a.: O'Reilly, 2005.

Danny Ayers, Andrew Watt: *Beginning RSS and Atom Programming*. Birmingham: Wrox, 2005.

Index

Printed in the United Kingdom
by Lightning Source UK Ltd.
121027UK00001B/193